Indexing Systems

Alberto Cevolini

Indexing Systems

The Evolution of Knowledge Organisation in Modern Society

palgrave
macmillan

Alberto Cevolini
Department of Education
and Humanities
University of Modena and Reggio
Emilia
Reggio Emilia, Italy

ISBN 978-3-032-13812-5 ISBN 978-3-032-13813-2 (eBook)
https://doi.org/10.1007/978-3-032-13813-2

Cover credit: Book cover image is a property-released photogram by Andrea Cevolini

This Palgrave Macmillan imprint is published by the registered company Springer Nature Switzerland AG
The registered company address is: Gewerbestrasse 11, 6330 Cham, Switzerland

To my father

Acknowledgements

This volume was published with the support of the 2024 University Research Fund (FAR) for departmental research development plans—Department of Education and Humanities, University of Modena and Reggio Emilia, CUP: E93C24000560005.

Contents

About the Author

Alberto Cevolini is Associate Professor at the University of Modena and Reggio Emilia, Italy. His research focuses on sociological theory and intellectual history, with particular attention to social system theory, the development of note-taking practices, and the invention of filing cabinets in early modern Europe. He is the author of *De arte excerpendi. Imparare a dimenticare nella prima modernità* (Florence, 2006) and editor of *Forgetting Machines. Knowledge Management Evolution in Early Modern Europe* (Leiden and Boston, 2016). He also edited the English translation of Thomas Harrison's *Ark of Studies* (Turnhout, 2017).

CHAPTER 1

Introduction

The use of search engines has become a common practice in our daily lives. The more society extracts information from digital archives, the more indispensable search engines become. The success of these memory structures can be regarded as an improbable outcome of socio-cultural evolution. However, we must exercise caution and refrain from making overly hasty generalisations. Labelling our society as a 'search engine society' (Halavais 2009) is to use one part to describe the whole. Such generalisations are not uncommon in modern society (consider similar self-descriptions such as 'industrial society' and 'information society') and serve to simplify the complexity of a description that would require more abstract and connection-rich conceptual tools (Luhmann 1997a, p. 1088).

Scientific research, on the other hand, has primarily focused on two crucial issues: a technical one and a moral one. On the technical side, a large and sophisticated body of literature has developed, commonly referred to as *information retrieval*. Search engines are a highly effective solution to the problem of organising access to information. Yet, the solution itself is a problem: search engines are not flawless; the complexity of stored knowledge is continually increasing; the variety of user queries makes it exceedingly difficult for machines to generate relevant results.

The manner in which search engine technology has addressed these self-generated problems has also raised moral concerns. The criteria for

A. Cevolini, *Indexing Systems*
https://doi.org/10.1007/978-3-032-13813-2_1

discriminating between what is retained and what is discarded remain opaque; search engines often present a biased picture of reality; the dramatic selection of what is deemed relevant inhibits curiosity and discourages the exploration of different perspectives. These concerns add to the array of criticisms that society has levelled at communication technologies—from writing (Plato) to printing (Trithemius)—and are intriguing largely for that reason alone.[1]

This book adopts a different approach. The fact that search engines have become indispensable conceals the far more significant fact that they are highly improbable. By shifting the focus to this improbability, the investigation follows a different trajectory. Since improbability is a defining characteristic of evolution, search engines should be understood as a technical solution intertwined with the evolution of society and its communication technologies. Only within this evolutionary context is it possible to explain how the use of indexing systems to organise information access has become so probable as to be perceived as normal. The improbability of search engines becomes more precisely defined when considering their function.

Strictly speaking, search engines are indexing systems. They are used to explore the knowledge contained in archives with the aim of finding information relevant to potential users. This implies, first and foremost, that knowledge is entrusted to external containers rather than being stored in the minds of those involved in communication. Secondly, an indexing system is effective if it can sift through vast amounts of data, retaining only what satisfies users' information needs. Finally, no one would memorise the catalogue of a library or the register of an archive. For all these reasons, archives accessible through indexing systems function as forgetting machines.

Forgetting, on the other hand, constitutes the primary function of memory (Esposito 2002). Essentially, it involves discarding the irrelevant past to continually liberate the system's limited capacity for processing information. Within this theoretical context, search engines can be investigated as an empirical case substantiating the sociological hypothesis that evolution, which inherently favours the implementation of functions, also favours forgetting.

[1] See only Pariser (2012, p. 219): "Something *is* wrong with our media" (italics in text).

Strange as it may seem, the introduction of new communication technologies also complicates the process of forgetting. Without writing and printing there would be nothing to archive and, consequently, nothing to index. However, these very communication technologies enable the retention of far more content than an individual mind could ever retain.[2] Forgetting, therefore, fuels the generation of novelty. This is why, as Henry Wheatley (1878, p. 13) already argued, "an Index is a standing warning against forgetfulness, and accurate reference to forgotten work is almost equal to a new discovery".

The aim of this book is to explore the interplay between evolution and social memory, beginning with the pivotal role that archiving and indexing systems have come to play in modern society.[3] If the main hypothesis posits that evolution favours forgetting, it becomes necessary to explain not only how this occurs but also what makes it possible. These are the two core questions addressed in this book.

In Chapter 2, I show how historical research on the success of indexing systems in early-modern society can be reframed within a neo-Darwinian theory of evolution. This approach unravels the ambiguity of an evolutionary novelty whose structural characteristics reflect both continuity and discontinuity with the memory practices of late-medieval scholars. The method adopted for this theoretical re-contextualization is functional analysis.

Following a proposal by Niklas Luhmann (1958, p. 98ff.), the concept of function is used to denote a viewpoint that regulates which possibilities can be regarded as equivalent from that functional viewpoint. Beyond the inherent circularity of this definition, the remarkable aspect of this concept of function is that starting from the viewpoint, it becomes possible to compare as *equivalent* (in strictly functional terms) possibilities that are concretely *different* (Luhmann 2005e, p. 17f.). In addition to serving as an analytical tool, function represents a fundamental evolutionary principle driving structural change. It is on the basis of function, in fact, that evolution evaluates available structures and modifies them when it proves advantageous for the system in terms of adaptation.

[2] Conversely, individual minds remember much more than what is stored in archives.

[3] In a recent article, Abbamonte and Kallendorf (2023, p. 465) argue that "the idea of the index has a history that is worthy of investigation [...], but there has been surprisingly little research on [this] topic until recently".

In Chapter 3, I examine early-modern readers' relationship with substitute memory systems such as commonplace-books, filing cabinets, and libraries. These external repositories of knowledge share a common prerequisite: the necessity to distinguish between the organisation of the repository and the organisation of knowledge itself. This necessity goes hand in glove with a curious ambiguity: early-modern educated men were simultaneously obsessed with the problem of order and inclined to praise disorder. My hypothesis is that underlying the problem of order was a concern related to time, and that emancipation from the constraints of traditional taxonomic knowledge organisation was primarily aimed at addressing an open future—namely, the increasing complexity of ever-expanding knowledge.

In Chapters 4 and 5, I deal with the mechanisation of indexing systems. When manual procedures are automated, semantic issues turn into statistical problems. To provide relevant answers to unpredictable queries, the machine must be designed to adapt to the user. Within the interaction between user and machine, the true black box is the user. Navigating an archive is less frustrating when the users' search behaviours are translated into signals, enabling the machine to make conjectures about their respective information needs. Thus, the interaction between users and the machine takes the form of a feedback loop whose function, like any cybernetic mechanism, is to minimise deviation from a desired state. In this case, the desired state is the relevance of the results.

In Chapter 6, my focus shifts to new methods of categorising resources stored in digital archives, such as social tagging and folksonomy. Both memory practices offer users the opportunity to directly intervene in the selection of metadata, thereby combining automatic indexing with personalised categorisation. These practices, closely reminiscent of the choice of subject headings by early-modern scholars, not only allow for the provisional categorisation of resources but also transform this categorisation into a form of second-order observation. The ontologies emerging from this social labelling should therefore be understood as an index of social memory rather than as a correlate of individual user memories.

Finally, in Chapter 7, I address some issues arising from the permanent maintenance of archives. On the environmental side of the distinction between system and environment, this maintenance involves decisions concerning archiving practices. On the systemic side, it pertains to indexing systems. In the former case, a key issue is technological obsolescence. In the latter case, the challenge lies in preventing search engines from becoming overly efficient. In a society seemingly capable of remembering everything, people are rediscovering the benefits of forgetting. However, since the digitisation of archives makes it difficult, if not impossible, to act directly on the vehicles of information, those who wish to be forgotten must act upon indexing procedures. Various strategies have been developed to organise the inaccessibility of information, aiming to scrub away traces of a troublesome past while preserving future possibilities.

Underlying all the chapters in this book is the hypothesis that the crucial role indexing systems have come to play in modern social memory can be explained by combining evolutionary theory with the theory of complexity.[4] As complexity increases, social systems must find ways to maintain their adaptation to the conditions brought about by the increased complexity. Consequently, they evaluate which of the available functional equivalents is best suited to the complexity achieved at any given time. In such cases, the system can co-opt old structures to perform a previously secondary function. The structural change resulting from this co-optation enables the system to reorganise its way of remembering and forgetting.

In archives, this reorganisation generates both higher selectivity and greater complexity. Increasing complexity is thus both a prerequisite for and a consequence of evolutionary advancement, without being either a cause or a goal of evolution. Such a conclusion should be taken into consideration not only within archival studies but also in the context of a socio-evolutionary theory of social memory. This book seeks to provide an empirical foundation for this theoretical conclusion.

[4] The exploration of this combination is suggested by Luhmann (1992e, p. 796).

CHAPTER 2

Indexing Systems as an Evolutionary Advance

2.1 Memory as the Organisation of Information Access

From a sociological standpoint, research on indexing systems can be regarded as a contribution to cultural memory studies. To properly delineate the subject of this research, it is therefore useful to begin with a definition of social memory.

Since indexing systems become indispensable when knowledge is archived, social memory can primarily be understood as the *organisation of information access*.[1] This definition should not be conflated with the more common notion of *information storage and retrieval*. Memory is not a closet of recollections, and information cannot be stored. Even the literature on archives only sporadically acknowledges that access to information presents conceptual challenges far more complex than they may seem.[2] One reason for these difficulties, I argue, is an insufficient understanding of the concept of information.

Information is not an entity with objective properties independent of the observer. When a system interacts with its environment, this interaction is informative if it makes a difference between what the system

[1] Luhmann (1993, p. 118). The reference book on social memory is Esposito (2002).

[2] See, for example, Swanson (1988, p. 92). I return to this point at greater length in Sect. 5.2.

A. Cevolini, *Indexing Systems*
https://doi.org/10.1007/978-3-032-13813-2_2

knew before and what the system knows afterwards (MacKay 1969, p. 10 and 158; Garner 1962, p. 2; Sommerhoff 1974, p. 381). Information thus implies both a temporal difference and a difference in the state of the observing system: the observer *already knows* something *afterwards* that it *did not know before*. Moreover, at least one difference must exist between two possibilities (head/tail, male/female) for the selection of one and the exclusion of the other to have information value.[3] Hence, in Gregory Bateson's (2000, p. 493) well-known definition, information is "a difference that makes a difference".

Both of these differences are not external but internal to the observer (Luhmann 2009, p. 31). The possibilities in relation to which an outcome appears as a selection (and therefore holds informational value), as well as the probability assigned to each of these possibilities, depend on the system rather than the environment. Both an increase in the number of possibilities and a decrease in the probability assigned by the observer enhance the element of surprise in selection, i.e., its capacity to be informative (MacKay 1969, p. 11 and 57; Atlan 1972, p. 8; Luhmann 1997a, p. 71). In both cases, the fact that a particular outcome is informative depends on the state of the system. Otherwise, it would not be possible to explain why the *same* event can be both informative and non-informative for *different* observers, or why redundancy produced by a sender may come as a surprise to the receiver. Information, therefore, always depends on the observing system.[4] The environment, on the other hand, is what it is—it does not contain information (Foerster 1987c, p. 158).

The phrase *information storage and retrieval* is ultimately misleading precisely because it treats information independently of the observer.[5] Information cannot be objectively measured, nor can it be stored in a repository as if it were a tangible object. What can be stored, at most, is the vehicle of information. It is based on this distinction that indexing

[3] To calculate the amount of information contained in a message, the mathematical theory of communication opted for a binary base. See Shannon and Weaver (1963).

[4] Cf. Luhmann (2005c, p. 38). See also Glanville (1984, esp. p. 658). In this regard, Eco (1962, p. 96f.) describes information as an *additive* quantity whose element of novelty depends on the "recipient's system of expectations". According to Maturana (1986, p. 25), because information is the construction of an observer, Shannon's theory is not only useless but also misleading.

[5] Foerster (1971) pointed this out more than fifty years ago. See also Foerster (1987b, p. 136f.).

systems fulfil their function, as they are not designed to retrieve vehicles but rather to facilitate access to the information potentially conveyed by them. And since the information that even a single vehicle may potentially convey is, in principle, unlimited and dependent on the user's perspective, which is by definition unpredictable, indexing systems are tasked with solving a seemingly unsolvable problem.

If one opts for a definition of social memory as the organisation of information access, the primary issue becomes *organisation*. The function of memory is to discriminate, in the available past, between what is worth retaining and what can instead be discarded (Luhmann 1997b, p. 365; Esposito 2001, p. 13; 2002, p. 27f.). This discrimination always takes place in the present. It does not depend on the past, which may have already been forgotten in the meantime, but rather on what is currently available to recall the relevant past. This is why, as Niklas Luhmann (1993, p. 118) argues, organisation is far more important than what actually happened in the past.

For the user of any archival system, this means that *metadata* take precedence over *data*. First, because users engage with metadata before they access the data. Second, because metadata must be determined before data are stored; otherwise, data—even though stored—are unretrievable. This difference between data and metadata implies a duplication of the order of reality.[6] A particularly interesting case in point in terms of socio-cultural assumptions is the list.

A prerequisite for lists is some form of writing (Goody 1981, p. 89ff.; 1989, p. 219ff.). Moreover, lists do not passively record the natural properties of reality and their relations. Rather, every list separates itself from what is ordinarily experienced as the "natural unity of the perceptual world" (Goody 1981, p. 123) and establishes an order that is not immediately perceived in concrete reality (one does not encounter objects in everyday life arranged in alphabetical order). The compilation of a list is therefore a "creative act": the inclusion of elements within the list, as in a table, presupposes both their de-contextualisation and their re-contextualisation according to selective criteria established by the compiler (Goody 1977, p. 205ff.; 1981, p. 65ff.).

In making this selection, the compiler engages in a process of abstraction and classification that enables the creation of semantic groupings

[6] For Petrucciani (1998, p. 154), indexing "*creates* [...] *an order* that did not preexist".

that would otherwise remain unexplored. There is, thus, more organisation in a list than in the concrete reality from which the listed items have been drawn.[7] Yet, whereas the order of concrete reality is given, the organisation of the list must be constructed. This opens up a space of possibility that necessitates choice. The problem of ordering the world is not resolved, but it can at least be addressed in a non-arbitrary manner.

Although the creation of metadata may seem an inefficient process, it is fundamental to social memory (Esposito 2001, p. 100ff.; 2002, p. 161ff.). Data are precisely what is forgotten over time. The system cannot, therefore, rely on immediate access to what it intends to remember. In fact, if data were always present, there would be nothing to remember, as nothing would ever be forgotten.[8] Moreover, unlike data, metadata can be technically managed. This advantage was already evident in the rhetorical art of reminiscence. The latter was a technique for managing semantic associations that could be reactivated to recall contents for communication.[9] However, unlike the art of reminiscence, where mnemonic cues must be memorised, metadata can themselves be forgotten.

Metadata allow the archive to be explored in a highly selective manner: of all that is contained, metadata retrieve only a fraction and discard everything else. In making this distinction, metadata do not even need to remember what has been excluded from selection. Pointing out what has been overlooked would sabotage the process of selection itself. Finally, metadata, like all categories, do not need to retain granular data, even though they enable their retrieval. As Geoffrey Bowker (2005, p. 21) puts it, "we classify in order to be able to forget". Metadata, in short, enable the forgetting of both data and metadata themselves.

[7] The list, as Eco (2009, p. 131) points out, "gives order, and thus a hint of form, to an otherwise disordered whole". Cf. also Gese (1958, esp. p. 131), who argues that the practice of ancient Oriental lists was the correlate of a "science of order", and Soden (1965, p. 29 and 32), who maintains that the practice of compiling lists was not merely a lexical or grammatical exercise but reflected a precise "will to order".

[8] Cf. Jonker (1995, p. 234): "Forgetting is an essential element in the process of remembering".

[9] Cf. Aristotle (*De mem. et rem.*, 1, 450b 20–27; 2, 451a 20–21). The iconic example is the image of the milk bottle used to recall the season of autumn.

This general framework aligns with the social systems theory assumption that the primary function of memory is forgetting.[10] Cognitive systems, in general, must discard anything superfluous to prevent their limited resources from being rapidly depleted and to ensure that further information can be processed. Memory does not *supply* the system with as much information as possible but, on the contrary, *buffers* the system from the excess of information constantly generated by any interaction with the environment.[11] This is why the organisation of access to information is so crucial. Since the only way to access data is through metadata, the selection and structuring of metadata cannot be left to chance.

In semantic cataloguing and indexing methods, highly selective access to the past available in the present depends on the categories through which the past has been classified. These methods are crucial but also challenging because, as Bowker (2005, p. 153) argues, "in general, what is not classified gets rendered invisible". The system must therefore take care of its memory in advance[12] by assessing, in the present, what past might be required in the future. Only the retrievable past can suggest connections for further operations and structure the future. The system, therefore, prefers to keep track of a past that can be re-used in the future, without forcing the future to repeat the past.[13] What governs the process of discarding and retention is not what has actually happened, but rather the anticipation of potential future uses of the present (understood as a future past).

[10] The seminal research is Foerster (1948). See also Luhmann (1995a, p. 45; 1996, p. 307ff.; 1997a, p. 579; 2000, p. 172); Esposito (2002; 2010, p. 181ff.).

[11] The distinction between *supply* and *buffer* is drawn from Simon (1971, p. 44). Empirical studies have confirmed that the 'channel capacity' of an observer, that is, the limitation imposed on its ability to process information from the variety of environmental stimuli, averages approximately 2.6 bits. This threshold is also believed to mark the boundary between the variety that the system can retain (i.e., remember) and that which it begins to discard (i.e., forget). On this topic, see Miller's (1956) seminal contribution.

[12] Luhmann (2011, p. 161). Lübbe (1994, p. 191ff.) similarly speaks of 'preception' (*Präzeption*), i.e., the present anticipation of the future reception of the past.

[13] The available past "should be impregnable" (Bowker 2005, p. 7). Not everything said in a meeting is recorded, nor is everything that happens during a scientific experiment, on board a ship, or in a hospital written down or measured for future reference. Cf. also Daston (2017b, p. 329): "The archive is the physical expression of how present science creates a usable past for future science".

Geoffrey Bowker refers to this as *memory practices*. The system does not passively allow events to dictate what is worth remembering; rather, it selects in a pre-categorised manner what might be useful in the future. This means implementing "proactive forgetting"[14]: the system retains a highly selective record of events, discarding almost everything except the small fraction that might be useful again. This has a relieving effect: not only does the system selectively register what deserves attention, but it also prevents time from being wasted later on dealing with irrelevant material.[15] Memory practices, therefore, do not merely function as *tools for remembering* but also as *tools for forgetting*.[16] Indexing systems are, precisely in this sense, forgetting tools whose remarkable success should be understood as a result of socio-cultural evolution.

2.2 Indexing between Historical Continuity and Discontinuity

Many historians have explained the development of indexing techniques as a consequence of the printing industry. Others, however, have pointed out that the habit of indexing books was already widespread in late-medieval manuscript culture. Because both perspectives are valid, scholars investigating the development of indexing systems face an apparent contradiction, which remains an unresolved question for historians.

Those who argue for the modernity of indexing techniques point out that it was only about a century after the invention of the printing press that the alphabetical subject index became the norm. In the Middle Ages, educated readers preferred to compile concordances. Moreover, indexed works were generally a minority, and there is often a sense that their compilation was carried out with a certain degree of carelessness (Witty 1965, p. 141ff. and 144ff.; 1973, p. 193ff.; Rabnett 1982, p. 100f.). Finally, only the high standardisation of printed books could justify the effort required for meticulous and painstaking indexing.

[14] A concept drawn from Bowker and Star (1999, p. 257).

[15] Time and attention are resources whose scarcity depends on the amount of information that the system must deal with. Cf. Simon (1956, p. 129ff.; 1971, p. 40ff.; 1997, p. 4f.).

[16] Cf. Bowker and Star (1999, p. 277 and 280): "Classification systems [...] operate as tools of forgetting".

This judgement is based on the technical characteristics of printed books and takes as a benchmark something that could not have been a choice for late-medieval readers. Hence, the weakness of the standardisation argument (Eisenstein 1979, p. 88ff.; Ong 1986a, p. 177). Historical research has shown that late-medieval scholars, mostly working in monastic and university milieus, experimented with sophisticated text-sorting techniques to produce indexes and concordances that did not rely on pagination and could not benefit from the mechanical reproduction of books, yet were no less effective than the indexes of printed books. These techniques were themselves the result of a certain standardisation of textual material, which allowed for unambiguous and fairly generalised cross-references, especially when dealing with canonical texts. All this suggests that indexes in printed texts had a long tradition behind them (Wellisch 1986, p. 76; 1994, p. 3).

The contradiction arising from the historical evidence is not resolved but can be partially explained if one adopts a socio-evolutionary approach (Cevolini 2014). Evolution always combines *continuity* and *discontinuity* simultaneously. This simultaneity must be kept in mind when considering whether evolutionary novelties arise gradually, through an uninterrupted succession of small changes, or abruptly, in leaps and bounds (Eldredge and Gould 1972, p. 82ff. and 109ff.; Gould 1989, p. 121ff.). Since every evolutionary advance implies both continuity (what evolves must persist as before, since only what continues to exist can also evolve) and discontinuity (what evolves must not continue to exist as before, otherwise there would be no structural change), it follows that every evolutionary novelty arises both gradually and suddenly (Luhmann 1997a, p. 505).

Evolutionary novelty is, indeed, one of the most challenging problems in evolutionary theory (Bock 1959, p. 194). The issue primarily concerns the explanation of so-called 'incipient structures', i.e., those rudimentary structures which, in the early stages of their development, cannot yet perform the function for which they are destined once fully developed (5% of a wing cannot fly).

Darwin argued that structures within an organism can either be used or fall into disuse. While overuse leads to hypertrophy, prolonged disuse may result in atrophy: the organ becomes increasingly rudimentary and may eventually be lost.[17] However, not all structures that fall into disuse

[17] Cf. Darwin (1952, Ch. 14, p. 225ff.) on the basis of Lamarck (1809, Ch. 7, p. 218ff., esp. p. 235ff.). For Lamarck, it was crucial that the change in conditions

are eliminated; some can be repurposed to perform a new function (as in the case of the penguin's atrophied wing, which has adapted as a flipper). Evolution thus exploits the fact that the same structure can perform multiple functions, just as the same function can be performed by different structures (Darwin 1952, Ch. 6, esp. p. 87f.).

During the prolonged period of latent preparation that precedes the emergence of an evolutionary novelty, a given structure primarily performs one function while serving another only secondarily. Structural change occurs when a previously secondary function becomes primary, while the former primary function regresses, gradually becoming secondary or disappearing altogether. The structure is thus *co-opted* to perform a function for which it was not originally designed. In this sense, a new structure is usually an old structure co-opted to fulfil a new function.[18]

The fact that evolution takes advantage of the multifunctionality of certain structures, albeit at a later stage (Darwin 1952, Ch. 6, p. 88; Ch. 14, p. 227), compels the theory to abandon the notion that evolutionary advancements follow a blueprint, that is, that they are goal-directed. On the other hand, it leaves open the question of the conditions under which a structure is co-opted for a new function. The hypothesis is that this occurs when the system strives to maintain its adaptation under conditions of increasing complexity. The next section explores this hypothesis in greater detail.

2.3 Morphogenesis of Complexity

The concept of complexity is not easy to define. Following a suggestion from cybernetics, social systems theory adopts the distinction between elements and relations (Klaus and Liebscher 1969, p. 307; Luhmann 1984, p. 45ff.). A system experiences complexity when it recognises that not all available elements can be interconnected, nor in every

requiring an adjustment of the system's action (or inaction) is not merely temporary but potentially permanent. Action (or inaction) must, in other words, become a habit. Time was, therefore, a crucial factor. See also Cope (1896, esp. p. 352ff.).

[18] Cf. Gould (1985, esp. p. 236; 2003, p. 1537ff.); Gould and Vrba (2008, p. 36ff.). On the principle of functional change, see the valuable contribution of Dohrn (1875, p. 60ff.). Cf. also Bock (1959, esp. p. 201 and 208f.); Mayr (1960, p. 360ff. and 377); Pievani (2009, p. 139ff.). For the use of these concepts in social systems theory, see Luhmann (1997a, p. 505ff. and 511).

possible way.[19] Compared to what the system can effectively do, there is, therefore, an excess of possibilities that remain unactualised.[20]

When considering the relationships that can link elements, the system is confronted with the difference between full connectedness and selective connectedness. These two sides of the same distinction are mutually implicated: any actual connection appears selective against the backdrop of a theoretically complete connectedness, while the very idea of complete connectedness emerges only in contrast to the selectivity of actual connections. In this sense, complexity is a "closed schema", as Luhmann (1976, col. 940; 2005b, p. 62) puts it.

The crucial point is that the distinction between complete connectedness and selective connectedness exists as a unity *within* the system, even though it affects systemic operations as a difference. As complexity increases, the system does not simply expand its structures but instead implements more selective structuring (Luhmann 1992b, col. 377f.; 2005a, esp. p. 258 and 268). This is where complexity theory meets evolutionary theory.

A long-standing thesis, which still finds supporters today, posits that evolutionary development tends towards increasing complexity. Evolution is assumed to progress from homogeneity to heterogeneity, from undifferentiated to differentiated states, and from uniform to multiform systems. In any case, the trajectory of change is always regarded as being "towards greater complexity".[21] Darwin (1952, Ch. 4, esp. p. 60ff.; Ch. 11, p. 176), however, had already challenged this thesis: both simple and complex forms can arise as outcomes of the evolutionary process, provided they maintain adaptation to their respective environmental conditions. Moreover, evolution does not follow a direction—neither in terms of an "upgrading adaptiveness" (Maturana and Varela 1999, p. 98ff.

[19] Gottinger (1983, p. 12) distinguishes, in this regard, a *structural* complexity (that of elements) from a *computational* complexity (that of relations).

[20] As the number of elements increases, the configurations of relations between these elements increase exponentially. Cf. Luhmann (1980, col. 1064; 1992a, p. 794; 2005a, p. 257). Cf. also Levins (1973, esp. p. 113 and 118): a system of 100 elements that can have two states is confronted with 10^{30} different configurations.

[21] Cf. Spencer (1898, p. 352; 1937, § 116, p. 295). This simplified description of evolutionary development has been widely accepted in the social sciences. Cf. Freeman and Winch (1957, p. 462ff.); Pringle (1951, p. 175f.); Heylighen (1999, p. 25ff.).

and 109), nor in terms of increasing complexity.[22] From the perspective of the conservation of adaptation, one could argued that simplicity and complexity are functionally equivalents, and that evolution has no reason to favour one over the other.

However, this does not rule out the possibility that evolution may, in some way, engage with complexity. It would not be reasonable for evolution to discard its achievements and start all over again. Every evolutionary advance entails a transition from one form of organisation to another,[23] thereby enabling the system to build upon prior developments in order to structurally manage greater complexity (Gould 1994, p. 86ff.). It is therefore inevitable that an increase in complexity will be observed in the course of evolution, even if such an increase is not the purpose of evolutionary change.

The main hypothesis is that the complexity attained over the course of evolution determines the form in which problems arise, for which different solutions can be considered functionally equivalent (Luhmann 1997a, p. 508). Even when different solutions fulfil the same function (such as the rhetorical storehouse and the archive, both serving the purpose of forgetting), one may prove more advantageous than the other in terms of complexity. Evolution, therefore, not only tests the suitability of various solutions to a given problem but also evaluates their respective benefits (Luhmann 1997a, p. 506).

In abstract terms, the primary advantage of evolutionary novelty is not merely that it *increases complexity*, but rather that it *increases reducible complexity* (Luhmann 1997a, p. 507). More precisely, the purpose is not to simplify an ever-greater complexity, but to increase the complexity that the system can manage through its own selective performances. Underlying this achievement is the amplification of deviation.

Every evolutionary advancement originates in a deviation, that is, the emergence of a difference from previous conditions. This deviation does

[22] According to Radcliffe-Brown (1947, p. 80), the idea of evolution "is a neutral scientific concept and does not imply movement in a desirable direction". Cf. also Luhmann (1997a, esp. p. 447).

[23] In this regard, Stebbins (1969, p. 109ff. and 124ff.) speaks of "conservation of organisation".

not go unnoticed[24] and compels the system to choose between reinforcement and removal. In the first case, the system 'activates' the structural change that leads to the realisation of an evolutionary novelty. In the second case, the system 'inhibits' this change. Evolutionary theory refers to these processes as *morphostatic* and *morphogenetic*.[25] They always affect the system's structures, as elements themselves do not persist long enough (precisely because they do not endure) to undergo change.

Whereas morphostatic processes involve the static preservation of given structures and a dynamic resistance to structural change, morphogenetic processes bring about modifications to pre-existing structures through the very operations that the pre-structured system continues to reproduce. The catalyst for this change is complexity. The structural changes underpinning the emergence of evolutionary novelties not only enable the system to cope with increasing complexity but also to generate greater complexity (Luhmann 1992a, p. 795). Evolution is thus the result of a "morphogenesis of complexity" (Luhmann 1997a, p. 415). The relationship between complexity and evolution, however, is not one of cause and effect. Increasing complexity is both a pre-condition and an outcome of evolution, without being the cause or the goal of the structural changes that drive evolutionary advancement. Building on these theoretical assumptions and the available historical evidence, it is now possible to explain indexing as an evolutionary achievement.

2.4 Facilitas Inveniendi

Between the 12th and 13th centuries, scholars experimented with various technical devices to facilitate the retrieval of topics to be used as subjects for communication. In the language of the time, these tools were often referred to with phrases such as *statim invenire* (to find quickly), *facilitas inveniendi* (ease of finding), *presto et sine labore habere* (to find quickly

[24] When it is argued that variations are 'blind' or 'unjustified', what is meant is simply that the system does not know how it will end up. Cf. Campbell (1960, p. 380ff.; 1969a, p. 73f.; 1969b, p. 207f.); Luhmann (2011, p. 351 fn. 58).

[25] Literature on this distinction is extensive. Cf. Maruyama (1960; 1963a); Buckley (1976, p. 72ff. and 77ff.); Gierer and Meinhardt (1972); Luhmann (1984, p. 480f.).

and effortlessly).[26] Some of the most frequently used techniques included organising text layout, compiling concordances, arranging subject matter alphabetically, numbering pages, and constructing inverted indexes.

Historical research has traced the origins of these innovations to the intellectual activity of mendicant orders and the early European academic institutions (Rouse 1976, p. 124f.). For the scholars of the time, these innovations were either entirely new techniques or adaptations of older methods to new situations (Rouse 1976, p. 131; 1977, p. 115ff.; Rouse and Rouse 1979, p. 42ff.). Compelling historical evidence suggests that the development of these tools began in the mid-twelfth century but truly 'took off' in the thirteenth century. Recent studies, however, have shown that many tools were used much earlier in legal texts, cartularies and account books. This finding tempers the impression that these tools emerged *ex nihilo* in response to an increasingly complex written culture and supports the hypothesis of an incremental adaptation through successive technical expedients and refinements.[27]

A fundamental innovation was the division of texts into parts. Based on the principle that what is divided is easier to find, the layout of manuscripts was structured to clearly identify their constituent sections. This initial phase of *ordinatio* was then followed by the so-called *compilatio*—the drafting of concordances and florilegia, in which the compilers' skill was not measured by their ability to produce original content (since the entire manuscript consisted of excerpts from existing works) but rather by their capacity to organise contents in a way that facilitated their reuse.[28]

[26] Cf. Rouse and Rouse (1982a, p. 202ff., esp. p. 207); Parkes (2008, p. 66); Kosto (2016, esp. p. 290ff.). Rouse (1977, p. 133), and Rouse and Rouse (1979, p. 40) point out that the use of these tools was often justified in terms of utility (e.g., "ad utilitatem predicandi", "utilem et salutarem scientiam apprehenderis"). This is evidence that the perception of inherent advantages was strong.

[27] Cf. Kosto (2016). Rouse and Rouse (1982a, p. 206) argue that many of these devices were not new; rather, what was new was their systematic and increasingly sophisticated use during the thirteenth century. The paragraph mark itself had, according to Rouse and Rouse (1979, p. 30), been "co-opted" (sic) between 1180 and 1200 to perform a new function—that of distinguishing the sections of a text. To achieve this, the mark was moved from the margin to within the columned text and was adapted in shape and colour to enhance its visibility.

[28] See the seminal studies of Parkes (1976; 2008).

To aid in *ordinatio,* readers could also resort to sophisticated systems of conventional symbols placed in the margins of the text to help locate specific topics (such as 'Trinity' and 'Original Sin' in theological writings). The use of these mnemotechnical devices had already been codified by Quintilian by the end of the first century AD. Quintilian encouraged the use of marginal *notae* as veritable 'active images' (*imagines agentes*), which orators could store in their rhetorical storehouse (*thesaurus*) to recall the topic they were meant to talk about (as the image of an anchor recalls the topic of navigation).[29]

It is not clear how Quintilian's use of *notae* as marginal signs related to his use of *notae* as active images. Most likely, these *notae* were designed to perform both functions simultaneously. Technically, the use of marginal signs facilitated the retrieval of topics, which could then be memorised through the same signs employed as active images. In this way, educated readers could construct their own "mental filing system" (Carruthers 2008, p. 136).

Medieval scholars, however, took Quintilian literally and used marginal *notae* to compile concordances—often referred to as *tabulae*—which functioned as inverted indexes. The benefit was evident: the reader did not have to go through the text from cover to cover. Marginal *notae* could be used to create a kind of "running index" (Blair 2000, p. 72) that provided highly selective access to the content of the manuscript.

A well-known example is the *Tabula* compiled by the Franciscan Robert Grosseteste between 1230 and 1235. This table contains nine general themes of theology (*distinctiones*), which are in turn divided into subjects, each accompanied by its own conventional sign (*nota*). Altogether, the table contains 400 subjects. While the first pages of the *Tabula* simply present the preliminary list of subjects that Grosseteste intended to use to compile his personal 'filing system', along with their respective *notae*, the subsequent pages contain the concordance proper. Here, arranged in a fairly orderly manner next to the marginal sign and subject heading, are the *lemmata* of the works that Grosseteste and his collaborators read and 'recorded'.

[29] Cf. Carruthers (2008, p. 135f.) with reference to Quintilian (*Inst. orat.*, XI, 2, 29). To prove the effectiveness of this method, Quintilian (*Inst. orat.*, XI, 2, 22) observed that with only 12 zodiacal signs, Metrodorus was able to memorise as many as 360 commonplaces.

Although no one knowns exactly how Grosseteste carried out this work, it is reasonable to assume that he first compiled the list of subjects and then devised a suitable *signum* for each of them (e.g., a triangle for the 'Trinity of God', a dot for the 'Unity of God', and so on). Once committed almost to memory, these signs were apparently placed in the margins of the texts scrutinised by Grosseteste and his collaborators to create the kind of running index that would later be used to record the cross-references (usually the number of book and chapter) that make up the entries of the *Tabula*. Since the final concordance appears particularly orderly and polished, it is likely that the *lemmata* were first recorded on index cards (which medieval scholars termed *cedulae* or *schedulae*) before being transcribed into the *Tabula*.

It is not easy to determine what Grosseteste intended to achieve with his *Tabula*, which remained unfinished. What is certain, however, is that the structure of the subjects had been determined in advance. This structure is hierarchical and closed, so it was not designed to be expanded at will.[30] Such closedness encourages, if not compels, reiteration. The commonplaces into which the main themes (the *distinctiones*) are divided are not arranged in alphabetical order, as a modern compiler might do, but rather in topical or hierarchical order, as was the custom of medieval learned men.[31] This does not preclude the possibility that the *Tabula* could also be used as a 'filing system'. However, it is more likely that this function remained secondary to its primary purpose as a memory aid.[32]

These few insights alone illustrate the sophistication of the knowledge organisation techniques developed by educated readers in the late Middle Ages. Nevertheless, it would be reductive to describe the long transition from the late Middle Ages to the early-modern period merely as a narrative of continuity, in which existing technical devices were simply adapted and improved. Historically, tracing the precise origins of an evolutionary

[30] The structure begins with God (first distinction), moves on to the Word (second distinction) and descends from there to creatures (third distinction), the Church (fourth distinction), and Holy Scripture (fifth distinction). Finally, beneath the creatures are the vices (sixth and seventh distinctions), certain properties of the physical world surrounding man (eighth distinction), the soul and its virtues (ninth distinction).

[31] Note that the memorisation of 400 places from 9 distinctions approximately corresponds to Metrodorus' mnemonic performance (360 places from 12 distinctions) mentioned by Quintilian.

[32] More extensively on Grosseteste's *Tabula*, see Cevolini (2017c). Duncan (2022, p. 75) argues that the *Tabula* was "the search engine of the thirteenth century".

advancement is always challenging. Innovations cannot be pinpointed through clear-cut breaks that definitively separate a 'before' from an 'after'. Continuity must be considered alongside discontinuity—namely, structural change driven by a functional transformation of pre-existing structures which had previously performed different functions. One way to grasp the complexity of this transition is to examine the ambiguous attitude of medieval scholars towards alphabetical order.

2.5 Alphabetical Order

According to a widespread opinion in cultural history, the alphabetical ordering of knowledge is a distinctive feature of the modern age, and particularly a consequence of the printing press. As we have seen, medieval scholars preferred to arrange subject matter in a way that mirrored the familiar order of Creation. Such an arrangement underpinned reminiscence. For this reason, placing 'Angel' before 'God' simply because the letter 'a' precedes the letter 'g' in the alphabet would have been counterintuitive for the medieval mind (Rouse 1976, p. 131). Similarly, scholars preferred to place 'Adam' before 'Abel', as Adam was the first man created by God.

Historical research has shown, however, that as early as the late Middle Ages, particularly from the mid-thirteenth century onwards, scholars experimented with alphabetical order both in the compilation of indexes and in the arrangement of subjects in encyclopaedias.[33] By the early fourteenth century, alphabetical indexes had even become a fairly common paratextual tool, at least in major university towns.[34] Yet, the success of alphabetical ordering can be traced even earlier, as demonstrated by the *Flores paradysi* of Villers (c. 1216–1230), which provides evidence of learned experimentation with alphabetical indexes in the first half of the thirteenth century.[35]

33 Cf. Rouse (1977, p. 115); Rouse and Rouse (1979, p. 4). For Rouse and Rouse (1990, p. 228), one would underestimate the inventiveness of medieval scholars if one believed that the alphabetical index was merely a product of typographic culture.

34 In these towns, the production of manuscripts was more intense and therefore also highly specialised. Cf. Rouse and Rouse (1990, esp. p. 219).

35 In the second part of the prologue, the compiler of this florilegium explains that he has included an alphabetical index to facilitate access to the contents. The advantage is that

The presence of alphabetical indexes in medieval books, however, does not imply that their use was widespread. On the contrary, the fact that compilers often felt the need to justify their inclusion suggests that the index was still a technical device that could not be taken for granted. When Vincent de Beauvais, for example, prepared an alphabetical subject index for his *Speculum historiale* (c. 1247), he deemed it necessary to explain its function—namely, that the index facilitated topic retrieval by allowing readers to browse entries arranged in alphabetical order—thus legitimising a technical tool that might otherwise have seemed incomprehensible.

That de Beauvais was nonetheless convinced of the utility of this tool is evident from his final exhortation to readers not to give up if they did not immediately find the passage they were seeking.[36] The indexing work of de Beauvais was not an isolated case. Around the same time, Albertus Magnus concluded his treatise on animals by appending an alphabetical index of noteworthy topics. Yet, like de Beauvais, he too felt compelled to justify a tool that might have been dismissed as a non-scientific manner (*modus non philosophicus*) of accessing knowledge, even though it had the great advantage of ensuring a rapid retrieval of subject matter (*facilitas doctrinae*) according to the reader's specific information need.[37]

The embarrassment betrayed by these justifications stems from the fact that every evolutionary advance originates from a deviation. Evolution, in fact, explains how the improbability of a change occurring at a given point can turn into the probability of it maintaining itself (Maruyama 1963b, p. 256A; 1976, p. 203). A technical innovation can be tested in isolation and with some hesitation until, for some reason that needs to be explained, it begins to be widely adopted, triggering profound changes that would have been highly improbable under the initial conditions. And since evolution never starts from scratch but is a cumulative process that builds upon previous achievements to experiment with new variations,

the reader will be able to effortlessly make use of what the compiler has so painstakingly gathered. The prologue can be found in Rouse and Rouse (1979, pp. 231–235).

[36] Cf. Brincken (1972, p. 901ff.). In 1320, Jean de Hautfuney compiled a new alphabetical index of the *Speculum historiale*, adding references to the location of topics within each chapter by means of a vertical division of the text into sections marked with letters (from A to G). Cf. Weijers (1995, p. 20f.).

[37] Albertus Magnus (1519, Book XXIII, p. 184r). On this work, see Meyer (1991, esp. p. 322).

the improbabilities that become probable tend to increase as evolution progresses (Luhmann 1984, p. 485ff.; 1997a, p. 413f.).

Within this theoretical framework, the distinction between *natural* and *artificial* could also be reinterpreted. This distinction does not merely concern what is characteristic of technical innovations. Alphabetical order is undoubtedly as artificial as the alphabetic writing that makes it plausible, even if, at some point, its use may become so stabilised that it appears as a natural fact. What is striking about evolutionary novelties—and initially somewhat puzzling—is their improbability. It is in the face of this improbability that a certain hesitation among contemporaries is entirely understandable. Moreover, the more improbable the preconditions for an evolutionary novelty, the stronger the impression that it is something 'artificial', and the greater the resistance to its adoption, despite the advantages it offers over available alternatives.

And conversely, when the sense of artificiality fades and what was previously unacceptable (or barely acceptable) comes to be taken for granted, evolutionary novelty can be said to have stabilised. This is perhaps the only trend in evolution that can be conceded: making the improbable probable. But this trend cannot be interpreted as a goal-directed process—it is too unlikely that evolution knows in advance what improbabilities it will have to address.

Late-medieval scholars exploited the advantages of alphabetical order not only to create inverted indexes but also to incorporate the indexing structure into the encyclopaedic work itself. The abstract order of the alphabet thus became the order of the subjects, sparing the compiler the burden of duplicating the organisational structures with which the reader had to engage (along with all the resulting complications and perplexities). This possibility gave rise to numerous collections of exemplary tales and florilegia, which for medieval scholars functioned as a kind of 'duplicate' of their personal memory. Their widespread diffusion, particularly between the 12th and 14th centuries, was largely due to the work of preachers.

Thomas of Ireland's *Manipulus florum* (c. 1306), for example, consisted of 266 topics arranged in alphabetical order, each containing memorable passages that Thomas had extracted from his readings. Historical research has shown that the *Manipulus* contains approximately 6000 entries—a number clearly daunting even for a well-trained memory. This suggests that the florilegium was conceived from the outset as a kind of large-scale archive, intended to refresh personal memory and to provide material for the occasional composition of new sermons (Rouse and Rouse 1979, esp. p. ix).

An anthology such as the *Manipulus* was obviously not designed to be read sequentially from cover to cover, but rather to be consulted in a cross-cutting manner. If a preacher needed to talk about the love of Christ, he could draft his sermon by consulting the first and last entries in this repository (Christ was abbreviated as 'Χρς'). The alphabetical arrangement of the subject matter was nothing more than an ingenious and particularly efficient means of organising information access.[38] Since the anthology itself was the result of a selection from a given library,[39] its search tools functioned as a form of second-order selection.

To perform the same function, highly modern technical tools were introduced, such as *cross-references* pointing to similar or related topics located elsewhere under different entries. In this regard, alphabetical recording proved particularly effective, as it made it possible to identify each excerpt with absolute certainty (when the number exceeded 23, the letters of the alphabet were doubled: aa. was the 24th excerpt, ab. the 25th, and so on). Cross-references not only addressed the problem of *multiple storage*—since the same excerpts, relevant to different subjects, would otherwise have to be copied multiple times—but also provided the repository with a self-referential closure, which, in turn, could enhance the complexity of search results.[40]

Such a structure encouraged a combinatorial rather than a sequential reading of the anthology's contents[41] and, as has been noted, represented the state of the art of the technical tools devised for information

[38] Rouse and Rouse (1979, p. 3f.) describe the *Manipulus* as a "research tool" designed "to gain access, to locate, to retrieve information".

[39] Thomas of Ireland explicitly acknowledges this selectivity in his preface: no one has the time required to sift through the "mare magnum" of authors, so it is preferable to "have at hand" (*promptu habere*) the finest sentences of the wisest men. In this way, one avoids wasting time reading what is superfluous. Among the various editions available, see Thomas of Ireland (1494, p. aiir).

[40] Cf. Thomas of Ireland (1494, p. aiiv). The topic 'Studium', for example, contains 34 quotations from various authors, including Augustine of Hippo, Gregory, Isidore of Seville, and Hugh of St. Victor. At the end, it refers to several related topics such as 'Curiositas', 'Doctrina', 'Labor', 'Ingenium', 'Sapientia', 'Sobrietas'. The cross-reference to 'Sapientia', in turn, contains the records h., i., ag., ak., which point to specific excerpts listed alphabetically under the entry 'Sapientia'.

[41] Moss (2002, p. 81) speaks, less accurately, of "oblique thinking".

processing at the time.[42] However, late-medieval scholars maintained an ambivalent attitude towards alphabetical organisation: while they recognised its effectiveness as a device for accessing knowledge, they also saw it as a threat to the memorisation of knowledge. Compared to topical and hierarchical orders, alphabetical order was inherently subversive, and those who adopted it were perceived as "abdicating" their responsibility to structure their texts in accordance with the logical and rational order designed by the Creator (Rouse 1977, p. 134; Rouse and Rouse 1979, p. 34f.; 1982a, p. 211; 1982b, p. 80; Martin and Vezin 1990, p. 463; Clanchy 1993, p. 181).

However, when the problem of knowledge organisation is examined from the perspective of social memory, a form of *functional competition* emerges. On one hand, alphabetical order was recognised as an efficient tool for facilitating the occasional retrieval of relevant content based on user instructions. On the other hand, it was also acknowledged that this technical device encouraged forgetfulness. Those who consulted the *Manipulus* could selectively retrieve the most relevant excerpts while disregarding everything else, and the material selected to prepare a sermon, once used, could be forgotten without being lost.

Underlying the competition between a topical-hierarchical order and an alphabetical order was the issue of functional primacy. The *ordo rerum* mirrored the structure of Creation and served as an excellent memory aid for recalling the contents the orator sought to retain. Conversely, the *facilitas inveniendi* fostered a peculiar relationship between the user and external knowledge containers which could, in principle, function as personal archives or filing cabinets. This relationship underpinned a selective reproduction of information.[43] For this reason, alphabetical registers were often employed for mundane realities, such as stones or animals—that is, things that were not deemed worth the effort of committing to memory.

Although these two functions were in competition, they were not mutually exclusive. Rather, they could be performed simultaneously by the same structure, albeit with one being the primary and the other the secondary function respectively. And historical research, as we have seen,

[42] Moss (2002, p. 77ff.), with reference to Rouse and Rouse's (1979) research.

[43] On this opposition between *ordo rerum* and *facilitas inveniendi*, see the valuable contribution of Meyer (1991), who explicitly suggests a functionalist approach, albeit without resorting to any theory of function.

supports the hypothesis that the *facilitas inveniendi* remained subordinate to the need for mnemonic assimilation of knowledge until the early-modern period.

Multifunctionality was sometimes achieved by integrating topical and alphabetical orders within the same anthology, demonstrating that the advantages of competing solutions are usually tested in transitional stages. In Pietro Capuano's *Alphabetum in artem sermocinandi*, for example, written between the late 12th and early 13th centuries, the entries are arranged, as the title suggests, in alphabetical order, but each commonplace is then internally organised in topical and hierarchical order, progressing from subjects concerning God, angels and the heavens to those concerning man, animals and the earth, and finally to those concerning the abyss (Rouse and Rouse 1982a, p. 219f.; Weijers 1995, p. 14).

It is evident, however, that the innovative potential of alphabetical order remained largely unexplored in the Middle Ages. Moreover, the mere presence of a deviation does not, in itself, suffice to trigger a morphogenetic change. Technical innovations, in such cases, remain confined to marginal use. In this instance, the inhibition can be attributed to medieval scholars' preference for mnemotechnical aids. Learned men were certainly not lacking in ingenuity and intellectual capacity. But their approach to knowledge was primarily one of memory-based assimilation, aimed at making scholars 'autonomous', that is, independent of external aids. The alphabet itself could be employed as a mnemonic hook to recall subjects, following the principles of the art of reminiscence. Individual letters could be transformed into active images which, when manipulated correctly, could re-actualise what had been forgotten.[44]

Under these conditions, it is clear that a topical and hierarchical order was, as Olga Weijers (1995, p. 13) argues, "more suitable for memorisation" than the more mechanical use of alphabetical order. The latter was ultimately too abstract and better suited to functioning as a kind of search engine for navigating extensive and, for that very reason, rather opaque encyclopaedic collections.[45] However, the idea of transforming

[44] This method dates back to Aristotle (*De mem. et rem.*, 2, 452a17ff.) and is often repeated in manuals on the art of memory up to early modernity (see, among many others, Dolce 2001).

[45] Duncan (2022, p. 28) argues that to accept alphabetical ordering required a *leap into arbitrariness*. I would rather argue that it required a *leap into (higher) abstractness*.

these collections into secondary memories was still too unconventional for a culture like the medieval one, burdened by the need to preserve the past through the assiduous training of personal memory.[46]

Ultimately, it could be said that alphabetical order was adopted rather reluctantly in the late Middle Ages and never truly became the norm.[47] It is telling, in this respect, that medieval scholars, when compiling an alphabetical index, did not feel compelled to adhere to strict alphabetical sequencing: they were still guided by hierarchical criteria (e.g., *pater* before *filius*), or by oral pronunciation instead of written spelling (*homo* was placed under the letter 'o' because the letter 'h' is silent in pronunciation) (Pellegrini 1995, p. 137).

This should not, however, be interpreted as a lack of rigour in the compilation of indexes. The late-medieval scholars' approach to alphabetical order may appear inconsistent only from the perspective of a modern literary culture that has fully internalised the advantages of typographic technology. That of the late-medieval man, in other words, was not a form of incoherence but rather a coherence of a different kind.

It was only in the course of the early-modern period that alphabetical order was fully normalised—a slow and laborious process, as evidenced by the fact that those who adopted it continued to justify their choice.[48] It was not until the mid-seventeenth century that alphabetical arrangement was systematically applied to the subject matter of encyclopaedic works and introduced, albeit from a historically distorted perspective, as a technical innovation.[49] Yet, involutionary resistance to this knowledge management system persisted well into the first half of the seventeenth

[46] Historical research has shown that, between the 13th and 14th centuries, collections of exemplary tales arranged topically were numerous, while those arranged alphabetically were rare. Cf. Welter (1927, p. 214ff. and 290ff.).

[47] Rouse and Rouse (1982a, p. 211f.). For the Rouses, this is evidence that alphabetical order was the manifestation of a "different way of thinking" (p. 212). One might even say of a "different way of remembering and forgetting".

[48] Robert Cawdrey, author of the first monolingual English dictionary, still found it necessary to explain to readers how to use alphabetical order and what its benefits were. He apparently assumed that this order was still unfamiliar to them. Cf. Cawdrey (1604, To the Reader, fol. A4v).

[49] Cf. Moreri (1683, Preface, s.n. sed ê4r): the author hopes that the reader will appreciate his historical encyclopaedia not so much for its content, which is by no means original, but rather for "la nouveauté de sa methode & de son ordre" (the novelty of its method and organisation).

century, and it was not until the second half of the eighteenth century that arguments in favour of its plausibility began to prevail.

A case in point is the monumental collection of excerpts that Theodor Zwinger had inherited from Conrad Lycosthenes, later expanded and published in 1565, though not before converting Lycosthenes' original alphabetical arrangement into a synoptic order based on the Ramist method of dichotomous divisions. The problem was that for readers unfamiliar with this order, Zwinger's encyclopaedia proved challenging to consult: they would be "paralysed" by an excess of structure (Ong 1976, p. 116) and able to access the stored knowledge only by meticulously following the rules of its branching system. Such an order, in short, was only suitable for those who already knew where to look for what they sought (whatever was located at the deepest levels of its extensive ramifications could only be retrieved by scrupulously retracing the entire hierarchy of the subject matter and could only be reinforced through repetition).

Zwinger was well aware of these difficulties. He therefore appended a register which, in the third edition of the work (1586–1587), reached an exceptionally large size (an entire in-folio volume of over 200 pages, containing approximately 23,000 entries) (Zedelmaier 2007, p. 235ff.; 2008, esp. p. 120ff.). This alphabetical register allowed users to consult the encyclopaedia as if it were an archive. In other words, rather than being constrained by its internal order, users were given the freedom to access the content according to their information needs. The final order thus became the outcome, rather than the prerequisite, of the interaction between the user and the archive.

Ironically, the Belgian theologian Laurens Beyerlinck republished Zwinger's *Theatrum* in 1631, reverting the systematic order back to alphabetical. It was evident to contemporaries that such a pedantic subdivision of subject matter placed an unbearable burden on readers, who had to expend enormous mental effort merely to familiarise themselves with the encyclopaedia's internal structure before being able to look up anything.[50] Moreover, such a rigid structure was only suitable

[50] See Morhof (1747, Tome I, Book I, Ch. XXI, p. 241), who observed that "inprimis molesta est tam anxia & sollicita rerum divisio", which "distrahit […] animum et oculos inquirentis" (such an obsessive and scrupulous division of matter, which distracts the attention and gaze of the user searching for something, is first of all burdensome and annoying). Morhof then praised Beyerlinck's alphabetical order, considering it more suitable ("accommodatior"). The question, of course, is: more suitable for what?

for preserving knowledge that did not allow for expansion—precisely the opposite of what the printing industry had made possible, if not indispensable.

Despite its apparent advantages and plausibility, alphabetical order struggled to become the norm until at least the mid-eighteenth century. This is evident both in Ephraim Chambers' *Preface* to his *Cyclopaedia* (1728) and in the famous *Discours préliminaire* (1763) of the *Encyclopédie*.[51] In the latter, D'Alembert emphasised the need to distinguish between the "production" of knowledge and its "representation". The former, according to him, is inherently haphazard (those who seek knowledge proceed through trial and error throughout history), whereas the latter requires a structured organisation if knowledge is to be made useful in any way. The "encyclopaedic tree" should therefore be constructed according to a method that cannot be derived from the "genealogical tree". Otherwise, the disorder inherent in the latter risks rendering the former completely ineffective.[52]

Traces of this shift towards a more improbable organisation of knowledge can also be detected at the semantic level. In his *Discours*, D'Alembert employs a remarkable variety of concepts to address the problem of order: knowledge can be represented as a "tree", the encyclopaedia as a "system", and the contents of the sciences and the arts as a "labyrinth", in relation to which the encyclopaedia itself seeks to provide an overview, like the "map of the world" in relation to the territories that can be explored.

For the editors of the *Encyclopédie*, however, users and their (selective) information needs were paramount.[53] This is why alphabetical order was ultimately preferred. This order was clearly at odds with the encyclopaedic order inspired by Bacon's division of knowledge into disciplines derived from the faculty of memory, those derived from the faculty of reason, and those derived from the faculty of imagination. The encyclopaedic order, in turn, was only one among many possible orders, and not necessarily the

[51] Regarding the ambiguities in Ephraim Chambers' stance on systematic and alphabetical order, Yeo (2001, p. 141ff.) argues that they resulted from a "historical [re]assessment of the state of knowledge". Here, however, I explore the possibility that they were instead a consequence of a knowledge management evolution.

[52] D'Alembert (1894, p. 58f.): "Ce désordre [...] anéantirait entièrement un arbre encyclopédique dans lequel on voudrait le représenter".

[53] For D'Alembert (1894, p. 133), it was a matter of seeking the order "plus commode et plus facile pour nos lecteurs qui désirant de s'instruire sur la signification d'un mot".

best.[54] The reconciliation between a contingent order and the "prétendu désordre de la succession alphabétique" (D'Alembert 1894, p. 133) was finally achieved by pointing, at the beginning of each entry, to the discipline to which it belonged, but above all "by inserting cross-references" to establish multiple links with other articles, whether within the same discipline or across different disciplines (D'Alembert 1894, p. 72f.).

The use of cross-references was Chambers' innovation. He was aware that "the technical or alphabetical" order of the articles in his *Cyclopaedia* might seem incomprehensible to readers accustomed to exploring subjects "in their natural order of science" (Chambers 1728, vol. I, The Preface, p. i). In principle, these references were intended to help restore the natural order that the alphabetical arrangement had dismantled. In practice, however, they functioned more like hypertext references. Cross-references could establish a "connexion" not only between topics belonging to the same discipline, but also between topics spanning different disciplines. They thus opened up "a communication" across various sections of the work, creating search paths that allowed readers to move "from more to less complex, and from less to more [complex]".[55]

However, references alone were insufficient to make the encyclopaedia fully 'navigable'. This is why, in 1780, Pierre Mouchon published two volumes containing an analytical index of the *Encyclopédie*'s subjects.[56] The purpose of this index was to help readers discover numerous connections absent from the encyclopedic entries. But it was also, if not primarily, intended to satisfy readers' curiosity without requiring them "to leave" the work (Mouchon 1780, Avertissement, s.n.). This 'closure' was made possible by the circularity of the cross-references. If the index pointed to the encyclopaedia's contents, the contents in turn referred to other contents and ultimately back to the index. The resulting explorability provided the work with a degree of autonomy, while simultaneously transforming the reader into a user (in the modern sense of the word).

When evolution normalises what was previously perceived as deviant, it also gradually conceals the improbability of the innovation. The technical (i.e., artificial) expedient eventually comes to appear as a natural fact. It is

[54] Cf. D'Alembert (1894, p. 62), where the author acknowledges that "arbitrariness" reigns in every division.

[55] Chambers (1728, vol. I, The Preface, p. i). On the use of cross-references in Chambers' work, see Mamiani (1983, p. 52ff.).

[56] In keeping with classical conventions, this index was referred to as a 'table'.

only once an evolutionary advancement stabilises and the use of an innovation has become the norm that one begins to wonder how something so commonplace today could once have seemed so extravagant.[57]

The improbability underlying the normality of achievements can only be fully recognised, once again, when examined through the lens of sociocultural evolution. In the case of the alphabetical index, the hypothesis is that the invention of typography played a crucial role in legitimising a tool that had previously been employed with caution, ultimately leading to the gradual shift of a once secondary function into a primary one. This hypothesis will be explored in greater detail in the following section.

2.6 The Use of Printed Books

From its very inception, the printing business in Europe developed as an industry selling products—books—to potential buyers. Supply sought to anticipate (if not generate) demand through pricing strategies based on what the public was willing to pay. In this way, a market gradually emerged. In the light of these economic aspects, it is noteworthy that between the late 15th and early 16th centuries, printed books prominently advertised the inclusion of a "rich index", which alone was claimed to justify the price of the volume. This advertising seemingly contributed to better sales.[58] Why?

Prefaces announcing the presence of an index explicitly referenced the *facilitas inveniendi*. The latter was deemed indispensable for works that could hardly be learnt by heart, such as herbals, but also for more traditional works of general interest, including theological treatises. Fifteen years after the invention of printing, for example, Johann Fust and Peter Schoeffer (the publishers of Gutenberg's Bible) printed an edition of Augustine's *Ars predicandi*. Although the booklet comprised only 22

[57] This is what made Wheatley (1902, p. 5) wonder: "It is strange, however, to find how long the world was in coming to this very natural conclusion"—namely, that the index of a book should be alphabetical. Walter Ong was among the few to emphasise that communication technologies are always artificial, even if this artificiality becomes second nature to those who use them. Cf. Ong (1986a, p. 121ff., esp. p. 124; 1986b, esp. p. 32).

[58] Cf. Wellisch (1978, p. 81ff. and 87; 1994, p. 4 and 9). This marketing strategy was continued into the early nineteenth century. Lund (1998, p. 24ff.) has calculated that between the 18th and the 19th centuries, more than one thousand books advertised the presence of an index.

in-folio pages, the editor had compiled an extensive alphabetical index, occupying no fewer than 7 pages of the entire volume (fol. 17b to fol. 20b). As the book was not paginated, the index entries do not refer to page numbers but rather to the paragraphs into which the text had been divided and which had been ingeniously—if at first glance rather cumbersomely—marked using letters of the alphabet. Additional features included cross-references (*remissiones*) and detailed instructions guiding the reader to the relevant passages (*post principium*, i.e., after the beginning; *circa medium*, i.e., about halfway through; *versus finem*, i.e., towards the end).[59]

The zeal with which these paratextual tools were developed from the earliest years of the printing industry seems to confirm Elizabeth Eisenstein's (1979, p. 93) view that printing offered learned men and clerks new opportunities to realise old goals. Yet this does not fully explain why these goals only became a priority after the invention of printing. My hypothesis is that printing technology significantly changed readers' relationship with the book, and that it was precisely this new relationship that transformed structures of knowledge management.

The earliest printed books in Europe were well-known and widely read texts among those who could devote themselves assiduously and diligently to studies. The novelty for readers, therefore, lay not in the *text*, but in the *book*. For medieval scholars, the manuscript was not only a highly personalised object but also an essential memory aid. Printing technology, by contrast, transformed this "memorial" culture into a "documentary" one.[60] Knowledge became increasingly independent of individual consciousness, and those who wrote for print had to address an anonymous readership.

This transformation, of course, did not happen overnight. Initially, those who produced books had the techniques of the amanuensis as their only reference model. Consequently, they printed texts that not only imitated manuscripts but often even required manual completion, such as the addition of page numbers—which was necessary, among other things, to make the subject index usable.[61] Printing itself was

[59] Cf. Augustine of Hippo (1467). On the index of this booklet, see Wellisch (1986, p. 75ff.).

[60] This distinction is drawn from Carruthers (1990, p. 8).

[61] Cf. McKitterick (2003). See also Martin and Febvre (1977, esp. p. 77ff.).

regarded by contemporaries as an *ars artificialiter scribendi*, a "technique of artificial writing", as if handwriting were something natural. The paradoxical outcome was that, for the first 50 years of the printing industry, books looked like "mechanically produced manuscripts" (Barbieri 2016, p. 100). Only in the early sixteenth century did people begin to conceptualise the book as something distinct from the products of the medieval amanuensis.

Readers, who no longer had to copy books by hand but could purchase them in a highly standardised format, began to perceive the book as an autonomous "object".[62] This shift corresponded to an increasing differentiation between oral and written communication. The book was regarded less and less as a record of a conversation (Thomas Aquinas, for instance, still expounded theology through a series of oral disputes [*quaestiones*] between two opponents defending competing viewpoints) and more and more as an object from which information could be extracted.[63]

The technical refinements of printed books contributed to an increasing separation between communication designed for the eye and communication designed for the ear. This is evident even in what might seem a trivial grammatical requisite, such as punctuation. Here, too, one can speak of functional change. What was once conceived as an aid to declamation was now addressing an anonymous public of readers, who were increasingly accustomed to silent reading. Correspondingly, reading became less intensive: the reader was no longer expected to "ruminate" on the text in order to assimilate it by heart.[64] Punctuation was inserted before the text was printed and primarily performed logical-syntactic functions. It was expected to provide "clarity" by marking "distinctions" in the text, thereby facilitating the comprehension of sentence structure and meaning.[65] In typographic culture, punctuation was, in short, a *simplification-for-understanding* rather than a *simplification-for-recall*.[66]

It was not until the late 17th and early 18th centuries that the separation between orality and writing became definitive and was widely

[62] In this regard, Ong (1961, p. 156ff.) speaks of "reification" (p. 167).

[63] Ong (1986a, esp. p. 179). Luhmann (1992d, p. 39) speaks of handwritten texts as objects treated by readers "as frozen language, as aids to memory".

[64] On the distinction between *intensive* and *extensive* reading, see Hirsch (1977).

[65] Bartoli (1844, Ch. XVI, § 1, p. 146f.). On punctuation, see Cevolini (2009).

[66] This distinction is drawn from Ong (1958, p. 89).

accepted as a hallmark of civilisation. Whereas, in predominantly oral contexts, those who secluded themselves to read were perceived as asocial, in a society that had fully internalised the printing technology, this value judgement was overturned. The possibility of acquiring knowledge "in silence and solitude", as Condorcet (1989, p. 224ff., esp. p. 227) put it, came to be regarded as a safeguard not only for freedom—meaning emancipation from the constraints of face-to-face interaction—but also for the dissemination and preservation of educational resources (Eisenstein 1979, p. 132). Instead of being educated by others, it now became possible to implement a form of self-education by means of books.

The 'reification' of the book brought about by the printing industry also made it clearer that communication is an operation distinct from consciousness. Writing alone could not achieve this awareness because its use was still subordinate to oral performance. With printing, books instead became "routine means of communication" (Luhmann 1990, p. 601). As such, they referred to other books, within an increasingly standardised and self-referential universe of publications[67] that simultaneously restructured the relationship between the past (what had already been published) and the future (what stood out from existing publications and therefore had a chance of being published).

Such a differentiation between society and interaction did not restrict the possibilities of communication; rather, it multiplied them, thereby also increasing the complexity that readers had to face when engaging with knowledge. Precisely because the universe of printed texts was closed and recursive, it was infinitely open to topics which could be explored in publications. For those seeking access to knowledge, it was therefore advisable not to rely on personal contacts, but rather on meticulous bibliographical research[68] (which did not exclude the possibility of turning to a well-informed person for reading suggestions).

[67] Striking evidence of this differentiation of non-interactive communication can be found in Drexel's *lemmata* method. Readers were supposed to record only bibliographical references in their notebooks, rather than the notes themselves. This method was viable only if readers had access to a well-stocked (public or private) library of printed books—and if the notebook was used as a tool for forgetting rather than memorising the stored material, since no one would commit to memory a potentially endless list of bibliographical references.

[68] For Fabricius (1752, p. 52), those who want to become learned men in modern society cannot do without books.

Bibliography, on the other hand, also circulated in the form of publication. Since the second half of the seventeenth century, the neologism *bibliographia* was used to denote a veritable literary genre consisting of annotated guides to the available literature on a given subject.[69] Lists of books had always existed, of course, since writing had vastly increased the number of noteworthy texts. But as the volume of circulating publications grew to the point that it was no longer manageable, the need for a new kind of selection arose.[70] The abundance of books (*copia librorum*) could only be managed through information about books (*notitia librorum*). This information, in turn, was made available through publications. In this way, a kind of "secondary memory"[71] was embedded in social systems, functioning as a veritable "search engine".[72]

The growing success of print-based communication led to a slow but irreversible decline of the ancient art of reminiscence (Berns 1993, p. 67ff.). Just as all unused organs eventually atrophy, so too does the ability to remember as reliance on external media increases. In early-modern Europe, it gradually became clear that training personal memory to select content for the success of oral communication was no longer worthwhile, since it was rather the success of printed communication that determined which content was retained in social memory (Luhmann 1990, p. 157). This shift was not simply a degeneration of the *individual*'s psychic capacity to remember (Hume 1975, p. 241), but a structural change in how *society* remembered and forgot. The invention of printing ultimately established a model of memory structured in the form of an archive.[73]

69 Previously, the classical term *bibliotheca* had been used. Cf. Blum (1980, p. 19ff.).

70 For Nevizzano (1525, p. diiir), the challenge was how to prune (*resecare*) the products of the printing industry, knowing that it is difficult for an educated reader to resist the temptation to read everything available.

71 A definition by Balsamo (2000, p. 5).

72 Krämer and Zedelmaier (2014, p. 324), referring to Gessner's bibliographical encyclopaedia.

73 On this memory model, see Esposito (2001, p. 151ff.; 2002, p. 237ff.). Here, 'archive' does not refer to the institution but, more abstractly, to a model of social memory.

2.7 Coping with Intransparency

Structural changes usually bring about semantic shifts that are not always immediately recognised by contemporaries. As early-modern intellectuals became accustomed to working with filing systems, the concept of 'artificial memory' acquired a new meaning. Whereas, in rhetorical culture, it referred to a set of technical aids that orators could use to avoid relying on chance or personal talent whenever they wished to recall something, in early modernity, the same concept came to denote a 'substitute for individual memory' that the user could *irritate* to observe the machine's *reaction* (Cevolini 2006, p. 39ff.; 2017a, p. 13ff.).

The novelty of this semantic adjustment is that, whereas in rhetorical culture consciousness was placed on both sides of the distinction between natural and artificial memory, in the modern understanding of this distinction, consciousness was withdrawn to the side of natural memory, while the opposite side came to be occupied by something increasingly perceived as a black box.

An early form of this kind of knowledge archiving system were the monumental anthologies produced in the early-modern period. In both form and size, these could be consulted as if they were account books, so much so that the intellectual activity involved in their production was described by contemporaries as a form of "scholarly accounting" (Placcius 1689). Whereas medieval florilegia were conceived as promptbooks to refresh the reader's memory (Carruthers 1990, p. 16 and 174ff., esp. p. 176), early-modern collections of commonplaces instead functioned as archives through which information could be produced in a highly selective manner. This function required appropriate structural changes.

The old mnemotechnical aids designed for interaction with handwritten books were no longer sufficient. Printed books were issued for an unknown readership. It could therefore no longer be taken for granted that the reader was familiar with certain re-activation procedures, such as marginal marks or abbreviations,[74] which depended on individual imagination and were, at best, shared by a small circle of people belonging to the same socio-cultural milieu. The printed book had to be self-sufficient, and the rules for accessing its content had to be conventional enough to allow for generalised use.

[74] On the use of abbreviations in medieval texts and their gradual disappearance following the invention of printing, see Cevolini (2017b, p. 135ff.).

One of the first adjustments made to printed books was pagination. In the Middle Ages, there was not even a verb to denote this kind of book organisation. The verb *paginare* meant "to write briefly" (Du Cange 1886, p. 92), to summarise a subject in a few lines (*breviter scribere, summatim de re aliqua disserere*), and presupposed the use of *paginae*, a synonym for *schedulae*, i.e., loose sheets and temporary index cards used to take notes or prepare a concordance, as in the case of Grosseteste.[75]

The mechanisation of book production in the late 15th and early 16th centuries encouraged the experimentation and refinement of technical innovations which, while not unknown, had previously remained secondary. Some of these innovations worked particularly well in combination. When Aldo Manuzio published Giovanni Crastone's *Dictionarium graecum* (1497), for example, he saw no need to number the pages, since the dictionary's alphabetical order was sufficient for navigation. However, as the book contained an extensive alphabetical index of Latin headwords, Manuzio encouraged readers to number each leaf to facilitate the retrieval of content.[76] In this way, strange as it may seem, the book could be 'personalised' by hand, even though it was produced mechanically.

Pagination became the norm in the first decade of the sixteenth century. By the late fifteenth century, Manuzio had already introduced the numbering of individual pages (*semipaginae*) rather than leaves (*paginae*), and added continuous line numbering in the inner margin, thereby sparing the reader the effort of navigating the four columns typically present on an open folio.[77] In general, however, it seems that pagination

[75] To navigate the text, medieval scholars focused primarily on its *mise-en-page*. While page numbering was not unknown, it must have seemed of little use, as each manuscript was a highly personalised product. On page numbering, see Schmidt (1896, p. 13ff.); Martin and Febvre (1977, p. 97f.); Turner (1977, p. 75f.); Smith (1988, p. 54ff.); Vezin (1990, p. 423ff.).

[76] Cf. Manuzio (1975, vol. 1, p. 20f.): "Quo facilius quod quaeris invenire possis". On this illustrative case, see Vecce's (1998) valuable investigation. A leaf corresponded to the two pages placed side by side when the book was open, i.e., the *verso* of one page and the *recto* of the next page.

[77] See, for example, Perotti's *Cornucopia* (1499). In this case, the index was particularly indispensable, as the work consists of approximately 700 pages in folios. In the index, the page number is enclosed between two dots, followed by the number of the corresponding lines, separated by a dot. The 1513 edition of the *Cornucopia*, printed together with Terence Varro's *De lingua latina*, has an index spanning no fewer than 750 columns. In this regard, Schmidt (1896, p. 13ff.) observes that what is self-evident to us today was

was primarily introduced to facilitate indexing. Since evolution is guided by function in assessing which of the functional equivalents offers the greatest advantages, it is reasonable to suppose that publishers gradually embraced the technical expedient of page-numbers, as it allowed for a more effective implementation of the function.[78] In other words, editors and publishers did not create an index because the book was paginated; rather, they paginated the book in order to create an index.

Technical innovations of this kind increased the accessibility of the knowledge contained in books. At the same time, as printing allowed books to circulate far beyond the limitations imposed by manuscript production and use, the social visibility of knowledge increased. This visibility, however, went hand in glove with a pervasive sense of opacity. Precisely because everything was now in the public domain and no longer jealously guarded in a cupboard or library chest, modern readers often felt as if they were navigating an ocean of publications where shipwreck was a constant risk (Blair 2010). The overwhelming abundance of available knowledge created a lack of orientation that had to be compensated for in some way.

This is why contemporaries began to appreciate the benefits of indexing. For Thomas Fuller (1840, vol. 2, p. 460), for example, "an index is a necessary *implement*, and no *impediment*, of a book [...]. Without this, a large author is but a labyrinth without a clue to direct the reader therein".[79] In fact, this technical aid does not eliminate the opacity of the knowledge contained in books, but rather makes this opacity operationally manageable.

by no means so for readers of the late fifteenth century. For them, "the easiest thing [...] was the most difficult" (p. 29).

[78] Cf. also the valuable article by Smith (1988, p. 54ff.), who argues that, to understand the slow adoption of pagination, we should examine its function, i.e., the location of relevant passages within a book. Precisely for this function, there existed "rival systems" (e.g. foliation and text subdivision). I am grateful to one of the two anonymous reviewers for drawing my attention to this article.

[79] See also Leibniz (1903, p. 30ff.): without any information retrieval system, men would be like merchants who kept no account books, or like a library without a catalogue ("aut Bibliothecae quae indice caret"). Cf. Seifert (1983, esp. p. 113): the prevailing opinion among contemporaries was that those who do not know their own treasure of knowledge are as if they did not possess it—and they do not possess it precisely because they do not know it.

Opacity, on the other hand, is not an intrinsic property of a supposedly universal library but rather a user-dependent attribute. Like all repositories, the library merely stores objects that can potentially trigger communication. It is only in relation to readers with specific information needs that the repository comes to appear opaque. The meaningful connections available in the repository are invariably overwhelming compared to those the reader can actually activate. The concept of intransparency, therefore, pertains more to how an observer deals with complexity than to the design of the library itself (Luhmann 1988, p. 251ff.).

Compared to a hypothetical state of complete connectivity among all meaningful units of knowledge provided by a library, the user must necessarily rely on selective connectivity. It is precisely against the background of this selection that the excluded possibilities appear as complexity. Complete connectivity, in other words, is only the outer side of a distinction whose inner side is selective connectivity. No side exists without the counter-side. Like every distinction, also the distinction between selective and complete connectivity exists only as a two-sided distinction. The index does not function as the map of a territory; its structure is digital rather than analog. Instead, the index generates exploration possibilities that, in turn, reproduce the very complexity the user seeks to reduce through selection. The index, thus, creates a *complexity of control*—a complexity that the user can at least manage operationally.[80] It is, therefore, an indispensable tool whenever the user interacts with external memories.

2.8 Succedaneous Memory

Indexing systems were developed not only in printed books but also in those peculiar succedaneous memories that are the Renaissance commonplace-books. Here, too, a change in function went hand in glove with evolutionary advancement.

The practice of collecting excerpts in a notebook, later to be used as a hypomnematic tool, played a fundamental role in classical and medieval rhetorical culture. It was by no means a new practice when the printing

80 The distinction between *design complexity* and *control complexity* is drawn from Gottinger (1975, p. 131).

press was introduced in Europe.[81] What changed, rather, was that, in the face of a never-ending supply of new publications, each potentially containing something new and memorable, Renaissance readers designed their commonplace-books to store a theoretically unlimited expansion of knowledge.[82] Whereas, before modernity, florilegia were often the end product of a long period of study—representing, in a sense, "the contents of someone's memory" (Carruthers 2008, p. 218), even though they could serve to instruct the memory of others—, the Renaissance commonplace-book was structured from the outset to be expanded indefinitely. This implied a profound transformation in the relationship between redundancy and variety.

First, because no one can retain an unlimited amount of information. Medieval scholars were well aware of this risk: those who succumb to the urge to read too many books inevitably end up forgetting, just as the gluttonous sooner or later end up vomiting.[83] This concern was enough to justify a strong opposition to the pursuit of novelty and a corresponding preference for redundancy. Medieval scholars insisted that those who read too much ultimately learn nothing; a few well-assimilated books are far more valuable than many books read and then forgotten. That is why educated men should not chase after the infinite.[84]

This warning made sense in a culture such as the rhetorical one, where lifelong training of consciousness was indispensable to ensure the success of performances that took place primarily in oral communication. The mechanical reproduction of books, by contrast, made acceptable the once-deviant idea that forgetting—i.e., entrusting knowledge to an external memory—was more useful than exercising the art of memory.[85] This

[81] See the collection of studies edited by Morlet (2015). Drawing on these studies, Morlet concludes that the art of making excerpts is a ***universal invariant*** (p. 9). My hypothesis, instead, is that it is rather an ***evolutionary variable***.

[82] Commonplace-books became "a place for storing ***dilations*** and ***expansions*** of a theme", as Lechner (1962, p. 178) points out. See also Cevolini (2016b, p. 155ff.).

[83] Cf. Petrarch (1975, p. 90), repeating a well-known commonplace (Seneca, *Epist. ad Luc.*, 2). The primary distinction was between reading many books (***multa legendum***) and reading few books but intensively (***multum legendum***).

[84] Cf. St. Victor (1880, col. 796A): "Infinitus est librorum numerus: tu nolis sequi infinita"; Petrarch (1975, p. 102): "[…] Multitudo librorum multis ad discendum nocuit, et ex ***copia***, ut fit, ***inopia*** orta est" (italics added).

[85] When Bartoli (1845, p. 221) suggested that those "who do not have in their minds a living library collected after long-time study […] would do better to take and gather

subversion of mnemonic habits implied a different way of interacting with the notebook and, between the 16th and 17th centuries, became a pillar of education.

One source among many will suffice to illustrate this point. In an anonymous manuscript written in 1681, probably intended for scholastic use, the author responds to objections against the practice of note-taking by arguing that it is merely "common place against common places".[86] Rhetoric, the author concedes, teaches that one should nourish the mind rather than merely fill notebooks, that one should understand the subject matter rather than memorise the name of the book and the title of the chapter. Yet, if some misfortune intervenes, such as an accident or illness, one finds oneself bereft, like someone who has gone bankrupt and is finally forced to beg. Therefore, instead of relying solely on their mind, scholars should compile notebooks to serve as a substitute for personal memory. The soul, the author continues, requires these "external aids" and benefits from using them as a "succedaneous memory". To retrieve what is needed when necessary, it is sufficient to compile a separate subject index and keep it readily available at all times to make full use of one's "library".

That these instructions completely overturned Platonic concerns about the use of external supports is clear. What was new, however, was that deviation, instead of being rejected, was accepted and normalised. In the seventeenth century, those considered deviant were, if anything, those who persisted in practising the "foolish" art of memory based on the faculty of imagination.[87] In the long transitional period during which this normalisation of deviation was gradually achieved, however, the relationship with the commonplace-book remained rather ambiguous.

On the one hand, the commonplace-book was closely akin to the florilegium and fulfilled the same function as a hypomnematic aid. On the

from many dead books what they will need", thereby compiling a "forest" (*selva*) of memorable texts, he simultaneously implied that those who possess such a rich "forest" can easily dispense with the need to retain an entire library in their minds.

86 This manuscript has been published by Havens (2001). The author largely repeats what Fuller (1841, Book III, Ch. X ["Of Memory"], p. 165ff.) had already written drawing on the distinction between (psychic) *memory* and *notebooks*.

87 Cf. Drexel (1638, p. 258); Philomusus (1684, p. 3): "*Memoria puerorum est, excerpta virorum*" (Memory is childish, adults make excerpts). More extensively on this point, see Cevolini (2019a, p. 481ff.).

other hand, it was an excuse to neglect training the individual memory and instead to maintain a personal archive. For early-modern scholars, this amounted to a kind of pragmatic paradox: they claimed to store in their notebooks everything they wished to remember, yet the technical ability to retrieve everything through suitable indexing systems granted them the opportunity to forget (Cevolini 2020, esp. p. 76f.).

By the early seventeenth century, the shift in the function of commonplace-books had become self-evident. To those accustomed to using these notebooks, it was clear that they functioned as a *substitute* for, rather than an *aid* to, psychic memory.[88] For contemporaries, however, fully accepting this evolutionary advance was not straightforward. Although it offered undeniable advantages in terms of knowledge management, it still stood in apparent contradiction to long-established scholarly practices. Many traces of this hesitation can be found in sources from the time.

In an academic exercise published in 1684, for example, Andreas Stübel defined the notebook as a "secondary and subsidiary memory", thereby conflating two clearly conflicting functions.[89] The conceptual ambiguity in Stübel's definition was likely intended as a warning: readers should not see the use of external archives as an excuse to escape the effort of memorising contents while reading. At the same time, however, it hinted at an opportunity that was becoming increasingly difficult to resist. To persuade his audience, Stübel introduced a subtle ontological distinction: excerpts, he argued, are "*per se* [essentially] a memory aid" and only "*per accidens* [incidentally]" a "substitute". Thus, students should not take them as a justification for intellectual laziness.[90] The very necessity of such a clarification, however, revealed the advantages of deviation.

[88] Cf., for example, Farnaby (1659, p. 65); English translation in Nadeau (1950, p. 174): "That the mind may not be taxed by the manifold and confused reading of so many such things and in order to prevent the escape of something valuable, that we have read, heard, or discovered through the process of thinking itself, it will be very useful to entrust to notebooks, as though to a storeroom for provisions and as an aid substituted for memory, those things which seem noteworthy and striking". On this passage, see the valuable contribution of Lechner (1962, esp. p. 147f. and 170).

[89] Stübel (1684, p. 33). Note the modernity of the definition 'secondary memory'.

[90] Echoes of this distinction between a use *per se* and a use *per accidens* of excerpts are still to be found in the early eighteenth century. Cf. Sidelius and Schubart (1713, esp. p. 8).

In retrospect, one could say that socio-cultural evolution ultimately retained what Stübel had dismissed as a secondary possibility. The bewilderment of Renaissance educated readers stemmed from the fact that the *same* tool could actually fulfil two *different* functions. The commonplace-book was both a memory aid and a tool for forgetting. But, as we have seen, any functional change occurs precisely by prioritising what was once secondary to a primary function while relegating what was previously primary to a secondary role.[91] When the notebook became so densely filled with notes that it was no longer possible to remember them all, the change in function was definitive.[92]

This functional substitution affected the structure of succedaneous memory. As the notebook ceased to serve as a stimulus for personal memory and instead came to be used as a veritable archive, the index—originally designed to facilitate reminiscence—was adapted to facilitate access to the archive's content according to the user's information needs. At the same time, users could no longer rely on personal memory to retrieve information. Retrieval, therefore, had to function independently of the performance of the individual mind, without, however, excluding its collaboration.[93] In other words, even if personalised, the index had to perform its function impersonally. This is evident in the indexing system devised by John Locke and in the relatively simpler one developed by Obadiah Walker.

Locke's system consisted of an alphabetical register in which each letter was flanked by a grid containing the five vowels. Within this grid, the reader was supposed to record the page numbers where an entry could be found in the notebook. The entry itself was identified by the first letter and the first vowel of the corresponding subject heading. For instance, if the subject was *Epistle*, one should look in the index box E.i. Here, one might find the numbers 2 and 14.[94] However, a fundamental flaw in this system was that it turned the use of the index into something of a riddle.

[91] See Sect. 2.2.

[92] For Yeo (2014, p. 68), this "functional change" occurred during the seventeenth century.

[93] According to Placcius (1689, p. 111f.), those who are unsure whether they possess a divine memory should meticulously compile alphabetical indexes.

[94] On Locke's method (1686) there is a large literature. See Meynell (1993); Walker (2001, p. 114ff.); Dacome (2004); Cevolini (2006, p. 121f.); Stolberg (2014); Yeo (2020); Crupi (2021).

The numbers associated with a given alphabetical combination remained ambiguous: pages 2 and 14 might also contain entries for *Enigma* or *Evidence*. Consequently, the only way to ascertain whether *Epistle* was indeed recorded on those pages was by leafing through the notebook.

Walker's method, like Locke's, was based on the assumption that scholars would record memorable content sequentially as it emerged during reading (Walker 1673, p. 124ff. and 132). To quickly retrieve what had been excerpted, the reader had to number both the notes and the pages of the notebook. If multiple notebooks were used, each had to be marked with a letter. The index would then indicate, next to each entry, the letter of the notebook, the page number, and the number of the note containing memorable material on the subject.[95] Finally, next to each note, the reader was expected to indicate on which page in the index the corresponding subject heading could be found.

This circular numbering system had many advantages. It enabled notebooks to be consulted without losing sight of the correspondence between recorded content and the subject heading under which it was classified. It also allowed for the creation of internal cross-references based on numerical locations, thereby fostering a complexity within the archive that emerged through user selection. Finally, an indexing system such as Walker's ensured the complete autonomy of the personal archive: once the method was mastered, anyone could use it effectively.

Indexing systems such as those outlined above leave no doubt that succedaneous memories were structured to function as machines with their own self-referential closure. This closure addressed the problem of how-to-begin while simultaneously ensuring the archive's potentially unlimited openness—that is, its capacity, in principle, to accommodate any content.[96]

For early-modern scholars confronted with the possibilities of typographic technology, the use of succedaneous memories clearly offered advantages that were difficult to relinquish. However, all this occurred

[95] For example, *Virtue C.26.12* meant "If you want to find something memorable about virtue, read note number 12 on page 26 of notebook C".

[96] On this combination of closure and openness, see Cevolini (2016b). Hodannus (1713, p. 10) described the art of making excerpts as a "Methodus quasi Universalis omnium studiorum" (an almost universal method applicable to all fields of study). Similarly, Luhmann (1992c, p. 59) regarded his own card-indexing system as a "universal tool" for precisely the same reason. Cf. Cevolini (2018, esp. p. 416ff.).

within a context still dominated by rhetorical culture. This culture not only continued to be taught in schools but also shaped the technical language used to describe cognitive habits that were changing. The presence of involutionary resistance among those who rejected deviation, as well as the unintentional contradictions of those who accepted it, should therefore come as little surprise. In a sense, evolutionary advancement is often more perceptible in resistance than in retention.

Indexing systems largely rendered obsolete the habit of intensive reading, which had characterised classical and medieval intellectual activity. The index encouraged a more opportunistic approach to books. The ease of information retrieval, already valued by medieval scholars (though secondary to the mnemonic assimilation of books' content), was now criticised as an excuse to lighten the burden of reading or to avoid studying altogether (i.e., to forgo the practice of 'rumination').[97] It was therefore left to editors, convinced of the value of this new paratextual tool, to justify its usefulness.

This is what Johann Freinsheim did, for example, in presenting his monumental index to the complete works of Tacitus. Freinsheim's index entailed not only the most important reports (*res praecipuas*) but also the memorable words and expressions (*phrases et verba*) of the Roman historian, thereby combining ease of retrieval (*facilitas inveniendi*) with a kind of compendium of history, grammar and commonplaces.[98]

Freinsheim was aware that such an index could lead to a highly selective reading of history. The German historian therefore defended his tool, asserting that its purpose was not to encourage readers to neglect continuous reading of the text ("ut continua lectio negligatur"), but rather to prevent scholars from having to retain everything in memory when reading Tacitus' work in its entirety ("sed cum perlegerit, non sane exigimus ut omnia memoriter retineat") (Freinsheim 1638, fol. a4v). In other words, the availability of a *browsing system* irreversibly loosened the pre-modern cultural constraint that bound reading to memorisation

[97] Cf. Conrau-Lewis (2021, esp. p. 9ff.), with numerous references to contemporary sources. The seventeenth-century controversy surrounding *index learning* was grounded in the distinction between *memory* and the use of *reason*. It was, therefore, a controversy in its own way inherently tendentious. Cf. Glanvill (1661, p. 143).

[98] Freinsheim (1638, fol. a4r). The final result was an index comprising approximately 300 pages.

and created the conditions for a new, more information-focused way of reading.

Self-defences and justifications like Freinsheim's were not uncommon in the seventeenth century. Thomas Fuller, for instance, conceded that the index favours "a lazy kind of learning", yet cautioned against condemning it, if only because those who most despise it are often those who use it the most.[99] In a similar vein, Juan Caramuel (1664, § 3223) defended the index against the charge that it bears ignorant theologians who are relieved of the drudgery of reading the sacred texts in their entirety. The very criticisms to which these justifications responded, however, were themselves evidence of how indexing systems had come into common use, fundamentally transforming knowledge management.

Referring specifically to Freinsheim's indexing work and his conviction that indexes would render the commonplace-book superfluous, Jeremias Drexel dismissed this assumption as absurd. The German Jesuit knew from experience that when consulting other people's indexes, he rarely found, even after extensive searching, what he was looking for.[100] He therefore urged learned readers to persevere in their note-taking and to meticulously compile their own personal indexes, for "the best notes are one's own".[101] The issue, then, was not whether to *use* indexing systems, but rather how to *personalise* them. In short, Drexel's nuanced distinction confirmed an ongoing evolutionary advancement.

In the light of these reflections on a tool that baffled some and enthused others, it is striking that almost a century earlier, Conrad Gessner had addressed the same issue in a remarkably modern way. His arguments rested on two fundamental distinctions. First, Gessner

[99] Fuller (1840, vol. 2, p. 460). The Scriblerian satire on the abuses of *index learning* was, therefore, not only misdirected but also redundant. The underlying complaint was that index learning enabled the storage of unearned knowledge, thereby rendering the storage itself illegitimate. Cf. Lund (1998, esp. p. 19).

[100] However, it seems that Drexel benefited far more from printed florilegia than he was willing to acknowledge publicly. Cf. Janssen (2012, p. 389ff.). It is evident that the construction of a personal archive does not necessarily preclude the use of others' archives, provided that the sources are reliable. The decline of printed florilegia is thus due to more complex factors, which will be examined in greater detail in the next chapter. It is illustrative, however, that Drexel appears to have relied on printed florilegia for classical sources while making personal excerpts from modern books (see Janssen 2012, esp. p. 412).

[101] Drexel (1638, p. 72f.): "Notae propriae, notae optimae" (p. 73).

observed that certain books, by their very nature, are not meant to be read from cover to cover but rather consulted selectively, such as dictionaries, alphabetical catalogues, and indexes. These reference works are intended to "lighten" (*levare*) rather than "burden" (*onerare*) study.

Gessner was aware that this possibility might encourage the laziness of those who, by cunningly avoiding reading the work in its entirety, sought only the little they needed. However, he was also convinced that the misuse of the few should not overshadow the utility of the index for the many. Since life is short and the variety of studies immense (*vitae brevitas* and *studiorum varietas* were two well-established classical commonplaces), it is better to make use of indexes than to denigrate them. Their function is not only to *recall* what has been read, but also to facilitate the *discovery of something entirely new*—that is, in modern terms, to obtain information.[102]

The index could serve both functions, yet the impression is that information processing was taking precedence. To accommodate this shift, it was necessary to dismiss another fundamental principle of rhetorical culture—namely, that knowledge must be systematically organised if it is to be retrieved quickly when needed. This is the subject of the next chapter.

[102] Cf. Gessner (1548, sig. *3r; Book I, Tit. XIII, § 2, p. 20a-b): the distinction is between "quae quis legerit *reminisci*" and "nova primum *invenire*" (italics added).

CHAPTER 3

The Organisation of Knowledge

3.1 In Praise of Disorder

In the previous chapter, we observed that in organising the content of a book, medieval scholars prioritised the systematic arrangement of the subject matter (*ordo rerum*) over methods of indexing (*facilitas inveniendi*). To determine which order to adopt, medieval readers typically referred to the order of nature. This was understood as an order independent of observers, which readers sought to emulate when attempting to organise knowledge. The result was what Michel Foucault (1996, p. 31ff. [p. 34]) has described as a form of "specular reduplication": observers view the world in the mirror of their representations, but instead of recognising that the representation is a projection of the mirror, they organise their knowledge—their 'memory chambers' (Bolzoni 1995)—in such a way that it reflects the world they engage with. In this reciprocal mirroring, what ultimately vanishes are the observers themselves, caught between the representation of the world and the mirror.

The primary advantage of this specular reduplication was mnemonic: if it is assumed that the world was created in seven days, everything in the world can be organised into seven 'rooms', each containing everything created on that day, neatly arranged in relevant locations. Based on this assumption, an encyclopedia can be produced that is easier to memorise, as the order of knowledge replicates the order of reality, which is, in

A. Cevolini, *Indexing Systems*
https://doi.org/10.1007/978-3-032-13813-2_3

turn, reflected in the order in which knowledge is recalled.[1] This clearly illustrates how space functions as the primary criterion in this form of mnemonics.

Space can be divided into locations (rooms, corridors, streets, gardens) that cannot be confused, provided one is familiar with the space in which they move. What is on the right cannot simultaneously be on the left, what is above is not below, and what is near is not far. Navigating through space means testing one's sense of orientation, and orienting oneself inherently involves remembering. Space thus provides, in a manner that could be described as natural, a built-in consistency check, which is, by definition, a function of memory.[2]

Rhetorical culture exploited this property of space by advising educated readers to construct a repository (*thesaurus*) where they could store images to recall the content they wished to remember (Lechner 1962, p. 150; Bolzoni 1995, p. 247; Assmann 2003, p. 115ff.; Esposito 2001, p. 101ff.). This repository existed only in the consciousness of orators but was modelled on concrete spaces familiar to them. The premise was that whatever was placed in the appropriate spots within the appropriate locations would be easier to retrieve. For the orator, hunting for memories meant wandering through the repository in search of active images. The reactivation of knowledge thus took the form of an actual "local movement" (Lechner 1962, p. 151; Bolzoni 1995, p. 71) within a closed and finite space whose architecture, once conceived, could no longer be altered.

The idea that everything memorable could be gathered into a kind of "topography of knowledge" retained its plausibility until the seventeenth century and inspired many encyclopaedic projects.[3] Regardless of their actual completeness, the crucial principle underlying these projects was that a place could be found for everything and that everything could be kept in its proper place. In this sense, *topica universalis*, which typically assigned topics to specific locations where they were to be stored and from

[1] Cf. Citolini (1561, p. 19), who choose the seven days of Creation, convinced that "the most suitable place one could imagine for things was the World".

[2] Cf. Esposito (2001, esp. p. 98 and 102). On the mnemotechnical use of space in ancient advanced cultures, see also Jonker (1995, p. 35ff. and 44ff.).

[3] Like Campanella's (1998, p. 258ff.) City of the Sun. On this point, see Yates (1966, esp. p. 297f.).

which they could be "drawn out" as if uncovering something hidden,[4] constituted a genuine *taxonomy*. Its fixity reflected the stability of human nature and of Creation as a whole.

Printing had initially encouraged encyclopaedic projects of this kind because, for the first time, it made all available knowledge easily accessible. By stripping away the redundancy inherent in medieval manuscript culture, the ideal was to create a sort of 'book of all books' that would encompass all memorable knowledge, leaving nothing new to be discovered. This ideal inspired the encyclopaedic works of early modernity that aspired to achieve a *pansophy*. A particularly emblematic example of this Renaissance encyclopaedism is Comenius' project.

Comenius' goal was to produce a single book that could serve as a "compendium for universal education". This book would be a "mirror of the universe" (*speculum* was a widely used metaphor for medieval encyclopaedic works) and would function as a "catalogue" in the etymological sense of the term—that is, as an inventory where readers could locate everything contained in the vast repository of the created reality. In this compendium, knowledge was to be organised hierarchically but also systematically, ensuring "methodical" access to its contents through a carefully constructed system of tables, indexes, and cross-references.[5] For all those engaged in creating such encyclopaedic works, the imperative remained to scrupulously adhere to a pre-established order,[6] derived from the presumed order of Creation (after all, one navigates space effectively only when the space remains fixed as one moves through it).

However, during the same period—that is, between the second half of the sixteenth century and the first half of the seventeenth century—scholars, as we have seen, began to express a growing dissatisfaction with rigid schemes of knowledge classification and an increasing preference for more flexible methods, such as the alphabetical order in encyclopaedic works or the miscellaneous order in commonplace-books. In this regard,

[4] The reference is to the classic passage by Quintilian (*Inst. orat.*, V, 10, 20), where places are conceived as sites in which arguments are hidden and from which they must be drawn out. Cf. also Cicero (*Top.*, 2, 7–8).

[5] Comenius (1974, p. 515 and 520ff. [p. 522]). On Comenius' project, see Nakládalová's (2016, esp. p. 191ff. and 203ff.) thorough analysis. Cf. also Schmidt-Biggemann (1983, p. 141ff., esp. p. 145).

[6] Cf., among others, Dick (1564, p. 35): "Ordo attendendus [est]".

Elisabeth Décultot is entirely correct when she states that the main advantage of the *adversaria* lay in their emancipation from the pre-established structure of commonplaces.[7] Nevertheless, it remains to be clarified why, at the dawn of modernity, this emancipation was perceived by scholars as an opportunity rather than a threat.

Somewhat simplistically, one could argue that the preference for the lack of a specific order in the storage of knowledge was a consequence of the printing industry. While the medieval reader was accustomed to engaging intensively with a few books, striving to memorise them through repeated reading, the modern reader was enticed to consult a wide array of works made available by print. The printed book was no longer conceived as a 'book of memory' but increasingly as a consumer good. And since the production of publications was continuous, learned men began to feel the need for a method of discriminating memories that could accommodate a reading practice increasingly open to novelty, influenced by chance and the free selection of books.

Unlike medieval scholars, modern readers could no longer reliably predict what they would read and what they would memorise. In the Middle Ages, writing rarely served to introduce anything new, whereas in early modernity, printing increasingly focused on publishing works that could stand out from the highly repetitive transmission of knowledge. Unlike Grosseteste, who knew in advance *how many* and *which* books he would scrutinise, modern scholars faced the constant possibility that something new might be published every day—something from which they could "glean" memorable information to add to their notebook. Succedaneous memory, therefore, had to be structured not to accommodate what had been anticipated in the design of research, but rather the unpredictable.[8]

All this might explain why, between the sixteenth and seventeenth centuries, a kind of 'praise of disorder' emerged among scholars. Practically and epistemically, this manifested in the rejection of pre-established

[7] Décultot (2003, p. 16). A more detailed description of the *adversaria* method is provided in the next section.

[8] In a clearly hyperbolic manner, Drexel (1638, p. 87) claimed that his note-taking method made it possible to read even one hundred or six hundred books a day, in various languages. The excerpts derived from these readings, which were to be copied without concern for overall order, could then be retrieved using a meticulously compiled alphabetical register.

topical or hierarchical classifications and the adoption of note-taking methods that allowed readers the freedom to reorganise, at a later stage, what they had gathered during their studies. With some caution, and mindful of the usual ambiguity characterising phases of evolutionary transition, one might argue that in the early modern period, scholars gradually came to believe that the best order for storing knowledge was the absence of order. This conviction is particularly evident in the reflections accompanying the practice of *adversaria* and the use of loose index cards.

3.2 Order Out of Disorder

In early modernity, the maintenance of the commonplace-book became an object of didactic exercises and intense pedagogical reflection. As with all techniques for managing knowledge, various solutions, with different degrees of effectiveness, could be adopted. Regarding the storage of subject matter, in particular, readers could choose between a methodical order, an alphabetical order, or a miscellaneous order. The first two were considered different forms of *loci communes*, while the last was typically referred to by the untranslatable term *adversaria*.[9]

The methodical order involved dividing the pages of the commonplace-book in advance according to the structure of a particular discipline, often by literally copying the table of contents of a handbook. This method had both advantages and disadvantages. It preemptively solved the problem of where to place the notes that readers might extract during their studies, but it also bound them to a predetermined structure that could no longer be modified. If readers later encountered a noteworthy passage in a text that did not align with the predefined categories of the commonplace-book, they would not know where to insert it. Another practical disadvantage was that, if the pages allocated to certain categories filled up with annotations, readers would have to start a new notebook to continue taking notes, even if the old one still contained many blank pages.

[9] A brief overview of the various note-taking methods can be found in Stolberg (2013, p. 43ff.). The etymology of the term *adversaria* remains uncertain. According to Stübel (1684, p. 15), it referred to the practice of recording everything that "strikes" the reader's attention and should not be forgotten. Others, instead, suggested that the term derives from the practice of inserting notes on the pages of a notebooks that are "facing each other". Cf. Stolberg (2016, p. 249f. fn. 21); Beal (1993, p. 132f.); Chatelain (1997, p. 169ff.).

The alphabetical order required readers to divide the pages of their commonplace-book based on the number of entries they anticipated placing under each letter of the alphabet. Since the entries followed alphabetical order, an index was unnecessary, and the book could be consulted like a dictionary. However, this approach also had significant drawbacks. First, readers had to decide in advance how many pages to allocate to each letter of the alphabet. While this method offered greater flexibility in collecting material, as it was not bound to the methodical order of a discipline, it still posed practical challenges. As in the previous case, some sections of the book would quickly fill up, while others remained empty.

To address these inconveniences, which made both the systematic and alphabetical methods rather cumbersome, many readers opted for the alternative of *adversaria*. In this approach, annotations were inserted one after another, as they occurred, without concern for their specific placement. This method allowed memorable passages to be recorded following the often incidental and cross-cutting order of readings and reflections. As a result, at first glance, the pages of the commonplace-book appeared as an "indiscriminate hodgepodge" of annotations, a "vast and confused jumble" of excerpts copied "without any [pre-determined] order," as Sixtus of Siena (1566, Book III, p. 251B) described this type of anthology.

The practical advantage of this method was evident: readers did not need to set up their personal archive by deciding in advance on a structure for their memories. Nor did they have to spend time searching for the proper location before annotating a passage; it was sufficient to insert it on the first available page after the last excerpt.[10] The disadvantage, however, emerged later during the information retrieval phase. To locate what they were looking for, readers had to carefully establish an indexing system that could function effectively.

Here, scholars could choose from various solutions, ranging from more abstract to more sophisticated methods.[11] Undoubtedly, the *adversaria*

[10] Cf. Drexel (1638, p. 87) ("[...] Nihil attendendum ad ordinem: quo res loco venerit, eo recipiatur"). Apparently, the *adversaria* method was widespread not only in Jesuit milieus but also in the Anglo-Saxon world. Walker (1673, p. 132), for example, advised readers "*to write down confusedly* what in reading you think observable". The extraordinary success of John Locke's method was, therefore, no coincidence.

[11] See Sect. 2.8.

method reached its full potential when bound notebooks were abandoned in favour of loose index cards. This technical possibility was not entirely new—medieval scholars had occasionally used loose paper slips for their compilations. However, between the mid-sixteenth and seventeenth centuries, there was a growing reliance on paper slips for making extracts and taking notes. Through trial and error, this practice eventually led to the creation of the first filing cabinets with removable entries (Meinel 1995; Krajewski 2002; Krämer 2014; Considine 2015; Cevolini 2017a; 2021). But how, then, could one reorder disorder without reducing the disorder itself to a pre-established order?

A collection of annotations inserted one after another on an ad hoc basis would have been unusable unless the annotations were organised under categories and these categories were gathered in an alphabetical index (or register). The speed at which annotations could be recorded should not come at the expense of the ability to retrieve the collected information. Scholars were well aware that the functional relationship between two essential prerequisites—*expeditio disponendi* (the speed at which selected material can be stored) and *promptitudo utendi* (the readiness with which stored material can be retrieved and reused)—is inherently circular. Those who chose a rapid method of entering information later faced significant challenges when attempting to retrieve it at the appropriate moment. Conversely, those who prioritised reliable retrieval by pre-organising the material to be annotated had to contend with a structure that significantly slowed down the recording process and made reading particularly laborious.

Scholars addressed this problem by separating the order of the material collected in the archive from the order of the index that provided access to the information. On the one hand, there was no need to pay attention to the placement of an excerpt within the notebook, as it was sufficient to insert it in the first available space. On the other hand, maintaining a strict alphabetical order in the index of entries was essential.[12] While this suggestion was not particularly groundbreaking on a practical level, it was quite subversive from the perspective of the ancient mnemotecnique. It marked a clear departure from the principle of mirroring the order of reality in the order of knowledge and prepared the reader to engage

[12] So argues Drexel (1638, p. 87) ("in solo indice ordinata series Alphabeti observanda"), to complete the instruction introduced above in footnote 10.

with a repository of all that is memorable—a repository that effectively functioned as a genuine substitute memory.

From the perspective of social memory, the shift from a mirrored order to the duplication of order should be regarded as an evolutionary advancement with fundamental consequences for the administration of knowledge in early modernity. On this topic, a wealth of empirical material is now available on the emergence of modern archives. The term 'archive', in the modern sense of formal organisation, can only be applied, as Markus Friedrich (2013, p. 38) has noted, when the production of written documents acquires its "own dynamic" (*Eigendynamik*)—that is, when a reaction to a written document produces another written document, which in turn can only be addressed through the further production of written documents. This "autonomous functional logic" both presupposes and simultaneously results in the emergence of new professional groups, the establishment of specific work routines, and the implementation of coherent decision-making processes for the preservation and organisation of materials (Friedrich 2013, p. 38ff. and 43).

Historical research has also demonstrated that the increasing complexity of record-keeping activities in many European states between the sixteenth and seventeenth centuries made a drastic adjustment of finding aids indispensable. Archivists proceeded through trial and error but consistently moved towards increasing abstraction (Head 2019, esp. p. 54 and 138ff.). Initially, they abandoned inventory lists and transitioned to maps representing the ideal-topographical organisation of the documentation stored in the archive (Head 2003, p. 750ff.; 2007, p. 322ff.; 2014, p. 505ff.). However, when they realised that this concrete order, tied to a specific context, rendered much of the potential information contained in the documents 'invisible', archivists also abandoned the ideal-topographical organisation and began experimenting with more sophisticated registers.[13] By doing so, they decoupled access to information from the document itself (i.e., the vehicle) and its physical location in the repository. The different levels of abstraction in the registers accounted for the variety of user perspectives, thereby enhancing the potential to exploit the complexity of the available documentation for the production of information.

[13] Cf. Head (2019, p. 211): "As record-keeping became more complex [...], the limitations of ideal-topographical organisation became visible".

The profound transformation in the organisation of knowledge during early modernity affected all forms of succedaneous memory, from note-books and filing cabinets to archives and libraries. In this regard, it is particularly interesting to examine how scholars responded to these changes. The reflections of contemporaries reveal an unusual concern with the problem of order, which deserves to be explored in greater depth.

The initial impression is that scholars only now realised that order is an indispensable requirement without which memory cannot function.[14] For instance, Christoph Udenius (1687, p. 61) advised those making extracts to record everything in an orderly manner; otherwise, when needed, readers would no longer be able to find what they had annotated, and it would be as though they had never selected anything to remember, rendering all their effort wasted. Warnings became even more explicit when reflections turned to archives and libraries. The evidence on this subject is abundant and, as expected in a society already characterised by the rapid circulation of printed books, highly repetitive.

For Bonifacio, for instance, order is the soul of the archive; it serves to give shape to the formless and, as such, must be preserved. Similarly, for Clément, order is the soul of the library; for this reason, as Morhof observes, no library can function without some particular order. The reason, according to all, is that without order, what has been collected is unusable—just as a pile of beams, tiles, and bricks is not enough to build a house, and a gathering of soldiers is not enough to form a well-organised army. Ultimately, as Hottinger metaphorically put it, it would be like having a buried treasure that no one can enjoy.[15]

All these warnings reiterated a commonplace originating from Xenophon. One might therefore wonder why, at this particular moment, order once again emerged as a challenge. From a socio-evolutionary perspective, the reflections of early modern scholars acquire a significance that extends far beyond the apparent obviousness of their observations and should be interpreted as evidence of a profound transformation in their intellectual habits.

[14] According to Drexel (1638, p. 259), for example, order is the fundamental memory-aid ("princeps memoriae subsidium, ordo").

[15] Bonifacio (1632, p. 10f.); Clément (1635, p. 286); Morhof (1747, p. 34); Naudé (1627, p. 129ff.); Hottinger (1664, p. 3). These authors are, of course, not the only ones who addressed this point, but they suffice to illustrate the idea.

One of the greatest challenges faced by early modern readers, who could now benefit from the products of the printing industry, was managing the desire for abundance (*copia* in the rhetorical sense of the term). While in the Middle Ages, as we have seen, the fundamental rule was to avoid pursuing the infinite, as an excess of knowledge leads to forgetfulness, this attitude was reversed with the adoption of substitute memory systems. By the seventeenth century, the capacity of commonplace-books and filing systems to accommodate something new every day—continually adding to what had already been collected—was celebrated, thereby infinitely expanding the available material (Drexel 1638, p. 100; Placcius 1689, p. 70).

The overturning of a fundamental principle of rhetorical culture was only acceptable because substitute memory systems relieved the reader's personal memory and ensured the retrieval of stored material through more abstract procedures, which required neither special cognitive skills nor relentless training in reminiscence. During the transitional phase, however, this advantage was not immediately evident. For a long time, efforts were made to reconcile an old way of remembering—the *thesaurus*—with a new way of forgetting—the archive. Lambert Schenkel's experience in this regard is particularly emblematic.

In his extreme attempt to preserve the rhetorical repository as a tool for gathering knowledge, Schenkel was compelled to multiply places according to a system of 'Chinese boxes', allowing for the inclusion of everything made available by the printing press. For this reason, in constructing his *domus sapientiae*, Schenkel had to abandon the possibility of imitating a natural space, resorting instead to increasingly artificial virtual spaces designed to expand the repository's storage capacity. The paradoxical outcome of this potentially limitless expansion was, ultimately, the collapse of the repository.[16]

The duplication of order alone, however, was not sufficient. When scholars called for the necessary order to ensure the functioning of a private archive or a public library, they simultaneously emphasised the importance of maintaining the catalogue and alphabetical register, which activated the network of references indispensable for accessing the contents of external memory. In the rhetorical repository, orientation depended on the organisation of the space where the active images were

[16] On Schenkel's mnemotechnique and its contradictions, see Kuwakino (2016).

placed. In the archive model, by contrast, the concrete placement of each element within the container was entirely irrelevant.[17] The only essential requirement was that access should not be left to chance and should not become overly burdensome.

When contemporaries spoke of 'method', they referred precisely to this: deliberate access to the contents of the archive based on the user's interests and selections. For this to be possible, every piece of content must be connected to a network of references that enables one to recall what the archive allows one to forget. Anything not linked to this structure—such as a book on a shelf but not catalogued, or an excerpt copied into a notebook but not indexed—is effectively lost: it can neither be intentionally searched for nor retrieved.[18]

The catalogue thus acquired a function it previously did not have. Originally intended merely as a list of owned items, in early modernity, the catalogue gradually became an indispensable tool for enabling users to externally explore the internal content of a library. Rather than remaining a simple inventory, the catalogue evolved into a genuine 'search engine' without which the library would otherwise be unsearchable. The possibility of being catalogued does not, of course, guarantee that a book will be read or consulted, but it does at least ensure its retrievability. The organisation of social memory thus shifted from focusing on content to focusing on procedures: the question was no longer what to remember in advance but what rules could reactivate memories at the appropriate moment. Already a century after the invention of the printing press, Conrad Gessner suggested that 'to commemorate' and 'to catalogue' were synonymous and that the organisation of information access—and thus social memory—could only be enacted through an effective indexing system.[19]

[17] Cf. Kayser (1790, p. 10): "Der Ort, wo ein Buch steht, ist *höchst gleichgültig*. Will man eine Übersicht dessen, was die Bibliothek in einem Fache besitze, liefern, so verfertige man seiner Zeit einen sogenannten *wissenschaftlichen Katalog*" (The physical location of a book is *entirely irrelevant*. If one wishes to provide an overview of a library's holdings in a particular field of knowledge, a so-called *scientific catalogue* must be compiled in due time).

[18] Cf. Krippendorff (1975, esp. p. 17). But see Bonifacio (1632, p. 11), who, much earlier, distinguished between accidental discovery (*casu*) and intentional retrieval (*sponte*), identifying alphabetical indices as the essential technical device for transitioning from the former to the latter.

[19] Cf. Gessner (1545, p. 3v). On this point, see also Müller (1998, esp. p. 293f.).

Through the process of cataloguing, scholars gradually distanced themselves from the real-world order that rhetorical tradition had sought to mirror in the order of knowledge. In a society increasingly grappling with a critical mass of publications, the idea that the arrangement of materials within a library should reflect the order of the cosmos lost not so much its plausibility as its mnemonic effectiveness. With the advent of print, the complexity of knowledge grew too rapidly to allow all memorable material to be reorganised into a provisionally definitive encyclopedia. Consequently, the catalogue was no longer expected to 'map' reality but rather to 'map' knowledge. It is within this separation of two non-overlapping orders that observers, so to speak, insert themselves, bringing about far-reaching socio-cultural consequences.

By the mid-seventeenth century, it had become evident that, to be truly effective, a catalogue must account for the different interests and perspectives of readers—especially when these readers are unknown and their interests, therefore, unpredictable. To prevent users from wasting their time on irrelevant results, indexing systems need to be as differentiated as possible. A good catalogue, as Hottinger (1664, p. 4) argued, must be precise (*distinctus*) rather than generic (*confusus*), detailed (*contractus*) rather than vague (*diffusus*). In other words, a catalogue functions effectively if it manages to exclude almost everything except the small portion that may be relevant to the user at any given moment. For the same reason, it is advisable to multiply catalogues: the variety of indexing systems (*varietas catalogorum*) compensates for the variety of user requests, thereby providing the library with the variety needed to deliver results that meet everyone's information needs (Hottinger 1664, p. 117ff.).

All these technical adjustments and the reflexivity of the social system's memory, as implicit in discussions about cataloguing rules, provide evidence of how the invention of the printing press marked a departure from the rhetorical repository model toward an irreversible adoption of a form of social memory based on the archival model.[20] This substitution can only be understood within the context of an evolutionary advancement that can be described as the social system's reaction to increasing complexity. Evolution, after all, is not a problem-solving mechanism.

[20] On this transition, see Esposito (2001, p. 96f. and 152f.; 2002, p. 184ff.).

Rather, as we have seen, problems emerge during the course of evolution in tandem with the level of complexity achieved.[21] It is in relation to this complexity that the most suitable functional equivalent becomes evident. With respect to the administration of knowledge and information processing, what becomes clear in early modernity is that there is no comparison between the rhetorical repository and the archive.

From an evolutionary perspective, what is particularly interesting is that certain possibilities for 'archiving' knowledge had already been experimented with before the advent of the printing industry. The sophisticated indexing techniques developed during the late Middle Ages had achieved a high level of abstraction and aligned with the functional need for rapid and targeted access to information—something characteristic of interactions with succedaneous memories. However, it was only in early modernity that the functional advantage of indexing systems was fully recognised and appreciated. In the face of increasing complexity, these systems revealed the very problem for which they themselves served as the solution.

The evolutionary advancement is particularly evident in the fact that the question was no longer *whether* indexing is the right solution for managing complexity, but rather *which* method is best suited for indexing knowledge. In this sense, evolution does not imply an upgrading of adaptation but an upgrading of distinctions. For early modern scholars, this required a profound adjustment of their intellectual habits. The order they aspired to was not an alternative to prior disorder but a more improbable form of order.

Drexel's assertion that readers need not worry about the order in which they introduce their annotations, as an alphabetical index suffices for retrieval, implies that from the apparent disorder of notes, it is possible, in principle, to derive an infinite number of different orders. Over time, not only do the reader's selecting criteria change, but so do the contents of the archive. Notebooks and filing systems thus function as 'cybernetic systems': the results users obtain when interacting with the system are always a combination of order and disorder.[22] The further the note-taking process advances, the greater the overall disorder of the collected content becomes, but at the same time, the possibilities

[21] See Sect. 2.3.

[22] Luhmann described his filing system in these terms. See Schmidt (2015, p. 158).

of discovering new and surprising orders also multiply. The denser the forest, the easier it is to get lost, but the likelihood of finding unexplored paths also increases.

This structural shift did not occur abruptly, of course. During the transition, old and new cognitive habits overlapped, often in contradictory ways. The technique of 'twin books', for example, required readers to first collect their notes in a book of *adversaria* and then to rewrite them neatly in another notebook, this time arranged systematically.[23] Those who recommended this technique admitted that it was very laborious and time-consuming, as it involved writing everything twice. As an alternative, it was suggested to use a single notebook, leaving a wide margin on each page. In this margin, readers could insert a heading alongside their respective annotations. This running index would then serve to compile an alphabetical register. Ultimately, however, a chaos that could be reordered at will was preferred over a pre-determined order.

3.3 Subject Headings as a Choice

Practical advantages alone do not suffice to explain the success of the miscellaneous order. Nor are they sufficient to clarify precisely how this order deviated from the topical organisation of knowledge preferred by rhetorical culture. It is therefore necessary to examine what changes are triggered in the organisation of information access when knowledge is no longer stored according to a predetermined structure of *loci communes*. As always, the starting point lies in the articulation of the categories used to give structure to this organisation.

To always have memorable things at hand when needed,[24] Aristotle already suggested assigning headings to excerpts, such as 'Soul (of Man)', 'Vices and Virtues', or 'God'. The philosophers' opinions could thus be organised into lists, which, in turn, could be distinguished by their respective headings. This facilitated both retrieval and memorisation. Aristotle (*Top*., I, 14, 105b14-25) also recommended keeping separate notebooks

[23] This method, it seems, was widely employed among the Jesuits. Cf., for example, Sacchini (1613, p. 65ff.); Clément (1635, p. 479f.). On this point, see also Cevolini (2006, esp. p. 111).

[24] In these terms, a modern source defines the art of excerption (*ars excerpendi*): "Illa, quae occurrunt, memorabilia suo tempore in promptu habere" (Sidelius and Schubart 1713, p. 8).

based on subject matter—for instance, one notebook for ethical questions and another for questions concerning physics. The guiding principle, therefore, was differentiation.

The universal scheme of knowledge organised into topics (*topica universalis*) adopted the same method. Since early modern scholars were still educated according to the principles of rhetorical culture, they initially absorbed the traditional headings used to classify topics in a rather passive manner. After all, the semantics of learned culture rarely changes abruptly. However, starting in the second half of the sixteenth century, a growing concern emerged over the selection of headings. Underlying this concern was the need to overcome a certain threshold of improbability—namely, the recognition that headings had become a matter of choice.

Historical research has only marginally explored this novelty. About a decade ago, Ann Blair (2010, p. 88) observed that "given the central importance of the [indexing] process, it is remarkable how rarely pedagogues or note-takers discussed heading choice". However, a more thorough investigation of contemporary sources challenges this claim.[25] These sources provide striking evidence that headings were gradually evolving into keywords (or 'subjects') used to index the contents stored in personal archives, which were increasingly taking on the form and function of true 'information processing systems'.

Ann Blair (2010, p. 63) herself acknowledged, however, that in early modernity, the choice of headings became "more idiosyncratic to each note-taker, and no longer follow[ed] a set of headings" that printed florilegia readily provided. The impression, therefore, is that scholarly readers gradually began to orient their choice of headings towards their own perspectives and capacity for abstraction, rather than simply drawing concepts from the repository transmitted by rhetorical culture. As Richard Yeo notes, what gradually spread was an open-ended practice in which the selection of headings became far more personal than the categories Renaissance commonplace-book culture had circulated.[26] In other words, the learned readers distanced themselves from the redundancy—now, for

[25] A source among many others is Udenius (1687, Ch. 4): "Wie des Excerpir-Buches Register und Titul zu verfertigen" (How to compile the index and titles of the excerpting book).

[26] Yeo (2001, p. 112). Yeo refers to John Locke, but his observation may be generalised.

the first time, perceived as an obstacle—of the concepts that had traditionally structured the systematic order of a discipline.[27] Readers sought to adapt the retrieval of knowledge to their own memory, rather than conforming their memory to an established order of knowledge. In this way, learned men became accustomed to take themselves into account whenever deciding which category to assign to an annotation. The choice of headings became a form of *self-control*[28]: readers decided not only what to remember and forget but also how to do so. Rather than planning their memories, they organised their memory system.

A similar form of self-control was absent in *topica universalis* because knowledge was considered valid independently of the learned individual, just as the map of a territory exists independently of the explorer. However, as scholars grew accustomed to using notebooks and filing systems functioning as external memories, the modern reader assumed a more active role in organising access to information. When the primary function of the notebook shifted from *recalling* to *retrieving*,[29] the role of headings changed accordingly: from being *loci* in a mental geography of knowledge, they became 'keywords' used to trigger the reference network through which archived material could be retrieved.[30] The fundamental hypothesis, therefore, is that *the novelty in the choice of headings* designed to compile a working indexing system lies in the fact that, in modernity, *headings became a matter of choice* (Cevolini 2022).

The emancipation from the order of categories transmitted by rhetorical culture coincides with the replacement of a *topical* with a *categorical* classification of knowledge.[31] For early modern scholars, this transition marked a shift from a classification that excludes to one that includes the observer within the observed reality—that is, from a first-order to a

[27] Yeo (2001, p. 113) speaks of "*separation* of the commonplace method from its earlier nexus with *systematic ordering of knowledge*" (italics added).

[28] Cf. Frank (1905, p. 2), who considers note-taking, in general, a form of "self-control".

[29] This important distinction is drawn from Yeo (2004, p. 37).

[30] Cf. Moss (1996, p. 279): headings are selected as keywords that function as a search mechanism rather than a structuring principle (for the reader's individual memory). For this reason, moreover, the thoughtful assignment of categories to notes stored in the commonplace-book could become, as Stolberg (2013, p. 51) put it, a "creative act" potentially productive of new knowledge.

[31] This distinction is taken up by Ong (1958, p. 112), but it is employed here in an inverted manner.

second-order observation.[32] In the latter case, the categories used to classify knowledge are provided by the very knowledge being classified, which implies an inherent self-referential circularity. When headings become a matter of choice, readers engaged in indexing tasks risk, therefore, finding themselves going in circles. Meaning is semantically complex, and every categorical selection inevitably excludes many other equally relevant possibilities. As a result, readers may be left uncertain as to whether the reduction of complexity achieved is truly the correct one.

This problem is, in principle, unsolvable. The generalised scheme of knowledge (*topica universalis*) simply neutralised it by providing a taxonomy where everything had a place, and there was a place for everything. However, as the complexity of knowledge increases, so does the need for selection. For this reason, *topica* (which, incidentally, is functionally equivalent to a subject index) proved inadequate for addressing the problem of accessing archived material.

Those responsible for deciding which subject to assign to books to be catalogued in a library faced the same problem. Individuals tasked with establishing guidelines for the first public libraries in the mid-seventeenth century acknowledged that the issue was particularly challenging (*tractatio difficilis*). The reason, as Johann Heinrich Hottinger observed, was that deciding which category (i.e., which indexing term) to assign to a book is far more difficult than first extracting its content and then assigning a corresponding category (i.e., a heading) to it. The former is an exceptionally complex task, but, as Hottinger noted, it determines whether memory is greatly economised or significantly wasted.[33]

Similar concerns arose when it came to organising private archives, such as books of excerpts or filing systems. By the mid-seventeenth century, some readers explicitly recognised that the choice of headings is the crucial element of all intellectual work.[34] The risk, in this case, lies in forgetting what is concretely contained in the archive but remains

[32] This is precisely what Zedelmaier (1992, p. 52ff., esp. p. 65) means when he states that (in Gessner's bibliographical encyclopaedia), the topical classification was used not to thematise "the world as the totality of beings, but rather [to thematise] the world as a library".

[33] Hottinger (1664, p. 79): "Collocatio enim memoriae magnum est vel compendium, vel dispendium".

[34] Cf. Kerger (1689, p. 4r): "Nervum totius rei excerpendae" (the marrow of the entire matter concerning the practice of excerpting).

inaccessible through the system of references users are expected to reactivate to interact with the external memory. For this reason, many scholars worked diligently to define rules guiding the indexing process.

The first rule suggested was to use common sense—to proceed rationally (*cum judicio*)[35]—but such an advice is so generic that it is practically useless. Manuals on how to read and make excerpts from books, therefore, sought to provide more specific guidance: focus on the main subject of the annotation and choose the first word carefully, as it will determine access to the archive when consulting the alphabetical register of entries. For example, if one notes something about the origin of springs (*origo fontium*), the recommended heading would be 'Springs, origin of' (*fontium origo*), because the subject is springs, not origin. Similarly, if one annotates something about the incredible increase of divine grace, among all possible alternatives, the preferred heading would be 'Divine grace, incredible increase of', because the main subject is grace, and it is more likely that readers would search under this word in their commonplace-books (Kerger 1689, p. 4r; Drexel 1638, p. 135).

In addition to general rules, more detailed guidelines were also provided. A heading should express many ideas with a single word or just a few words (Quensted 1678, s.n., § 2). Put differently, the terms used for indexing can be simple (e.g., 'Father') or compound (e.g., 'Father caring for his newborn son') (Schubert 1699, s.n., Membrum V, § 8). The indexer's skill lies, in any case, in selecting the most appropriate term to denote a complex topic. Headings can also be structured hierarchically, distinguishing between universal titles and specific titles (Quensted 1678, s.n., § 3). Titles should preferably be written in Latin, but Greek or German terms may also be used if they better or more concisely express the content of the entry (Schubert 1699, s.n., Membrum V, § 8). Finally, metaphorical expressions should be avoided, and common words should be used instead, as the latter are easier to recall (Udenius 1687, p. 75).

The choice of headings remains, in any case, a challenging problem to resolve. Its management depends, among other factors, on the indexer's capacity for abstraction. Here, the active role of the reader in organising memory becomes evident. If the topic is 'Children against parents', one might alternatively choose the commonplace 'Parents against children',

[35] Drexel (1638, p. 136); Quensted (1678, s.n., § 5): "Titulus rei annotandae cum iudicio est formandus" (the heading of the item to be annotated should be formulated using judgement).

fully aware that the alphabetical placement in the register depends on the first letter, and that this introduces the risk of failing to find something that is, nonetheless, stored in the filing cabinet. Alternatively, the indexer might opt for 'Obedience', 'Family', or 'Conflict', with none of these choices being inherently right or wrong—because all of them are simultaneously both right and wrong.

The abstraction applied in the selection of headings contributes to the creation of a kind of "systemic boundary" (Luhmann 1992c, p. 59) between users and the archive. Since substitute memory is organised as a self-referential system of meaning, it functions as an autonomous observer endowed with its own capacity for abstraction—one that does not necessarily align with the user's capacity for abstraction, even when the user personally feeds the memory. Each time users query the machine, they cross a boundary of meaning and engage operatively with a horizon of references and associations that do not merely replicate the references and associations users can activate independently.[36]

The instructions devised by early modern scholars for formulating headings also addressed more practical issues. For example, many recommended keeping the index separate from the commonplace-book to make consultation more efficient (Udenius 1687, p. 62). Recognising that it is not always easy to immediately identify the most relevant category, some advised postponing the decision and writing a provisionally suitable category on a temporary slip (Udenius 1687, p. 74). This delay left open the possibility of revisiting the choice. In other words, readers allowed themselves time to gather additional information before making a definitive decision on which term to use for indexing.

All these instructions reflect the inherent difficulties of indexing the contents of an archive. The core issue lies in the complexity of meaning and the unpredictability of the future. To effectively organise the future retrieval of the available past,[37] some scholars suggested creating a hierarchy of general and specific, primary and subordinate headings. Although the concept of hierarchy was fairly traditional, its novelty lay in the fact that the distinctions had to be derived from the 'purpose' (*ratio finis*)

[36] As we will see later, aligning the machine's horizon with that of the user is not advantageous. Maintaining a difference, in fact, increases the likelihood that succedaneous memory will be surprising—and therefore informative—when consulted by the user.

[37] Cf. Erhardt (1716, p. 40): "Prompte, & facile invenire" (To readily and easily find [what has been excerpted]).

scholars aimed to achieve with their intellectual activity.[38] In this way, it was no longer necessary to adhere to a single, universal order of knowledge: different readers could set different purposes, from which they would derive the distinctions needed to structure their personal memory. This approach implied a new way of coupling the past with the future.

3.4 Combinatorics

The abandonment of a pre-established order and the preference for a disorder that can be reorganised at will and provisionally, based on user instructions, presuppose a profound transformation in the temporal structures of society as a whole. Between the sixteenth and seventeenth centuries, this transformation had a significant impact on methods of knowledge administration. Following the pioneering work of Francis Bacon, scholars became convinced that there are essentially two ways to organise information access: the first involves arranging material in a "systematic" or "methodical" manner; the second consists of collecting data "in a more loose and unconfin'd way" (Boyle 1772, p. 54). Both approaches have their advantages and disadvantages.

A systematic order is very useful for providing a compendium of a subject and, for this reason, serves as an important aid to memory. However, because (scientific) knowledge advances rapidly, systematic treatises quickly become obsolete. A loose order of notes may be less appealing than a methodical one, but it has the advantage of encouraging reasoning and, above all, facilitating the discovery of "latent truths".[39] In other words, order is reassuring but compels the present to repeat the past. Disorder, by contrast, offers numerous opportunities for comparison and aligns with the restlessness of those who wish to explore the unknown. The loosening of the constraints imposed by systematic orders thus corresponds to an orientation toward an open future.[40]

[38] Cf. Erhardt (1716, p. 43). On the function of purpose, see further below Sect 3.6.

[39] Boyle (1772, p. 55). Cf. also Chambers (1728, vol. I, The Preface, p. xxix): the primary advantage of a "promiscuous" order of knowledge where "numbers of things are thrown precariously together" is that "we sometimes discover relations among'em, we should never have thought of looking for".

[40] For Francis Bacon, the purpose of unorganised note-taking was "to unloose Men's minds being bound [to the past]". Cf. Rawley (1670, s.n.).

From this perspective, the true advantage of knowledge management methods such as *adversaria* collections and the use of loose index cards lies in the fact that entries do not preclude the possibility of adding further entries or establishing additional connections between existing ones. The very phrase 'miscellaneous order' is, in fact, an oxymoron. Learned readers who adopt this method do not aim to impose order on what has been collected in a disorganised fashion.[41] Rather, they aim to make the mass of annotations accumulated over time reusable in a way that is suited to the present situation.

A methodical or systematic order, by contrast, rarely allows for the addition of new elements without compromising the entire structure. For this reason, faced with the growing complexity brought about by the printing press, seventeenth-century scholars began to favour methods that enabled the fragmentation of knowledge into elementary units ("particulars"). This approach ensured that the task of rearticulation remained potentially open to any solution. Even for the Royal Society, this "neglect of order" in data storage was not to be criticised; rather, it was the result of a deliberate approach supported by well-founded arguments (Sprat 1667, p. 115).

The decision to collect "a mixt Mass of *experiments*" without organising the self-produced data of scientists into a predetermined structure was justified by the recognition that reducing science to a systematic order hinders the "growth" of knowledge. By contrast, the unlimited archiving of empirical observations and their proper indexing made it possible to leave room for others to "*change*, to *augment*, to *approve*, to *contradict*" what was already known at their discretion.[42] The empirical-experimental research activities of scientists such as Joachim Jungius, Martin Fogel, Ulisse Aldrovandi, and Francis Bacon, along with their concurrent adoption of note-taking methods that loosened the relationships between

[41] An exception is the 'twin books' method. See above Sect. 3.2.

[42] Sprat (1667, p. 116). The inspiration still came from Bacon (1876, p. 173), who distinguished 'method' from 'aphorisms' and pointed out that "aphorisms, representing a knowledge broken, do invite men to *inquire further*; whereas method, carrying the show of a total, do secure men, as if they were *at furthest*" (italics added). On this point, see Vine (2019, esp. p. 213ff. and 220ff.).

entries, demonstrate how this new temporal orientation had firmly taken root by the seventeenth century.[43]

The loosening of the available past into data or annotations represents only one side of the temporal relationship. The fragmentation of knowledge into elementary units compels the reader, even on a practical level, to selectively recombine what has been retained. In other words, this fragmentation creates a combinatory space that would not otherwise exist. This predisposition to recombination marks a profound shift in the intellectual habits of Renaissance scholars compared to those educated in rhetorical culture.

The ability to recall certain contents through combinatory operations represented an alternative method to the art of reminiscence, one that had already been experimented with in the thirteenth century by Ramon Llull. Rather than working with space and vivid images, Llullian mnemotechnics employed highly sophisticated rules that enabled users to obtain the correct answers to any questions they could formulate.[44] The peculiarity of this technique lay in the fact that scholars did not need to exercise their imagination to derive, through successive associations of meaning, the topics they were to discuss. Instead, they had to memorise abstract combinatory rules which, when applied correctly, would generate the desired results. In this sense, Llull's art functioned like a typical 'search engine' that could be reactivated through keywords.[45]

Despite these differences, Llullian combinatory art retained many aspects in common with the rhetorical art of reminiscence. First, it was

[43] On Jungius, see the valuable contribution of Meinel (1995). On Fogel, see Marten and Piepenbring-Thomas (2015, esp. p. 35ff. and 121ff.). Regarding Jungius' *History of Worms*, Morhof (1747, p. 439) observed that it had been compiled posthumously by simply assembling the author's paper slips one after another—something clearly evident in the printed edition (Jungius 1691)—without any selection and without attempting to arrange them in a coherent order ("e schedis sine selectu & ordine congruo"). On Ulisse Aldrovandi and Francis Bacon, see Krämer (2014) and Vine (2011), respectively. On the revival of the *sylva* genre in early-modern scientific circles, see De Bruyn (2001, p. 347ff.). As De Bruyn rightly points out, both the continuity and the discontinuity of the genre must be taken into consideration to fully grasp its novelty.

[44] On Llull's mnemotechnique, see Yates (1966, p. 175ff.); Fauvel and Wilson (1994); Rossi (2000, p. 66ff.).

[45] For Llull (2002, p. 84), the purpose of his art was to answer all questions, provided that one knows the meaning of the terms used to begin with ("respondere de omnibus quaestionibus, supposito, quod sciatur, quid dicitur per nomen").

finite: no matter how one turned the wheels of the Llullian mechanism, the combinations that could be generated were always the same. Anyone with sufficient time and energy to test all the combinations would eventually reach a point where there was nothing left to learn. The combinatory mechanism was not designed to explore the unknown but rather to exhaust all possibilities leading to the recollection of what was already known (but forgotten). Finally, Llull's art shared with rhetorical culture the assumption that the logical order of ideas reflected the metaphysical order of reality—that the structure of discourse (that is, of things within the soul) mirrored the coherence of the structure of the cosmos (that is, of things outside the soul). This ultimately justified the invariability of knowledge: since the structure of reality does not change, neither does the structure of knowledge.

These very assumptions had been sharply criticised by Descartes. Like the syllogism, Llullian art, according to Descartes (1902, p. 17), was merely a technique for extracting knowledge already implicitly contained in its premises. Despite this, such techniques still required a certain level of intelligence. Descartes' critique, however, was rooted in the idea that only when intellectual activity is freed from the exhausting labour of memorisation can cognitive energy be redirected toward the production of information. Combinatory activity serves this purpose only when it shifts from being a *closed* combinatory system, like Llull's art, to an *open* one. Achieving this required dismantling the topical architecture of knowledge. The loosening of knowledge into alphabetically ordered entries was already a step in this direction.

During the long evolutionary transition between the first half of the sixteenth century and the first half of the seventeenth century, *topica universalis* was gradually replaced by a "universal index upon all authors". Samuel Hartlib used this phrase to describe the *Ark of Studies* invented by Thomas Harrison around 1640.[46] In this cabinet, individual entries (or "commonplaces") were physically represented by plates placed on wooden beams fixed inside the filing cabinet. Each plate could be

[46] Hartlib Papers (30/4/47A, Ephemerides 1640, Part 2). Apparently, the expression was already in use in the early seventeenth century. Alsted (1610, p. 45), for example, defines commonplace-books as an *index* of principal authors ("*index* in praecipuos authores") that serves as a repository from which readers can draw a vast abundance of excellent material ("ingentem copiam optimarum rerum") for their conversations or written works.

removed and repositioned at will—either to make room for new plates or to allow the scholar to work with slips attached to a nail fixed on the plate.[47]

This particular method of storage involved fragmenting knowledge into elementary units, disrupting any pre-established order, and granting the reader the freedom to add and recombine at will the content extracted from books. A fixed geography of *loci communes* was thus abandoned and replaced by an alphabetical order of homogeneous entries[48] that could be infinitely multiplied. But what did the transition from *topica universalis* to a "universal index upon all authors" truly entail on an operational level?

Working with a filing cabinet like the one designed by Thomas Harrison in the first half of the seventeenth century primarily meant making a different use of attention. Rather than exhausting it on memorising the contents of books, scholars could use it to compare knowledge with itself. From this comparison, redundancies and inconsistencies could emerge, but so too could surprising connections that might otherwise have gone unnoticed.[49] For Hartlib, after all, the "combination and coordination of propositions" was one of the greatest advantages of Harrison's filing system (Hartlib Papers 30/4/47A, Ephemerides 1640, Part 2).

Since loosening was permanent, the combinatory potential could only increase over time. This, almost automatically, implied an increase in complexity which could be reduced through selective combinatory operations. From this perspective, the improbability of modern memory based on archives lay in the fact that, for the first time, memory was being used to produce information.[50] This information resulted from the machine's

[47] Cf. Harrison (2017). On this invention and its author, see Malcolm (2004) and Cevolini (2017a).

[48] The entries are 'homogeneous' because no entry is more important than another. Alphabetical order alone eliminates any hierarchy and branching structure.

[49] Cf. Yeo (2014, p. 120); Cevolini (2017a, p. 44f.). See also Leibniz (1903, p. 34): the use of indexing systems allows combinations from which "many new things emerge" ("multa nova exurgent") which we would not otherwise have thought of. This use of combinatory activity to generate information was still praised at the end of the eighteenth century as one of the key advantages of note-taking. See, for example, Meiners (1791, p. 91f.).

[50] Cf. Esposito (2001, p. 150). In this regard, Luhmann (1992c, p. 59f.) spoke of the "innovation effect" of the filing system, which arises from its ability to provide users with more information than they had originally sought in their query.

ability to respond in surprising ways to the user's input, suggesting connections that the user alone would never have discovered.[51]

In the interplay between the loosening and recombination of knowledge, the temporal horizons of the past and the future were loosely connected. For scholars, 'loosening' meant preserving a potentially relevant past without the obligation of repetition, while 'recombination' signified looking toward an open future in search of what was not yet known.[52] What unified these two temporal horizons was the present—the only temporal dimension in which concrete action can take place.[53]

For those engaged in the ambitious task of managing and reproducing knowledge in early modernity, the goal was certainly not to dispense with the past. Rather, it was to prevent the past from so saturating the present that it hindered research from progressing in innovative ways. Indexing provided a technical solution perfectly suited to this purpose. Through differentiated and interconnected indices, as suggested by Hottinger, learned men could explore the available past in a highly selective and contingent manner. This exploration did not exhaust the combinatory potential; on the contrary, it simultaneously reproduced and expanded it. Each exploration could lead to the discovery of new connections, which could be recorded within the filing cabinet to remain accessible for future inquiries. In short, indexing emancipated the present from a binding past, enabling it to respond to the unpredictable demands of an ever-changing future.[54]

Ultimately, the problem of the *order* of knowledge faced by scholars in early modernity was, at its core, a *temporal* problem. From a socio-evolutionary perspective, this temporalisation of knowledge management emerged as a response to growing complexity and as a functionally more adequate alternative to the externalisation that had previously characterised the generalised and comprehensive schemes of knowledge (*topica*

[51] Eco (1990, p. 180) observed that in a filing system, connections are always present—it is merely a matter of wanting to find them.

[52] The terms 'loosening' and 'recombination' are drawn from early-modern semantics but also hold conceptual validity within the framework of sociological media theory. On this theory, see Corsi (2001; 2023).

[53] On the loose coupling of past and future as a temporal structure of modern society, see Corsi (2014a, esp. p. 66; 2014b, p. 302ff.).

[54] Here, I draw on a statement by Bowker (2005, p. 230), who argues that "only an open past can unlock the present and free the future".

universalis). This shift also implied a more pronounced presence of observers in their own operations. Yet, if the future remained dependent on the available past, how could one determine in the present which past would most likely be needed in the future?

3.5 Forgetting Machines

The relationship that early modern scholars had with the past was undoubtedly ambiguous. One of the first effects of the printing industry was the widespread availability of knowledge that had previously circulated only through manuscripts. The mechanical reproduction of books represented a unique opportunity, as it relieved scholars of the laborious and time-consuming task of copying texts by hand and significantly accelerated access to publications. However, this social diffusion of knowledge also had unintended consequences: if everyone could access all available knowledge, what was the purpose of displaying a prodigious memory?

In its first two centuries of operation, the printing industry circulated a large number of 'sylvae' and 'polymathy' books that either reproduced (with some updates) or imitated medieval collections of commonplaces (*florilegia*). However, this very circulation rendered pedantic what had once been the product of laborious yet essential compilatory activity. During the sixteenth century, the genre of florilegia retained some appeal only insofar as it transformed erudition into a form of leisure for those seeking unusual answers to rather common questions (e.g., why humans have two legs and walk upright).[55] Yet, the inflation of this type of knowledge was inevitable. Faced with the vast number of publications readily available on the book market, the abundance of references to tradition began to be perceived as a form of artificial and contrived erudition—one that the emerging sensibility for the progress of knowledge made increasingly unconvincing (Ong 1970, esp. p. 101; Mertner 1972, esp. p. 54ff. and 68).

On the other hand, dispensing entirely with the past was not an option. First, because those who sought to present themselves as 'authors' with something new to say had to be aware of what had already been published—if only to avoid being perceived as ill-informed readers. Moreover, only the past (i.e., the content of a universal library) could indirectly

[55] On the rise and decline of this literary genre (including its commercial aspects), see Cherchi (1998; 1999).

point to what was not yet known. Learned readers could no longer justify their ignorance through external causes, such as the unavailability of a text. Like knowledge, ignorance could only be self-attributed. Publications thus became both indispensable and superfluous at the same time. On the one hand, they served to keep one informed; on the other hand, they represented a starting point from which to distance oneself, avoiding the risk of merely repeating what could be read elsewhere.

Without taking this particular temporal structure into consideration, it would be difficult to understand a warning like that of Muratori, who advised that only by "handling" many authors is it possible to identify what they have addressed "little or not at all [...], or poorly", thus offering a suggestion on what readers themselves might "address better and with greater success". For Muratori (1768, Second Part, Ch. XVI, p. 355), the principal rule for anyone wishing to publish a book was, consequently, to read widely and observe "what is lacking in the books of others".

In rhetorical culture, such an instruction would have been incomprehensible. First, because the reader's attention was focused on 'ruminating' the book's content in order to memorise it. Moreover, the idea that intellectual activity should aim at expanding and improving knowledge was foreign to a culture primarily concerned with preservation. Even the work of scribes was driven more by the necessity to safeguard a text than by a desire to circulate it. This logic of "treasuring" (Chartier 1999, esp. p. 25) also explains why, before the invention of the printing press, the preference was to replicate the same books rather than entice readers with the offer of new texts.

The modern library aligns with Muratori's instructions. In a hypothetical universal library, one can review everything that has been produced and, *precisely for this reason*, also discern what is still missing (Theisohn 2009, esp. p. 142). The marking of absence is a correlate of society's orientation toward the future. Printing, understood as the possibility of publishing, provides a supporting medium for this orientation. The motivation to say something new or to explore the unknown arises not so much from individual consciousness but from the medium itself, which ensures the recursive reproduction of communication.

Precisely when the future assumes the role of an inexhaustible reservoir of irritations, the ability to forget becomes crucial.[56] This does not mean dispensing with stored knowledge, as we have seen. Rather, it involves preventing the past from constraining the present's capacity to imagine alternative possibilities. There is a shift, so to speak, from a compulsion to repeat to a compulsion to combine. For this reason, it becomes essential to always have a memorable past readily available for an unpredictable future.

The modern maxim that "novelty is no small part of beauty" (Muratori 1768, Second Part, Ch. XVI, p. 355) cannot simply be explained as a rejection of redundancy. The past must be embraced in order to be rejected. Moreover, although it cannot change, it is always different; for this reason, it suggests new perspectives each time it is taken into consideration. As Luhmann (1997b, p. 368) states, "every new situation renews, with the then newly organised information, the difference of past and future as well". The value of indexing systems becomes clear when considering this contingent coupling. Precisely because it leaves the future indeterminate (a catalogue does not predetermine how and for what purpose users will use it), indexing enables the recursive reuse of redundancy in ever-new contexts and for new purposes. As such, it constitutes a fundamental structure of modern social memory.

The fascinating aspect of this structure is that it enables the operational combination of an open future with an ever-expanding past. On the one hand, as we have seen, information processing techniques such as notebooks or filing cabinets allow for the daily addition of new material to what has already been stored. This expanding past is preserved in an order designed to foster the production of possibilities while minimising constraints. In this sense, as Muratori put it, the past is "capitalised".[57] While methodical order relieved the reader of the need to determine meaningful connections—thereby drastically limiting the potential for exploring innovative links—a loose order of notes left entirely open the

[56] Cf. Esposito (2016, p. 338): "The more relevant the future becomes, the more the role of forgetting increases".

[57] Muratori (1723, Second Part, Ch. VII, p. 134). At the level of society as a whole, this 'capitalisation' also has a counterpart in the rejection of constraints attributable to external causes, such as one's family background—particularly when it comes to building an individual 'career' that depends on functional subsystems like the educational system. See Corsi (1993, p. 252ff.; 2014a, p. 65ff.).

combinations the reader might achieve. Rather than simply conforming the future to the accumulated past, the reader could instead adapt the past to an unpredictable future.

This form of capitalisation relied on effective techniques of forgetting—not only because the unlimited expansion of the past, by definition, cannot be fully memorised, but also because, in order to make use of the available past, the reader had to forget almost everything except the small portion that could serve to produce information. The inhibition of forgetting occurred selectively, based on the reader's purposes, yet it was not random, thanks to indexing structures. Precisely in this sense, succedaneous memories were primarily employed as 'forgetting machines'.[58]

3.6 Archiving and Indexing

The modern model of social memory is based on a crucial distinction: that between 'archiving' and 'indexing'. In the first case, the task is to decide what to retain and what to discard. In the second, the task is to establish the rules governing access to what has been archived. In both cases, discrimination is involved. Archiving distinguishes what will be available from what will be unavailable.[59] Indexing methods, on the other hand, distinguish what is accessible from what is inaccessible to the user interacting with external memory (Esposito 2016, esp. p. 340).

The consequences of these two forms of discrimination are very different. In the first case, what is discarded falls into oblivion. In the second, what is inaccessible cannot be intentionally retrieved and does not even appear in the user's searches. In a sense, it is as if it did not exist at all, even though it is stored somewhere in the archive and may be rediscovered by chance. In very abstract terms, one could say that archiving draws a boundary between an explorable space of knowledge and a space of non-knowledge that cannot be acted upon (the filing system forgets what the reader discarded when selecting something to remember). Indexing, on the other hand, draws a distinction between what becomes present whenever the user reactivates the search engine and what remains latent. The

58 See the contributions edited by Cevolini (2016a).

59 Regarding scientific archives, Daston (2017a, p. 1) speaks of a "third nature": the archive would be the repository of those findings of second nature which have been selected to endure.

unmarked space beyond the boundaries of the archive thus represents the 'dark side' of social memory.[60]

Two centuries after the invention of the printing press, it became evident that solving the problem of availability had created a concurrent problem of accessibility: users risked getting lost in an 'ocean' of contents, much of which was superfluous to their information needs. At the same time, it also became clear that the relationship between archiving and indexing is a circular one. While it is evident that one can only catalogue or index what has been stored, it is equally true that the index provides a network of references and connections that serve as vantage points for selecting what can be further archived.[61]

Here, once again, the importance of subject headings becomes evident. Taken together, they form a self-referential horizon of meaning that marks the boundaries of what is memorable for the observer (even when the observing system is society as a whole). Memory, after all, cannot be organised externally but only internally—that is, after the system has already begun to produce operations. The challenge lies in managing this organisation while acknowledging that, in relation to what is realised, there are always infinite alternative possibilities. In early modernity, this issue did not go unnoticed.

When the Jesuit Jeremias Drexel advised students to begin early in extracting memorable contents from books, he specified that the purpose of this activity was *to select and thereby prepare for meeting future needs*.[62] However, this approach merely pointed to the problem without solving it. Each time readers select some material, they must avoid preserving what is superfluous while also ensuring that nothing essential is discarded. If the question is "What is the best method for reading books profitably?" (Sacchini 1613), selection alone is insufficient. There must also be criteria to guide this selective activity—criteria that can only depend on the future, which, by definition, remains unpredictable.

On this matter, Muratori observed that the key "lies in knowing what one must or must not select [trascegliere]" and "in subsequently being

[60] The distinction between *unmarked space* and *unmarked state* is drawn from Spencer Brown (1979).

[61] In this regard, Luhmann (1987, p. 150) stated that he always read with an eye toward the possibility of filing notes.

[62] "Excerpe, & nota: selige, ac futuro para" (Drexel 1638, p. 290). Cf. also Cevolini (2019a).

able to arrange [that is, organise] the selected information with some method, so that it may be more easily at hand when needed".[63] However, Caspar Sagittarius (1703, § 8, p. 5) had already pointed out that determining what might prove useful in the future is difficult. Scholars who attempted to address this problem typically offered tautological solutions. No one, of course, questioned the necessity of selection.[64] Yet, when asked how one could know which content was memorable, the usual response was that the reader should choose the best material (*selectiora*) and note only what was worthy of attention. In doing so, they would preserve for future use what would later prove useful.[65]

Like all tautologies, these too resulted in an unproductive circularity. And, like all unproductive circularities, it could be interrupted (though not eliminated) by introducing a distinction.[66] The modernity of the solution proposed by seventeenth-century scholars lay in the fact that the distinction they introduced was a temporal one. They encouraged readers to keep in mind "the purpose of their studies" (Sacchini 1613, p. 63; Drexel 1638, p. 85; Sagittarius 1703, § 8, p. 5). This instruction is less self-evident than it appears and deserves closer examination.

A purpose is a future-related distinction that allows observers to refer to themselves without the risk of falling into circularity (Luhmann 2011, p. 162ff.). Purpose generates complexity—an excess of possible connections—while simultaneously reducing it. For instance, someone studying theology can disregard legal texts but must still engage with all the possibilities that theological texts present. This does not eliminate the productive role of chance, but it at least narrows the scope of what can initially be considered relevant. By keeping their study purpose in mind, readers can monitor themselves, asking, for example, whether what they are reading is essential and whether the text they are studying is worth

63 Muratori (1723, Second Part, Ch. VII, p. 136). Muratori did not provide any answer to these two questions, as he believed that this was not the appropriate place to address them. However, one might suspect that he simply had no answer to give.

64 Drexel's (1638, p. 2) book on note-taking methods opened with precisely this observation: "Legere, & nihil seligere, meo judicio, prorsus negligere est" (to read without selecting anything, in my opinion, is sheer negligence).

65 Cf., among others, Sacchini (1613, p. 62); Titius (1676, p. 2); Placcius (1689, p. 27); Sidelius and Schubart (1713, p. 8).

66 Here, I reiterate an argument made by Luhmann (1981, p. 32ff.).

being excerpted—not *in se* (i.e., inherently), but *per se* (i.e., in relation to themselves and the scope of their studies).

The encouragement to keep in mind the purpose of one's studies might, at first glance, seem to contradict early modern scholars' preference for loose annotation methods such as *adversaria*. Those who opted for a miscellaneous order did so to maintain the freedom to read in an occasional, interdisciplinary, and even chaotic manner. In this regard, Fred Schurink (2010, p. 453ff.) distinguishes between two types of readers—*goal-oriented* and *recreational* readers—and argues that there was significant diversity among educated classes of the time. However, this classification does not account for the function of purpose. Purpose does not constrain the unpredictable development of research; rather, it provides a structured framework for this unpredictability. Purpose is, therefore, one of the tools through which readers, rather than controlling knowledge, control themselves when engaging with learning.

The purpose of one's studies, however, is not the purpose of the filing cabinet. This distinction becomes evident when considering that, while studies may conclude once their purpose has been achieved, substitute memory systems can archive content indefinitely. In the semantics of the time, particularly in the seventeenth century, traces of this orientation toward an open future can be found in many concepts, including that of 'perfection'.

In the Old European tradition, the concept of perfection was closely associated with purpose within a teleological understanding of reality. The idea was that everything in existence has its own nature, toward which it tends as its final end, and upon reaching this end, it can be said to be 'perfect' (Aristotle *Metaph.*, V, 16, 1021b24f.; Foss 1946, esp. p. 8ff.). The notion of perfection thus implied a sense of completeness, whereby something imperfect lacks what is necessary to be fully realised. That which achieves its purpose has nothing more to add and finds in this fulfilment a state of rest (much like the completion of a building according to its design). In contrast, the absence of certain elements—that is, imperfection—motivates movement and corresponds to a state of restlessness.

In the administration of knowledge, this idea of immobility associated with the notion of perfection found its counterpart in the universal system of topics (*topica universalis*). Just as a physical territory typically remains unchanged, nothing usually needs to be added to its map, provided that the geography of the places has been accurately represented. Similarly, the contents of *topica universalis* retained their extra-temporal validity as they referred to a nature—Creation—which, by definition, is not subject to improvement. The knowledge transmitted by rhetorical culture was thus paradigmatic knowledge—that is, the result of inferring universal truths from particular episodes (*exempla*). This also justified a meta-historical interpretation of history: while singular and unrepeatable worldly events alternate chaotically over time (*tempus*), the lessons derived from them possess a stable and repeatable validity.[67] Like everything that pertains to eternity (*aeternitas*), this validity resists the passage of time and remains independent of the author who formulated the teaching.[68]

For all these reasons, the topical conception of knowledge did not allow for progress or improvement. This is why its organisation could take the form of a taxonomy. Perfection itself—by resorting to self-reference—provided a justification for resisting change: perfection is perfect by definition; one perfection cannot be more perfect than another, as perfection lacks nothing to be complete. For the same reason, infinity could not represent a form of perfection, as it can always have something more added to it (Thomas Aquinas *De Div. Nom.*, c. XIII, l. 2, § 964).

In early-modern Europe, this static conception of knowledge, which was thought to reflect the eternally valid order of the universe, began to be questioned. In the semantics of the time, a temporalisation of concepts, including that of perfection, became increasingly evident (Koselleck and Meier 1991, esp. p. 33ff. and 38ff.). This temporalisation was reinforced and accelerated by the restructuring of temporal horizons: the administration of knowledge was no longer driven by the distinction between *tempus* and *aeternitas*, but rather by the distinction between past and future.

Social memory adapted to this temporal restructuring through, as we have seen, a growing appreciation for methods of knowledge storage that left space for the addition of further content. The fact that something was missing from what was already known was no longer perceived as a flaw but rather as a precondition for encouraging scientists to explore what was not yet known. Substitute memory systems were thus designed to continuously accommodate something new. In other words, archiving

[67] In this sense, history is full of 'examples' (Cicero). Cf. Koselleck (1979, p. 38ff.).

[68] On the concept of 'classic', cf. Gadamer (1960, p. 269ff.). See also Curtius (1972, esp. p. 9).

and filing systems were structured not to preserve the past but to preserve the future.[69]

In the reflections of seventeenth-century scholars, this profound transformation in temporal orientation is evident in how it led to the overturning of the classical precept that the wise should not pursue the infinite. For readers dealing with the uninterrupted reproduction of potentially interesting publications, the idea of relying on a pre-structured commonplace-book became increasingly unappealing. This is why some manuals on the art of note-taking reassured readers, asserting that they need not fear multiplying the "classes" (i.e., entries) in their personal archives.[70] It was clear that this would promote forgetting. Yet, it was equally evident that the use of external memory systems would enable users to remember far more than even before.

Furthermore, given that reading the texts circulated by the printing industry could, in principle, continue indefinitely, the idea of having a finite space to store what was considered memorable began to appear contradictory. For this reason, Philomusus (1684, p. 32) admitted that, faced with such difficulties, he had come to appreciate those authors who instead advocated *numbering* commonplaces as a way of encompassing the "entire variety of knowledge" (*omnis rerum varietas*).

This numerical recording paved the way for the unlimited expansion of memory contents, with crucial implications for how those contents could be retrieved. The same applied to all those filing systems that, from the outset, were structured to function as "universal (alphabetical) indices of all authors". In both cases, the future-oriented structure of secondary memory systems was supported by filing methods that, more than any others, dismantled the topical organisation of knowledge. It is only against the backdrop of these profound structural transformations that we can fully grasp the enthusiasm of learned men like Hartlib, who saw the filing cabinet's inability to be perfect (and therefore its perfectibility) as the very reason for its perfection (Hartlib Papers 30/4/46A, Ephemerides 1640, Part 2). In the chapters to come, I will explore how 'mechanisation', which had already begun in some sense with the

[69] On the 'future-centric' nature of modern archives, cf. Pomian (1997, p. 4058). See also Cevolini (2016b, p. 169ff.).

[70] Cf., for instance, Philomusus (1684, Ch. VIII): "Non esse temere multiplicandas excerptorum classes".

filing cabinet, further transformed the processes of archiving and indexing knowledge after the advent of the computer.

CHAPTER 4

The Cybernetic Library

4.1 Mechanical Memory

To introduce the topic of this chapter, I would like to begin with a reflection extracted from § 463 of Hegel's *Encyclopaedia of the Philosophical Sciences*. In this section, Hegel (2000, p. 763) addresses the subject of mechanical memory and assumes as a given the fact that "a composition is, as we know, not thoroughly conned by rote, until one attaches no meaning to the words. The recitation of what has been thus got by heart therefore becomes accentless by itself. The correct accent, if it is brought in, suggests the meaning; but this meaning, the idea which is evoked, disturbs the mechanical nexus and therefore easily throws out the recitation. The faculty of conning by rote series of words in whose connection there is no understanding, or which are meaningless in themselves (for example, a series of proper names), is so supremely marvelous, because it is the very essence of the mind [Geist] to be *with itself* [*bei sich selbst* zu sein]; whereas, in this case, the mind is estranged *within itself* [*in ihm selbst* entäußert], and its action is like machinery".

This quotation contains at least two crucial observations. The first concerns the fact that mnemonic learning becomes easier when it is reduced to a mechanical activity. Meaning is inherently complex because any meaningful content opens up a space of references to potentially infinite further contents. This excess of possibilities is disorienting and facilitates forgetting. Mechanical connection, on the other hand, relieves

A. Cevolini, *Indexing Systems*
https://doi.org/10.1007/978-3-032-13813-2_4

reason of any particular involvement and makes recall of what has been memorised more immediate. The contradiction, at least as far as the individual mind is concerned, lies in the fact that a mechanical connection is best performed by a mechanism external to consciousness. When reciting a series of meaningless syllables by heart, the mind operates like a machine, thereby finding itself externalised within itself.[1]

Hegel was well aware that the ancient art of reminiscence (*Mnemotechnik*) relied on the imagination's capacity to fix meaningful associations in order to recall what had been forgotten in the meantime. But he considered this technique to be "the stuff of idiots", as it forced consciousness to torment itself with a number of images that, while referring to something, could just as easily refer to something else, ultimately leading to forgetfulness rather than recollection.[2] In line with the Enlightenment critique of reminiscence techniques, Hegel regarded as more authentic a memory that springs, as it were, from within the mind and proceeds by means of logical-rational connections—one that arises as the product of reason's activity.

The allusion to a relationship between mechanical activity and memory is nonetheless remarkable, as it suggests the possibility that the retrieval of memories could be entrusted to an external tool—a machine—that operates more efficiently than consciousness precisely because it is not hindered by the mind's self-reflective activity. The rehabilitation of the mechanical arts had begun two centuries earlier, when Francis Bacon (2002, p. 13f.) observed that, while the liberal arts had remained essentially unchanged over time, the mechanical arts had made significant progress and continued to advance day by day for the benefit of humankind. This perspective reinforced the idea that innovation in general (not just technical innovation) is inherently positive and that what adds something new to what is inherited from the past is better than what remains unchanged.

[1] It should be noted, however, that in his famous psychological studies on memory, Ebbinghaus (2011, esp. p. 19ff.) resorted to meaningless syllables precisely to prevent meaning from suggesting associations that could drive the retrieval of memories. By avoiding any use of language, consciousness could be investigated regardless of its structural coupling with communication. Cf. also Luhmann (1996, p. 317 fn. 16).

[2] Hegel (2000, § 462, p. 761). Hegel was familiar with Kästner's (1805) work. However, the critique of the ancient art of reminiscence was not novel, having already been widespread two centuries before Hegel. See Sect. 1.8

Behind this re-evaluation of the mechanical arts lay a far-reaching change in social structures that undermined the hierarchical difference between professions practised out of necessity for survival ('illiberal') and professions practised without this concern ('liberal'), such as that of the rhetorician. The success of printing technology and the increasing complexity of knowledge paved the way for a technologisation of knowledge management. The same filing cabinet invented by Thomas Harrison in the early 1640s was described, by the late seventeenth century, as a "machine for producing and collecting excerpts".[3] Commenting on the advantages of this filing cabinet, Samuel Hartlib explicitly referred to a "mechanical way for common-places with removable notes",[4] without this mechanisation of the process of storing and retrieving memorable notions being perceived as something particularly deviant.

However, this definition implicitly accepted the unprecedented idea that memory retrieval could depend on the interaction between the user and an external machine, rather than on the users' interaction with their own mind. And it definitively positioned consciousness on the side of natural memory, placing on the opposite side of the distinction—artificial memory—everything that could be structured as an external memory to be used as a substitute for individual memory.

The second remarkable observation in Hegel's reflection is that memory might function more efficiently when it is detached from the processing of meaning. Neither the filing cabinet nor the modern library achieves this result because they remain bound to a semantic indexing of their contents. It is true that, compared to the library, the filing cabinet allows for much greater flexibility in the abstraction procedures used to categorise knowledge. But this categorisation, as we have seen, still entails decisions that once again struggle with the complexity of meaning and the temporal circularity of concerns regarding access to archived contents. The true evolutionary saltation, therefore, occurs when

[3] Morhof (1747, p. 713) ("ad excerpendum et colligendum machina").

[4] Harrison (2017) himself, in fact, often refers to his invention as a 'machine'. Hartlib's observation dates back to 1655. Cf. Hartlib Papers (29/5/40B, Ephemerides 1655, Part 3).

accessing information relies on machines that operate according to predetermined rules but neither understand the meaning of what they do nor the meaning of the rules themselves.[5]

The relationship between evolution and technological progress should not, however, be misunderstood. It is not technology that drives evolution; rather, it is evolution that takes advantage of technological progress if, under certain conditions, it proves beneficial to the system of society. Furthermore, while technological progress can be planned to some extent, evolution cannot. It is therefore not search engines that have driven the evolution of social memory. Rather, it would be more accurate to say that the evolution of social memory has leveraged the advantages offered by search engines over other alternatives.

The difference between socio-cultural evolution and technological progress is also evident in the fact that evolution does not replace old communication technologies with new ones. People do not stop communicating orally simply because they have learnt to write, nor do they abandon handwriting when mechanical writing becomes available. Rather, socio-cultural evolution operates reflexively: when people learn to write, they come to perceive writing as an alternative to oral communication, thereby transforming orality into a possibility among available alternatives.

The success of search engines, therefore, does not depend solely on their technical properties.[6] Tim Berners-Lee (1999, p. 133) himself acknowledged that the Web is more a social creation than a technological innovation. From a strictly technical standpoint, in fact, the Web emerged from the integration of two pre-existing technologies—the Internet and hyperlinks. Once again, we can say that evolution has taken advantage of something originally conceived for other purposes,[7] without being intentionally designed to underpin the evolution of social memory.

[5] These rules usually take the form of algorithms. Cf. Luhmann (1966, esp. p. 45) and, more extensively, Esposito (2017b) and Burrell (2016, esp. p. 10). The algorithm, therefore, is the machine.

[6] This does not change the fact that search engines survive or die out depending on their quality, that is, their ability to make relevant selections within the available complexity. Cf., for example, MacCormick (2012, esp. p. 13).

[7] The same can be said of Google: its algorithm was developed by integrating common information retrieval technologies with well-known mathematical tools such as sociometry, graph theory and the analysis of citations in scientific publications. All these tools had been conceived in different contexts to solve different problems. See, in historical perspective, Mayer (2009, esp. p. 56 and 58ff.); Rieder (2012); Jones (2017, esp. p. 321ff.).

This does not exclude the possibility that, when faced with practical problems, those most familiar with them may provide valuable insights for developing appropriate technical solutions. In this regard, Heinz von Foerster suggested that the real question is not so much what technology can do for librarians, but rather what librarians can do for technology.[8] However, the evolutionary success of different technical solutions ultimately depends on how effectively they manage complexity.

The possibility of mechanising access to content stored in external memory systems began to be explored in the second half of the twentieth century. Although the term 'semantic computation' was somewhat misleadingly used between the late 1960s and early 1970s, the idea inspiring these experiments was the possibility of entrusting the machine with selection tasks that would otherwise have to be carried out by a human staff.[9] In executing this project, the renunciation of meaning was not a sacrifice to be accepted as a consequence of mechanisation; rather, mechanisation itself represented an advantage that could be exploited, provided operations could do without meaning. The machine could thus replace consciousness, relieving it of the burden of selection.[10]

From a strictly historical perspective, the preference for the automation of access to information arose precisely from socio-economic considerations. The Web had made it evident that manual indexing by specialised personnel was not only slow and laborious but also expensive and influenced by subjective factors, while traditional information retrieval techniques based on matching search terms with retrieved documents too often yielded poorly relevant results (Brin and Page 1998, p. 107f.). The alternative was therefore not merely between manual and mechanical indexing, but also (if not primarily) between effective and ineffective mechanical indexing. However, the precondition for achieving this mechanisation remained unchanged: people had to abandon the idea of the document as a compact form of communication, consistent with the traditional culture of the book.

[8] Foerster (1971). On this seminal article, see also Cevolini (2008).

[9] On this issue, see the valuable contribution of Maron and Kuhns (1960), who explicitly stated that their aim was to "mechanize a library" (p. 217).

[10] According to Luhmann (2011, p. 376), the computer, like all technical systems, is generally designed to relieve—if not entirely replace—self-reproducing systems, such as consciousness.

4.2 Processing Data to Obtain Information

The essential technical prerequisite for automating the retrieval of archived content is, first and foremost, the transformation of documents into data. This is the task of all those sophisticated computational procedures that constitute the core of search engine science.[11] At every stage—from text acquisition to transformation and the creation of an inverted index—the machine never processes meaning but merely converts documents into a data store that the machine itself can manage. These assumptions have two fundamental consequences: the definitive separation of information from the act of communication (*Mitteilung*), and a clearer distinction between document and information.

The habit of extrapolating memorable passages from books and then storing them loosely in a filing cabinet based on alphabetically organised entries had already depreciated the persuasive components of communication, bringing information to the foreground.[12] Samuel Hartlib observed, in this regard, that one of the main advantages of the filing cabinet invented by Thomas Harrison was that the use of paper slips instead of bound notebooks compelled the reader "to cut off all superfluitys and impertinencys from the propositions" (Hartlib Papers 30/4/47B, Ephemerides 1640, Part 2). The excerpting technique thus aligned with the practice of 'aphorisms' recommended by Francis Bacon. Assuming that in the great variety of books (*varietas librorum*) continually produced by the printing press, there was not only diversity in the way subjects were treated (*diversitas modi tractandi*) but also an infinite repetition (*repetitiones infinitas*) of content, Bacon (2002, p. 12) urged the educated reader to extrapolate only what was truly informative, discarding everything else. The method of aphorisms—that is, the preference for short annotations free from the author's interference and the cumbersome burden of rhetorical devices—was particularly well-suited to this purpose and ensured a swifter advancement of learning.

Only with the introduction of a machine, however, does the unity of understanding and the act of communication become lost. First, because

[11] Literature is very large. See only Büttcher et al. (2010); Croft et al. (2015); Lewandowski (2015).

[12] According to Luhmann (1997a, p. 1091), this preference for information over persuasion is an effect of printing technology.

one cannot reasonably attribute to a machine the intention of communicating anything.[13] Second, because the machine functions as a 'data processing system' in the sense that the outgoing data are never exactly the same as the incoming data, as they have been 'processed' in the meantime.[14] This implies that, in terms of information, the output is less than the input, either because inferences are drawn from the data and presented in place of the raw data, as in the case of statistical tables, or because the data are indexed. But it also means that the output can exceed the input, as processing may generate information that would not have been obtained otherwise.

The second consequence of converting documents into data that can be mechanically managed is that users' access to information becomes detached from the information vehicle.[15] This separation already implies a certain level of abstraction. The user no longer needs to ask, "Where is the answer to my question?" but rather, "What is the answer to my question?" (Foerster 1971, p. 786). The transformation of documents into data significantly enhances the overall combinatorial potential, as it leaves entirely open how users can interact with the data. As a result, the likelihood of generating surprising—and therefore genuinely informative—combinations increases proportionally.

The overcoming of the document as a vehicle for information is not a direct consequence of automated data processing. As we saw in the previous chapter, to cope with the increasing complexity of knowledge, modern society had already developed sophisticated indexing systems, abstract archiving procedures, and complex cross-reference structures that allowed users to 'navigate' the *mare magnum* of knowledge. From a functional viewpoint, all these tools anticipated the technical innovations represented by search engines. Their use, however, remained tied to a 'library', i.e., a collection of books.

In addition, those responsible for indexing the content of a library did not abandon the idea that knowledge could be organised according to distinctions independent of the user. The true technical advancement

[13] You do not talk to the computer; you use it. Cf. Esposito (1993, p. 350; 1995, p. 97).

[14] This was exactly what Simon (1971, p. 42ff.) meant when he spoke of *information processing systems*. Cf. also Luhmann (1997a, p. 309), referring to the computer.

[15] This important distinction between information and the vehicle of information has been suggested by Foerster (1969, p. 22; 1971, p. 789). See also Sect. 2.1.

with far-reaching consequences for the organisation of information access occurs only with the transition from a network of documents to a network of data.[16] Knowledge is thus 'atomised' into data linked by relational structures. This approach not only avoids redundancy, thereby addressing the issue of *multiple storage*, but also offers advantages beyond mere space-saving.

Databases allow stored data to be accessed from any entry point chosen by the users based on their information needs. The architectural structure of the rhetorical storehouse required the rhetorician to establish a single entry point, from which the exploration of the storehouse could proceed according to the order of *loci* designed to store active images. A database, by contrast, enables users to freely select their entry point from among the potentially infinite access points provided by its relational structure. Atomised and loosely connected data also allow for a theoretically unlimited recombination.[17] Both of these possibilities—the free selection of access points within the database and the possibility of recombining the available data at will—ultimately correspond to an open future and the inherent uncertainty of users' information needs.

Like the miscellaneous collections of excerpts produced by learned men in early modernity, databases are not merely chaotic repositories of data. The relational structure that loosely links the data represents an 'ordered chaos' that enables users to derive order from disorder, that is, to extract information from the redundancy that the machine stores in the form of something that is, precisely, 'given' (*datum*).[18] For this reason, the structure of relations is far more important than the individual data. A data point is what it is—that is, a difference. Each data point acquires informational value only when it is related to other data points, so that

[16] On this shift, see Bizer et al. (2009, § 1); Guerrini and Possemato (2013, p. 70ff.); Wood et al. (2014, p. 60ff.); Iacono (2014, p. 17ff.); Berners-Lee et al. (2001); Berners-Lee and Hendler (2010, p. 158).

[17] On the structural properties of databases, cf. Klaus and Liebscher (1979, vol. 1, p. 154); Gillespie (2014, esp. p. 171); Manovich (2002, esp. p. 275).

[18] On the apparent disorder of databases, see Manovich (2002, p. 281 and 291ff.). Cf. also Ernst (2002, esp. p. 116ff.). Retrospectively, it is interesting to note that Brin and Page's (1998) original intention when formulating the PageRank algorithm was to "bring order to the Web". By this, however, they meant the need to discriminate between search results so that the user would not waste time browsing through a myriad of irrelevant contents. In short, it was a matter of increasing the machine's capability to discard. I will return to this point later.

the difference can potentially make a difference to the observer. Moreover, each data point is accessible only insofar as it is embedded within this relational structure. For all these reasons, as Tim Berners-Lee (1999, p. 14) pointed out, in archives, "structure is everything".

While the input of data does not follow any particular selection criteria (no data are inherently better or worse than others precisely because they are 'given', regardless of who produced them), the choice of relationships that structure access to the archive cannot be made arbitrarily. Various projects aimed at facilitating a more efficient use of archived resources, such as *linked data* or the so-called 'Semantic Web', address exactly this issue. Unlike hypertext links, the guiding idea in both cases is to qualify the links by, so to speak, adding meaning to the relationships between data.

The machine, of course, does not understand the meaning of its own operations. Meaning plays a role either on the programmer's side—when, for example, the programmer determines the relation that should link a predicate to a subject (the so-called RDF: resource description framework)—or on the user's side. The goal of still unfinished projects such as *linked data* or the 'Semantic Web' is to create an ambient in which every piece of data is indeed linked, but not indiscriminately connected to every other piece of data, since this would make the ambient unexplorable. In other words, the issue is adding constraints that reduce the degrees of freedom in the relational structure—at the risk, however, of making the memory system more predictable.

The common ambition of these projects is to create a "global space of data linked to other data", making a decisive step toward the full realisation of the potential implicit in the Web.[19] The outcome would be a machine that is both transparent and opaque at the same time. The Web is opaque, by definition, simply because no user can explore the content of the machine from the inside (and even if they could, what they would see would be so complex as to be opaque). But the Web is, at the same time, transparent because the user's interaction with the machine does not aim to inform the user about the *contents* stored within it, but rather aims to inform the user about the world *through* interaction with the machine.[20]

[19] As Bizer et al. (2009) state in the conclusion of their article. Cf. also Wood et al. (2014, p. 239ff.).

[20] In this regard, Bizer et al. (2009, § 2) argue that the Web of data is "*a Web of things in the world, described by data on the Web*".

If the data space were global, the machine would, in phenomenological terms, be as extensive as the world itself, and any access to the world would—as in many cases it already does—first pass through the machine, with consequences for society that remain, at least in part, unexplored.

4.3 User Adaptiveness

To re-activate the relational structure of the archive, an index is first required. In the case of a machine, this index is the result of search engine operations, that is, of an automated system designed to index and retrieve content stored in the digital archive. From a functional standpoint, there is no fundamental difference between the inverted index generated by a search engine and one that can be produced manually, such as the alpha-numeric index devised by John Locke to access his collection of excerpts.[21] Between these two inverted indexes, however, there are differences that extend beyond the simple distinction between manual and automated processes.

The institutionalisation of the first modern libraries made it evident that, in order to be of *public* utility, a library must be able to meet the knowledge needs of a potentially infinite and inherently unpredictable number of *individual* users.[22] This apparent paradox arose from the definitive differentiation between social memory and individual memory. While medieval educated readers adapted their florilegium to their own scholarly attitudes, personalising what was meant to support their individual memory, the modern archive separates the realm of consciousness from the realm of communication. This separation makes the standardisation of information access procedures indispensable in order to facilitate their personalised use.[23] This increasing standardisation had, as we have seen, first affected the printed book and encouraged the introduction of technical devices now taken for granted, such as page numbering and the compilation of alphabetical indexes. The ability to store data in a

[21] See above Sect. 2.8.

[22] Cf. Hottinger (1664, p. 79): "Anyone who wants to make libraries available to the public must adapt to many minds" ("Qui Bibliothecas usui publico vult inservire, multis se debet accomodare ingenjis").

[23] On the fact that communication technologies promote personalisation through standardisation, see Esposito (1995).

computer, along with the corresponding automation of indexing procedures, has further reinforced this standardisation, thereby making the need for personalisation even more challenging.

Just as the queries addressed to a universal library are always particular, so too are the queries submitted to a machine inherently indeterminate. Search engines are specifically designed to accommodate this indeterminacy. Users' queries do not need to be formulated in a pre-classified manner, nor do they have to adhere to an order of knowledge that is independent of the users. The provisional nature of information needs renders any attempt at categorisation superfluous, though this does not exclude the possibility of reducing the complexity of queries through differentiated access to the archive. In the early 1970s, Heinz von Foerster (1971, esp. p. 792f.) observed that librarians would need to prepare to answer user questions formulated as riddles. Drawing on the algorithms pioneered by Paul Weston (1970), he further argued that this would only be possible by developing relational databases in which exploration would depend, first and foremost, on user input.

The defining characteristic of riddles is that they provide incomplete information, leaving the person who intends to solve the riddle with the task of completing the missing information through logical-deductive operations or semantic associations. By doing so, the residual uncertainty is gradually reduced until the final solution is reached. A riddle thus combines knowing and not knowing, making the latter dependent on what is already known (each riddle starts from different premises). Information, in other words, both reduces and generates uncertainty at the same time.

The HIRWON algorithm, developed by Weston, was designed to draw inferences from the initially incomplete information, either by leveraging existing relationships in incoming data, or by logically and deductively exploring unexplored search paths. In the latter case, the algorithm was trained to discard paths leading to contradictory conclusions and to retain those yielding consistent results. The outcome was an expansion of the relational structure, which the algorithm could then use to refine subsequent search operations and eventually achieve a complete result.

Such a machine had the advantage of not being rigidly bound to a predetermined correspondence between (user) questions and (machine) answers. It was, instead, designed to adapt to the user.[24] The primary challenge was not only to train the machine to solve riddles, but also to recognise, within the user's search behaviour, the riddle to be solved. The success of this evolutionary-technical advancement raises at least three fundamental questions: What is the purpose of adapting the machine to the user? How is this purpose achieved? And, ultimately, what is its significance for the evolution of social memory?

4.4 Minimizing the Deviation

Like all indexing systems, search engines are primarily designed not to present the correct results, but to filter out those most likely to be irrelevant to the user.[25] The fundamental problem remains the same: the time and attention users can devote to examining search results are scarce. The Web significantly expands data storage capacity, thereby increasing the potential for generating information, but it does not proportionally create more time and attention to devote to that information. On the contrary, it exacerbates the scarcity of these resources, making them increasingly difficult to manage. The paradoxical consequence is that users spend more and more time on the Web, dedicating greater attention to what it provides, while the time and attention they can allocate to its content are becoming increasingly scarce.[26]

From the perspective of social memory, however, the fundamental challenge for search engines remains their 'sorting out' function—namely, their ability to make a highly selective distinction between what is worth remembering and what is better forgotten. The unity of this distinction is rarely emphasized enough: one cannot retain something without discarding something else. Search engines not only consume users' time

[24] On this fundamental distinction between question/answer-systems, which are *machine invariant*, and cognitive memories, which are *user adaptive*, cf. Foerster (1971, esp. p. 793).

[25] For Halavais (2009, p. 57), a search engine is "a technology as much of ignoring as it is of presenting". On the other hand, the 'correct' results do not exist. The concept of relevance, as we shall see later, also implies this conclusion.

[26] This is why, according to many scholars, the real challenge for search engines lies in their ability to capture users' attention. Attention becomes a 'scarce commodity' that must be secured to ultimately make a profit. The literature on the attention economy is very extensive. In a more sociological perspective, see Halavais (2009, p. 69 and 77ff.); Introna and Nissenbaum (2000, p. 169ff.).

and attention as they engage with the machine's results, but they also save users' time and attention by sparing them the effort of consulting irrelevant content. In this sense, it is fair to say that search engines function as forgetting machines.[27]

As the need for sorting things out increases, so does the selectivity of selections, thereby enhancing the informational value of the latter. When interacting with the machine, however, users do not aim to optimize their information consumption; they simply seek to satisfy their need for information.[28] This distinction is crucial: users are not typically concerned with gathering all available information to form a comprehensive understanding of a situation. More often than not, they lack the time required to achieve this goal.[29] Instead, the search ends when users feel sufficiently satisfied with the results obtained—that is, when the uncertainty they were dealing with at the start of the search has been sufficiently reduced by the self-generated information, allowing them to absorb the residual uncertainty through a decision.

In rhetorical culture, attention was employed for different purposes. Orators wandering through their rhetorical storehouse in search of subjects not only had to pay attention to the architecture of the space to avoid losing their way; they also had to focus their attention on the images they encountered in order to trigger meaning associations that would lead to the retrieval of memorable things. This reminiscence activity was highly demanding in cognitive terms. Since attention was consumed in remembering, there was insufficient attention left for processing information. Only when users are freed from the need to commit things to memory, delegating even the task of indexing to the machine, can attention be redirected toward the self-production of information. The latter does not take place through the mere transfer of signals from one end of a channel to the other. The user-machine relationship is far more complex, taking the form of a cybernetic system.

[27] For further confirmation, see Vaidhyanathan (2011, p. 177): "Google is not just our memory machine; it is also our forgetting machine".

[28] On this important difference between 'optimization' and 'satisfaction', cf. Simon (1956, p. 129ff.).

[29] This does not rule out that the user sometimes has precisely this goal, as in the case of a scientist who wants to keep abreast of the available literature on a certain topic. But even when the topic is very specific, the amount of literature available is normally so vast that the user must stop before having consulted all that could be taken into consideration.

The typical function of a cybernetic system is to minimise the deviation from a difference—that between a desired state and the current state of the system.[30] The best-known case is the thermostat. To prevent the temperature from deviating from the preferred one, the machine turns the heating on or off based on the information it derives from the current temperature of the room. The cybernetic system is not the thermostat itself, but the circular interaction between the thermostat and its environment. Indeed, no system would exist if the machine did not treat temperature as a signal with informational value. Only when the thermostat 'couples' with its environment does a dynamic system emerge, exhibiting cybernetic properties.

The hypothesis derived from the scientific literature is that, in the case of search engines, the difference lies in the *relevance* of the results users obtain when performing a search.[31] What makes approaching this relevance particularly complex is the unpredictability of the questions users pose to the machine. Topical-rhetorical culture had circumvented this problem by organising knowledge around meaningful differences, which effectively reduced complexity but also drastically constrained access to knowledge. The ways in which a question could be framed, and consequently the possibilities of querying and obtaining consistent answers, were limited and highly repetitive. Variety was achieved not at the level of content, but at the level of content articulation.

Search engines, on the other hand, face the problem of the heterogeneity of user queries. Queries do not reach the machine in a pre-categorised form, so they cannot be processed by the machine in a pre-categorised way. While the geographies of commonplaces provided a kind of horizon of pre-understanding that pre-structured access to knowledge, search engines leave entirely undetermined the way in which users can irritate the machine to generate information. This indeterminacy coincides with the randomness by which individual instances scattered across the environment (i.e., user queries) are taken into consideration

[30] Sommerhoff (1974, p. 85). It should be noted that this cybernetic description is not only more appropriate than one based on the mathematical theory of communication, but also consistent with the socio-evolutionary approach adopted in this book. As Ashby (1956, § 1/2, p. 1) states, cybernetics is a 'functional' science whose crucial question is not "What *is* this?", but rather "*What does it do?*". In short, the epistemological approach of cybernetics is not ontological, but functional.

[31] On relevance, see Chap. 5.

to produce the desired knowledge.[32] Through the machine, the social system can thus tolerate far more uncertainty than before. In other terms, the irritability of the communication system increases as it relinquishes control over how the environment might surprise the system.

If, in cybernetic terms, we understand the minimization of discrepancy regarding the relevance of results as a form of 'regulation', then we can say that the introduction of the machine is a means for the social system to amplify its regulatory capacity in the face of an extremely heterogeneous and indeterminate environment.[33] From the perspective of social memory—understood as the organisation of access to information—this means that the system must be provided with far greater variety than before. Whereas a pre-packaged list of answers would be unsuitable for meeting the information needs of users posing the most diverse questions, a machine that adapts its responses to user queries, based on a pool of loosely connected data, is more likely to produce relevant combinations. The variety of results that the machine can produce is indispensable for 'breaking down' the variety of queries that may be submitted to the machine by the environment.[34] In this way, the social system preserves its adaptation despite the increasing complexity it has to tackle.

However, users' information needs are not only indeterminate; they are also unpredictable. This temporal aspect should not be underestimated. For the machine, the challenge is not merely to predict the unpredictable but, more fundamentally, to predict unpredictability. The machine, in other words, must operate under the assumption that it cannot know in advance what queries users might submit. For this reason, the machine must be designed from the outset to accept any question. In the light of this requirement, organising knowledge would not only be useless but also counterproductive: as with Llullian combinatorics, a pre-established order is suited to a scenario in which, whatever the topic may be, questions and answers are always the same. Yet, when memory is oriented toward the future, the management of knowledge becomes unpredictable for the simple reason that one cannot know what unknown users already know and what they do not yet know. While access to information can

[32] This hypothesis had already been put forward by Luhmann (1966, p. 63f.) with regard to early forms of automation of data processing within public administration.

[33] The concept of 'amplification of regulation' is borrowed from Ashby (1956, Ch. 14, p. 265ff.).

[34] On the principle of 'requisite variety', cf. Ashby (1958).

be organised, it is equally true that information itself cannot be stored; rather, it must be regenerated each time in a provisional way, based on the specificity of the situation. The loose manner in which data are interrelated in digital archives is a correlate of both the unpredictability of the future and the necessity of leaving open the possibility of querying memory in unexpected ways.

The amplification of regulation occurs through learning. Here again, learning is not a one-way process: users learn from the machine when they receive a list of answers to their questions, but the machine also learns from users when it detects redundancies in the variety of submitted queries. Learning takes place through signals that have informational value for the machine. The interaction between users and the machine thus exhibits a characteristically cybernetic circularity. Signals reflect the machine's capacity to inform itself based on the irritations (input) triggered by the environment. There is no transfer of information from the environment to the system. The increasingly sophisticated complexity of the algorithms that enable the machine to make conjectures is a direct consequence of the need to enhance the system's 'sensitivity', that is, its ability to accommodate greater indeterminacy in order to develop a more accurate understanding of the environment with which it interacts.

It is thus not only the archive that represents a black box for the user; the user, too, is a black box for the machine, which functions as a system for indexing the archive's content. To provide relevant results and meet users' information needs, the machine must, in turn, extract information from users' search behaviour. Only in this way can the machine address relevance issues and minimise discrepancies by implementing variations that serve a compensatory function (Sommerhoff 1974, esp. p. 78). Today, this process is carried out in a highly sophisticated manner through the social regulation of information access.

4.5 The User as a Black Box

Underlying the user-machine relationship, as we have seen, are two crucial issues. Indexing concerns the contents of the archive, not the information itself. Moreover, the machine does not understand the meaning of user queries. Even the relevance of results, as we shall examine in the next chapter, remains largely a conjecture based on user behaviour and cannot be definitively determined at either the beginning or the end of the search process. The technical mechanisms of search engines are designed to compensate for these limitations by generating a certain variety of results while ultimately reducing it.

The essential prerequisite, however, is that users and the machine are functionally 'coupled', thereby establishing a circular feedback relationship.[35] This coupling is, first and foremost, necessary to activate the machine. Like all heteropoietic systems, the machine can operate only if triggered from the outside. Furthermore, to fulfil its cybernetic regulatory function, the machine needs to acquire information about its environment via signals that determine the system's structural uncertainties. Only in this way can the environment become perceptible and less opaque. For all these reasons, as Kenneth Cukier (2010, p. 6) points out, the design of the *feedback loop* connecting users and the machine is crucial. The objective is not to achieve a specific goal but to enhance performance.

In the case of search engines, performance is no longer about ordering knowledge but about making conjectures. In technical terms, it still involves generating metadata to organise access to information. But when the succedaneous memory is no longer designed to provide redundancy but to produce information, the main opacity to be tackled is not only that of available knowledge—which, in its extreme complexity, remains intransparent—but also that of the user seeking access to knowledge. This opacity presents a problem without a definitive solution, which is why the search for a solution remains a never-ending challenge. For search engines, in other words, the ultimate algorithm does not exist. The environment is too heterogeneous, chaotic, and dynamic over time to be rendered fully transparent.

If user opacity cannot be reduced to transparency, efforts can at least be made to manage this opacity in a way that maximises the effectiveness of the user-machine relationship. For this reason, the machine must be continuously stimulated through signals that function as 'clues' through which the machine attempts to infer the user's actual need for information and selects, based on this inference, the content most likely to satisfy it.

The first clue, of course, is the user's query. The words in the query trigger the inverted index, thereby activating the structure of relations that constitutes the only internal order of the external memory. However, many additional clues can supplement this initial one, drastically reducing the variety of results that even a simple query could generate. The aim is

[35] On this concept of 'coupling', cf. Ashby (1956, § 4/6, p. 48f. and § 4/8, p. 51).

not to achieve complete relevance but rather to approximate relevance in the selected results (Gillespie 2014, p. 175; Croft et al. 2015, p. 280ff.).

Among the signals added to query terms are the context and the user's reaction to the results suggested by the machine. Context reduces uncertainty regarding the meaning of the query and, consequently, increases the likelihood of retrieving relevant results.[36] In verbal communication, this typically occurs through implicit, context-based assumptions. The question "What is more enlightening?" takes on a different meaning if it refers to the furnishing of a room rather than the insightfulness of an argument. Context increases situational redundancy, thereby reducing the degrees of freedom and refining the information that can be obtained.

Search engines cannot process the meaning of the frame surrounding each query, but they can take advantage of a number of signals (such as the physical location of the person submitting the query) that function precisely as clues and reduce the complexity of the situation (Pitkow 2002, p. 50ff.; Brewer 2001, p. 53ff.; Halavais 2009, p. 51). In this way, the machine can adapt to the environment without this adaptation resulting in a permanent state. What remains unchanged is the functioning of the signals. Like all cybernetic machines, search engines operate within a relatively indeterminate (i.e., contingent) situation, which is determined on a case-by-case basis through interaction with users. Contextual signals act, in this sense, as *structural uncertainties*: while the signal input is unpredictable, what can be anticipated is that the signal will provide useful indications for narrowing the variety of results.

Context is further refined through users' reaction to the results provided in response to their query. This feedback on the relevance of results is a typical tool of machine learning techniques already developed in the 1960s.[37] The underlying principle is that user reactions provide data which can be used to train the machine and enhance its performance. Just as a librarian might question the reader to better understand what could satisfy his or her desire for knowledge, the machine derives useful

[36] Meaning is a function of setting, as Maron and Kuhns (1960, p. 219) point out, but the machine has no access—or drastically limited access—to both meaning and setting. Hence arises the problem of semantic noise. On this problem, see further below Sect. 6. 1.

[37] See the seminal article by Rocchio (1971) based on a research project carried out in 1965. For a literature review on the concept of *relevance feedback*, cf. Kelley and Teevan (2003); Pasi (2014); Croft et al. (2015, p. 208ff.).

information from the outcome of the user-machine interaction to refine and optimise the interaction itself.

Feedback, as always, is reciprocal: from the difference between the results users discard and those they retain, the machine gathers information about the relevance of selected results and the irrelevance of those discarded. Similarly, users learn from the outcome of the interaction, for instance by rephrasing their query when the results are not particularly relevant. This rephrasing, in turn, feeds back into the machine as a signal that enhances its experience, enabling it to react to future queries in a more relevant manner.

Rather than producing the correct answer, the machine actually aims to generate an appropriate question.[38] The latter, however, remains a mere assumption. As Joseph Rocchio observed, if the right question were already known, the corresponding answer would also be known, eliminating the need for complex exploratory procedures. Search engines, by contrast, are designed to address the information needs of users who cannot adequately formulate their queries precisely because they do not really know what they are looking for. The absence of a pre-determined order in knowledge leaves entirely undetermined the criteria for its exploration. Yet, while such a form of looseness would have been inconceivable in a topical organisation of knowledge, in the case of cybernetic machines, this indeterminacy becomes an essential prerequisite for coping with the indeterminacy of the environment.

The feedback derived from users' reactions to search results reduces the discrepancy between the meaning of the query and the relevance of the answer by iteratively refining the query formulation. The circularity of feedback provides the machine with the ability to even anticipate what might be the most appropriate formulation. Feedback, in fact, leaves traces that the machine transforms into new connections and relationships. One could say that the machine learns not only from users' successes but also (perhaps even more so) from their mistakes. When users rephrase a question and obtain an answer they consider relevant, the machine links the previous (inappropriate) formulations to the relevant answer and uses this connection to suggest the correct query formulation to subsequent users (in the typical "Did you mean...?" format). The effect of this interaction is a gradual reduction in user opacity: not only does the

[38] Rocchio (1971, p. 7ff.) distinguished, in this regard, between an *optimal set of documents* and an *optimal query*.

machine gain a better approximation of what the user is searching for, but users also develop a clearer idea of what they actually want to know.[39]

Relevance feedback is also derived from users' behaviour when they select certain results from the list while discarding the others. The machine gathers information not only from the results that are retained but also from those that are ignored. If, for example, a user selects the third result in the list over the first and second, the machine learns by adjusting the ranking so that, in subsequent queries (all things being equal), the previously preferred result is ranked higher.[40] The machine learns, so to speak, that a less relevant result is more relevant because more relevant results are less relevant.

This ability to use past interactions as feedback to adjust future behaviour also affects the indexing process. The machine's learning performance depends as much on social factors as on temporal dynamics. These two dimensions do not operate independently but interact, thereby increasing the complexity of the situation that the machine can manage through the complexity of the algorithms activated by user queries.

In the indexing process, the machine can exploit the correspondence between query terms and selected results to expand the representation of resources in the inverted index. This is not merely a solution to the classic problem of multiple storage. Rather, it involves associating a heterogeneous set of metadata with the resource being searched, using submitted terms as training data for constructing the inverted index. The machine links to the resource not only the exact terms that immediately lead to the desired result but also incorrect terms that often prompt a reformulation of the query. The machine's performance can improve, in fact, if the indexing system also takes into account links between data and metadata that are *not* relevant (Amitay et al. 2005, p. 194ff; Brusilovsky et al. 2018, p. 226ff.). The search engine incorporates formulation errors (such

[39] Scholars speak, in this regard, of *query understanding*. Cf. Lewandowski (2015, p. 58ff.).

[40] On the information derived from users' *clickthrough* behaviour, cf. Joachims (2002, p. 133ff.) and Joachims and Radlinski (2007, p. 34ff.), followed by extensive subsequent research. The core idea was that any user behaviour can be treated by the machine as implicit feedback to refine and re-rank search results. For Granka (2010, p. 367), "user click behaviour is the most fundamental metric that search engines use to infer relevance". Through user behaviour, in fact, the machine derives an enormous amount of training data which it uses to continuously refine its selection process. Cf. also Lewandowski (2015, p. 106ff.); Brusilovsky et al. (2018, p. 232ff.).

as 'aquatic vegetation' instead of 'marine flora') as equally valid representations of indexed resources, thereby achieving the remarkable feat of learning to provide the right answer to the wrong question.

Such a performance is possible because, in search engines, it is the indexing system that adapts to the user, rather than the user having to adapt to the rules of the indexer.[41] The incorrect terms embedded in the index as 'pointers' to a particular resource enhance the functional capacity of the index, allowing the user-machine interaction to tolerate far more noise than traditional meaning-based indexes. This also prevents the search process from being interrupted: while a pointer leading to nothing forces users to suspend the search until the correct pointer is found, a wrong pointer leading to the right result enables users to satisfy their information needs even when their query formulation is inaccurate.

With the automation of indexing processes, the index is no longer merely a prerequisite but simultaneously becomes the result of the search, which is then used again as a prerequisite for subsequent searches. This means that the indexing process undergoes continuous restructuring. The user-machine interaction functions as a *historical machine* in the cybernetic sense: each user irritation changes the state of the machine, which then reacts to subsequent irritations through the changed state (Foerster 1971, p. 793f.; 1985, p. 131; 1987a, p. 128f.). As a result, the machine exhibits a certain degree of unpredictability, despite functioning in a fully deterministic manner, as its operations ultimately depend on the past, that is, on the consequences of previous search behaviours.

The widespread distinction in the literature between *static* and *dynamic* index should be reconsidered in light of these reflections. In modern culture, the index is the same for everyone and is laboriously updated over time without disrupting the underlying architecture of the indexing system. With the automation of data processing, by contrast, not only is the inverted index continuously restructured, but it can also be personalised according to the user profile. This alone sweeps away the idea that a perfect and ultimate index for the organisation of knowledge

[41] See the pioneering research on *adaptive indexing* carried out by Furnas (1985, p. 131ff.).

exists. The permanent updating of the inverted index is merely the counterpart of a memory primarily oriented toward an open and indeterminate future rather than a closed and largely predefined past.[42]

A typical outcome of this dynamism is what could be termed *performative lists*: instead of being the result of a categorisation process that applies independently of the observer, the list is the result of the interaction between users and the machine, depending crucially on the instructions provided through search behaviour. This kind of performativity implies a shift from a single actual list to an infinite number of potential lists (Esposito 2017a). Instead of merely serving as a tool to facilitate searching, the list also becomes a technical product of the search process itself. Consequently, the world presented in the form of a list appears differently depending on the conjectures generated contingently over time by the cybernetic interaction between users and the machine. The order of the list is, therefore, only provisionally valid, as are its results, which remain subject to continuous change.

Access to information is reorganised accordingly, shifting from *cognitive* to *reactive* strategies. While an observer-independent order forces the observer to become familiar with it—i.e., to memorise it—before being able to use it rapidly and efficiently, the absence of a predetermined order and the interaction with a user-adapting machine foster a search process that reproduces complexity through selection. Early-modern learned men, as we have seen, had already sought to emancipate themselves from the constraints of a predetermined order that compelled them to follow the same paths of inquiry. The loosening of notebooks into entries organised alphabetically, or left not-organised altogether, required readers to reconstruct the order of discourse based on contingent selections made by navigating the apparent chaos of their personal archive. Yet, this had not dispelled the ambition to establish a structure capable of organising the knowledge collected in an encyclopaedia or a universal library.

When transitioning from a semantic to a mechanical organisation of information access, this ambition fades, albeit with some residual resistance and occasional re-evaluations. Since the machine does not process meaning, any sense attributed to the results of its operations is merely an attribution. Operationally, the main challenge lies in imposing constraints

[42] On the difference between *static* and *dynamic* ranking, see also Sect. 5.3.

on the data structure to ensure that not everything theoretically possible is also operationally feasible. These constraints remain invisible to the user. What users see each time they perform a search is how the machine reacts to their input. In this interactive relationship, a semantic index becomes unnecessary: rather than retrieving data from a precompiled list, users construct the data they may be interested in by combining their own selections with those made by the machine (Hesse 1996, esp. p. 31; Nunberg 1996, p. 126; Esposito 2001, p. 240; 2002, p. 334f. and 357).

The space of possibilities for recombining available data at will and contingently constructing personal memories thus expands significantly. The search strategy becomes 'reactive' precisely because the outcome of the search cannot be anticipated until the user interacts with the machine. In a sense, users cannot know what they are looking for until they see what they find. While in a representational memory model, such as the topical-rhetorical one, people had to know before acting, in a performative memory model, such as that developed by search engines, they must act before knowing.[43] In the next chapter, I will examine how this highly improbable interaction between users and the machine is based on constraints and conjectures.

[43] A similar case is that of *sensemaking* in formal organisations. Cf. Weick (1995).

CHAPTER 5

The Relevance of Relevance

5.1 Constraints and Conjectures

In the previous chapter, we observed that the relationship between users and the machine takes the form of a cybernetic system aimed at minimising the deviation of results from a desired state. When the machine is a search engine, the desired state is relevance.[1] Achieving such a state is challenging due to the high complexity of the environment in which the system operates. The machine does not eliminate this complexity; rather, it generates *its own* complexity and manages it operationally.

The problem of relevance emerged in the second half of the twentieth century.[2] Of course, retrieving relevant results had always been a challenge. But only when attempts were made to automate the procedures

1 According to Luhn (1958b, p. 159), the purpose of automating access to the content of a library should be "to save a prospective reader time and effort in finding information in a given article or report".

2 An excellent literature review is provided by Mizzaro (1997), who examines about 160 publications divided into three periods: before 1958 (the year in which the concept of relevance was first proposed as one of the fundamental problems of information retrieval), between 1959 and 1976, and from 1977 to the late 1990s. Cf. also Mizzaro (1995, p. 361ff.; 1998, p. 305ff.). His conclusions are not encouraging: ultimately, the concept of relevance is too "complex", "not well understood", while its definition in formal terms remains "problematic, if not impossible" (Mizzaro 1995, p. 362).

A. Cevolini, *Indexing Systems*
https://doi.org/10.1007/978-3-032-13813-2_5

that enable users to explore the content of an archive did it become clear that discarding irrelevant results and retaining only those with genuine informational value for each user is an extremely complex task. In other words, people realised that the use of computers introduces problems that, in turn, require computational capabilities to be solved.

One of the main advantages of automation is that it relieves human personnel of cognitive tasks that the machine can perform faster. Another key advantage is the machine's ability to manage a far greater variety of data than individual human minds can process. However, this increased capacity also amplifies the need for selection, particularly when users are given the freedom to formulate their queries at will. While the machine can avoid many common human errors, it also introduces a new category of errors that it must, in turn, be capable of correcting.

Underlying these challenges is once again the previously explored distinction between archiving and indexing.[3] The introduction of the machine does not definitively resolve the problem of archiving; rather, it provides a different and more economical way of preserving what is deemed memorable. Yet, precisely when it becomes possible to store virtually anything that can be reduced to data, a new challenge arises: how to selectively retrieve, each time, only what may hold informational value for the user. The computer, understood as an information processing system, must filter incoming data (input) so that the user only receives, as output, what is genuinely relevant. As Vannevar Bush (1992, p. 1/46) already argued, with the introduction of the machine, the primary challenge is no longer knowledge preservation but its *selection* based on user instructions.

With the automation of knowledge retrieval procedures, relevance becomes a challenge primarily because the machine must forgo meaning—and with it, all those forms of complexity reduction (such as the organisation of knowledge) that meaning makes possible. Compounding this difficulty is the fact that, for the machine, the user remains a black box that cannot be made more transparent through conventional communication processes. On a mechanical level, alternative forms of interaction must be implemented to effectively achieve selective performance. As we have seen, the interaction between users and the machine takes the form of a cybernetic system based on a

[3] See Sect. 3.6.

circular exchange of information.[4] Users do not directly inform the machine; rather, they enable the machine to self-inform itself based on user-generated irritations. This, in turn, triggers a feedback mechanism through which the machine can regulate itself and enhance its performance.

The primary advantage of this type of interaction is that, with their search behaviour, users provide the machine with a vast array of stimuli that the machine can use for self-training. The drawback is that these stimuli are ambiguous, 'noisy', precisely because the machine cannot understand the meaning of users' behaviour. Based on the data it uses for self-training, the machine can only make conjectures. The latter refer not only to users' current behaviour but also to their future decisions. Cybernetic systems can minimise deviation from a desired state only if they can anticipate how their environment will behave.[5] From this perspective, setting up a cybernetic mechanism is considerably easier in the physical world than in the social world, where complexity is significantly greater.

In the natural environment, predictability is often based on deterministic principles, leaving only a small margin of uncertainty. By contrast, the social environment is far more chaotic and unpredictable. To operate effectively in this environment, the machine must not attempt to reduce chaos to a deterministic state (users cannot be compelled to submit only pre-classified queries) but rather manage chaos in a non-chaotic manner. To achieve this, the machine relies on users' behaviour. By learning from past interactions, the machine seeks to improve future interactions, in a potentially never-ending deviation minimising process.

For this circular process to function, as we have seen, the machine must detect user behaviour as a signal. Machine and users are coupled

[4] In the literature on information retrieval, it is common opinion that the user-machine interaction is effective only if it works *iteratively*. Cf. Brin and Page (1998); Pasi (2014, p. 8). The organisation of information access is, therefore, structurally contingent, i.e., it depends on the current state of the user-machine interaction system.

[5] To hit a target, for example, one must minimise not the error between the pointer position and the *current* position of the target, but rather the error between the pointer position and the *future* position of the target. Achieving this requires first understanding how the target moves (e.g., how a duck flies). See Wiener's (1948, p. 12 and 133) classic book on cybernetic.

together, in a cybernetic sense, precisely because a constant flow of information occurs between them.[6] Here, it is evident that the true black box between the two is the user. It is not the user, in fact, who is interested in uncovering the machine's regularities to predict its behaviour. Rather, it is the machine that is structured from the outset to detect patterns in users' behaviour, rendering them, to some extent, calculable and thus predictable.[7] By identifying external regularities, the machine can draw inferences about a supposed internal order (that is, users' personal needs and preferences). More importantly, the machine can discern irregularities against the backdrop of established structural regularities, treating these deviations as information to continuously adjust its behaviour and further refine its operations. In doing so, the machine improves its ability to respond more pertinently to future queries. The process of minimising deviation does not lead, therefore, to a static equilibrium but instead perpetuates a dynamic learning loop in which the machine adapts to an ever-changing environment.

The set of inferences the machine can draw from the data provided by users constitutes the individual 'profile' through which the machine continuously adjusts its selective performance. In cybernetic terms, this profile is a form of *functional description* that does not define the internal nature of the object being observed (the user) but merely makes assumptions based on externally observable behaviour.[8] Added to this is a reasoning typical of statistical inference, namely, that patterns observed in the past will likely recur in a similar manner in the future. The machine, therefore, does not react immediately to user queries in a simple input–output relationship. Rather, any response to a given query first passes through the machine's reaction to the user's profile—thus, through the machine's reaction to itself.

When the machine can construct a working description of the user, the discrepancy regarding the relevance of returned results can be minimised. To achieve such a description, the machine must process both outputs and inputs as inputs (Glanville 1982, p. 1ff.; 2009, p. 158ff.). For the machine, therefore, there is no difference between external and internal.

[6] Cf. Ashby (1956, § 6/17, p. 110). Licklider (1960, p. 4ff.) spoke of "man-computer symbiosis".

[7] This is, indeed, the meaning of 'black box' in functional terms. Cf. Ashby (1956, § 6/5, esp. p. 89f.).

[8] So Glanville (1982) in a remarkable article on the cybernetic meaning of black boxes.

This distinction can be used by an external observer to describe the relationship between users and machine. For the machine, instead, the difference between inside and outside only makes a difference if it is internally articulated through the processing of signals with informational value. The user profile is thus a 'construction' of the machine operating as an observing system.[9] As such, each profile remains a working fiction, at least as long as the machine is able to deliver results that users find satisfactory in relation to their information needs.

What the machine attempts to detect in users' behaviour are patterns, structures—in short, redundancies. Only in this way can the machine make conjectures as to what other users may want when submitting similar queries under similar conditions (Brusilovsky et al. 2018, p. 214ff.). This is why, in the most sophisticated techniques for organising access to information, any user behaviour is potentially valuable: what would otherwise just be a single data point within an indeterminate background of countless possibilities can be treated as a clue if it repeatedly correlates with other behaviours that the machine can detect. By recording these correlations, the machine learns to recognise data clusters and relationships, leveraging this redundancy to deal with the variety of stimuli triggered by the external environment.

On the other hand, the black box is not the description of the black box. By definition, the inner order of the box (assuming there is any) remains inaccessible to the observer. The fact that predictions about the box's behaviour are accurate does not prove an equivalence between its internal structure and its external description. All that an external observer can determine when observing the interaction between two black boxes (such as a user and a search engine) is whether the interaction functions. If it does, the impression arises that the machine understands users better than users understand themselves. Indeed, the machine not only detects errors and suggests corrections, but also anticipates users' information needs before users have even come to formulate them properly. However, the assumed transparency of the user is only an illusion. The predictive power of the machine is always provisional, as it is based on assumptions (Glanville 1982, esp. p. 3). Yet, as long as the results are satisfactory, the interaction maintains its own equilibrium and goes largely unnoticed.

[9] Again Glanville (1982, p. 2): "The black box is a construct of an observer".

The search for redundancy in user behaviour is essential. A completely chaotic environment would be unpredictable and would undermine any cybernetic system (Ashby 1956, § 7/17, p. 131). If an observer, on the other hand, detects that variations are not entirely random and exhibit interdependencies, it becomes possible to establish relationships that, for the observer, assume the sense of constraints and conditions. In highly abstract terms, this means recognising that the set of actualities is merely a subset of the overall set of possibilities, so that every actuality excludes countless alternative possibilities (Ashby 1956, § 7/8, p. 127; 1962, p. 257).

Constraints reduce the uncertainty that observing systems have to deal with. The world thus becomes more predictable. At a traffic light, one can reasonably expect that green is followed by yellow (rather than blue, purple or grey) and that after red, green eventually returns. In this way, not only are the possible events (the colours of the traffic light) drastically limited, but so too are their relationships. This selectivity significantly narrows the space of possibilities to be considered, based on the implicit assumption (valid only provisionally) that selectivity will repeat over time. In short, constraints reduce uncertainty regarding what the observer should expect and, in this sense, perform a structuring function for the observing system.

Constraints, however, do not belong to the observed reality but to the observer. They are not in the environment but within the system, although, of course, an environment is necessary for the system to observe anything at all. At any given moment, reality, especially social reality, can manifest itself in surprising ways, forcing observers to adjust their expectations—precisely what a learning machine continuously does based on the behavioural data provided by users.

With the automation of indexing and information processing systems, the search for constraints has merged the social dimension with the content dimension. Using its enormous computational power, the machine identifies recurring patterns within vast volumes of data and employs them to organise information access for prospective users. The paradox of this form of automation is that search can become increasingly personalised through continuous monitoring of anonymous user behaviour, which is then incorporated as a constraint shaping the machine's selective processes. In other words, by *socialising* the organisation of memory, it becomes possible to *personalise* access to information.

This development has also raised criticism and concerns. According to Eli Pariser, for example, the personalisation of search results isolates users within 'filter bubbles' that present only what is consistent with their existing ideas while excluding anything that might challenge them. In doing so, users' exposure to potentially informative content would be drastically narrowed to what confirms their preconceptions, thereby reinforcing their self-perception and understanding of reality. As a result, information consumption on the Web becomes a kind of "invisible auto-propaganda" that stifles curiosity and makes genuine learning impossible (Pariser 2012, esp. p. 15ff. and 82ff.).

Pariser's criticism essentially reiterates an appeal to the culture of suspicion (what are search engines hiding from us?), echoing concerns about mass media manipulation that predate the Web. Therefore, his argument is just as questionable as the idea that the mass media distort our perception of reality. The concerns he raises conflate the personalisation of search with the personalisation of search results, thereby confusing the issue of relevance with the potential for serendipitous exploration of digital archives. Yet, this exploratory potential is technically ensured by hyperlinks, which remain viable regardless of the selectivity of search engine results. There is no empirical evidence, therefore, supporting the claim that the Web has shifted from a "discovery-oriented" system to a "search and retrieval-focused" system (Pariser 2012, p. 103).

It is also very unlikely that users would willingly accept irrelevant answers to their questions simply for the sake of being exposed to topics "outside their normal experience" (Pariser 2012, p. 235). The use of search engines, in this case, would likely lead to annoyance and disappointment. The issue, therefore, is not so much with the search engine itself as with how users choose to use it. In this regard, Laura Granka (2010, p. 372) aptly observed that "search engines do a lot to ensure that interested individuals have the ability to acquire whatever they need, but are not useful for bringing new knowledge to those who lack the desire to ask for it".

Finally, it remains unclear how the world 'outside the bubble' should be selected. Beyond what is filtered, there exists an overwhelming abundance of information that must, in turn, be sorted out and presented in a relevant manner. This process could not be left to arbitrariness but should again be subject to technical control. The real challenge one should focus on, therefore, is not an excess of relevance but rather the insufficiency of relevance in the results delivered by automated indexing systems. Considering the challenges involved, one might even ask whether the core problem ultimately lies in the very notion of relevance itself.

5.2 Solving an Unsolvable Problem

If we examine the problem from a functional perspective, we must bear in mind that social memory does not immediately deal with content but rather with the need to distinguish what is worth remembering from what can be forgotten. Memory, therefore, operates through a distinction. The present past is the result of enacting this distinction.

When the task of selection is delegated to a machine, users expect it to sort out what is relevant while discarding everything else. The challenge is not only how to extract content holding informational value for the user, but also how to disregard everything that does not pertain to the query. In the literature, however, the problem of relevance is never framed in terms of difference, nor is it investigated from a functional perspective. The very question, "How does the machine select what is relevant?" assumes that relevance is an *inherent property* of stored documents—something that merely needs to be located within the vast repository of the digital archive. This assumption underpins the idea that relevance can, in some way, be measured. It is precisely this notion of measurement that informs the widely used concepts of *recall* and *precision*.[10]

While the concept of *recall* measures the ratio of relevant documents retrieved to the total number of relevant documents available, the concept of *precision* measures the ratio of relevant documents retrieved to the total number of available documents. In the first case, the implicit concern is how many relevant documents were missed in the search. In the second case, the focus is on the machine's error in attributing relevance to documents that, actually, are not relevant to the user's query. In both cases, the underlying assumption is that the machine makes mistakes: search results may include false positives (a retrieved document proves to be irrelevant), or false negatives (a relevant document was overlooked). Most importantly, both measures rest on the premise that the set of relevant

[10] Recall and precision are two well-known concepts in the science of information retrieval that go under the heading *effectiveness measure*. Cf. Saracevic (1975, p. 321ff.); Büttcher et al. (2010, esp. p. 407); Croft et al. (2015, p. 308ff.); Lewandowski (2015, p. 215ff.).

documents can be objectively determined as a subset of the overall set of available documents.

All these metrics assume that relevance is a property independent of the user who deals with the search results, and that the purpose of the search is to retrieve documents possessing this property. However, this assumption is questionable. While it is true that memory has a sorting-out function, it is equally true that this function is not performed in the context of an observer-independent reality. On the other hand, if the object to be measured is absent, measurement itself becomes impossible. In short, relevance should not be understood ontologically, nor should it be treated as an objective property that can be simply located within archival records. This assumption makes the notion of relevance far less relevant than is usually assumed when it comes to assessing the effectiveness of machines designed to organise access to information.

This, of course, does not mean that the so-called *library problem* is not (and does not essentially remain) that of providing relevant results whenever a user submits a particular query. If the machine were unable to solve this problem, users would give up using it. The fact that they continue to rely on it suggests, instead, that the problem is being solved in some way. The question, however, is "How?", given that relevance is not an inherent property of the documents the machine selects, and that the machine itself cannot even understand the meaning of the questions it is expected to answer—consequently, it cannot establish a semantic match between a query and the documents it retrieves.[11]

Rather than being treated as an objective property, relevance should be understood as a *relational* one. Like information, relevance is not a property that a document possesses inherently (*in se*), but one it acquires in relation to a user (*per se*). This relation is always contingent—both in the sense that it depends on the observer engaging with the search results, and in the sense that it is merely one possibility among many, subject to constant change over time. This contingency alone could be enough to undermine the notion of relevance and might explain why search engines inevitably deliver results that are sometimes unsatisfactory (or not entirely satisfactory). A document may be relevant to a decontextualised query, yet irrelevant to a real user's current information need. Moreover, upon

[11] Cf. Maron and Kuhns (1960, p. 217): "The heart of the problem does not concern *size* [of documents in the library], but rather it concerns *meaning*" (italics added).

reviewing the results, users may modify their query or shift their perspective, thereby reshaping their own information needs.[12] In both cases, any verdict on whether the results are relevant can only be returned after the search has taken place, not before.

These challenges have not gone unnoticed in the science of information retrieval, but they have not been sufficient to prompt a reformulation of the concept of relevance. The only notable exception is represented by Don Swanson's research, who, as early as in the 1970s, advocated replacing the term *information retrieval* with the more appropriate *document retrieval*. This substitution implied that any judgement on the relevance or irrelevance of a document should be left suspended until a particular search has actually been carried out (Swanson 1977, p. 128ff., esp. p. 130). Swanson's proposal also strongly suggested that the inadequacy of the notion of relevance primarily stemmed from a flawed understanding of the concept of information itself.

Like the science of information retrieval, the notion of relevance was also founded on Shannon's mathematical theory of communication.[13] The crucial premise of this theory, as we have seen,[14] was to treat information as a quantifiable variable. The challenge was to identify an appropriate measure for this quantity. Once the probabilistic estimation of the logarithm on a binary basis of the reference variety was established as the fundamental metric, the mathematical theory of communication could precisely determine the informational content of a message.

Subsequent research questioned whether information can genuinely be treated as a measurable quantity independently of the system that observes an event as information (MacKay 1969, p. 9ff. and 156ff.; Atlan 1972, esp. p. 7ff.). If the observing system is included in the calculation of the information contained in a message, then measuring information becomes impossible—at least until both the structure of the system and its current state are known. Information thus ceases to be a static entity

[12] Cf. Doyle (1963, p. 3f.). Cf. also Morville (2005, p. 53): "Information retrieval is an uphill battle".

[13] Maron and Kuhns (1960, p. 220f.) pointed out that "the problem of explicating the notion of relevance (which is the basic concept in a theory of information retrieval) is similar to that of explicating the notion of amount of information (which is the basic concept of information theory)".

[14] See Sect. 2.1.

and instead becomes a dynamic construct, always constituted relationally. Consequently, no information exists until this relation is operationally established—that is, until the system compares its internal state with the external correlate of its own observations.

A crucial consequence of this approach is that the variety upon which the information value of a message depends lies within the system rather than in the environment. And because the observing system always operates in a provisional and unpredictable manner, it is not feasible to provide the machine with fixed rules for determining the informational value and corresponding relevance of the results it selects in response to a particular query. If relevance is to be understood as a combination of meaning and information, it should also be borne in mind that information does not last. Consequently, a document may cease—at least partially—to be relevant precisely because it has been selected due to its relevance to a particular query.

Added to this is the fact that what is informative for a user also depends on how the user structures the information request. If the message received is "John sleeps in room 10"—to repeat an example suggested by Donald MacKay (1969, p. 97)—the information obtained is different depending on whether the question being answered is "Who is sleeping in room 10?" or "Where is John sleeping?". Once again, it is evident that asking whether a document is relevant or not makes little sense if relevance is narrowly understood as the ability of a document to satisfy a user's information need. Rather than treating relevance as an intrinsic property of a document, one should instead address relevance as a property that is constructed only in the interaction between users and the retrieved documents.[15]

Relevance, however, is not solely a problem of information, it is also a matter of meaning. The machine must be able to select results whose meaning corresponds, at least to some degree, with the meaning of the query. However, the machine's inability to process meaning makes the issue of relevance considerably more complex. The mathematical theory of communication itself had acknowledged that the fundamental problems it must address can be divided into *technical* and *semantic* aspects, yet it had deliberately neglected the semantic dimension in favour of the

[15] Cf. Swanson (1977, esp. p. 137 and 139). For Morville (2005, p. 55), "like beauty, relevance exists in the eye of the beholder".

technical one.[16] This has led to some confusion in subsequent research, at least on a terminological level. Meaning and information should, in fact, be kept separate at an analytical level, even though they remain closely interconnected in social communication.

This separation is indispensable because, first of all, an event can be informative even when its meaning remains undetermined. Machines, for example, process vast amounts of differences that make a difference (and therefore have an informational value) without being able to determine the meaning of this processing. Likewise, a text retains its meaning even if it ceases to be informative for a reader who is already familiar with its content. Finally, re-reading a familiar text merely reproduces redundancy and may aid memorisation, but does not multiply the information conveyed by the text (MacKay 1969, p. 76ff. and 83ff.; Atlan 1972, p. 18ff.).

These reflections suggest that the problem of relevance cannot be resolved a priori. Relevance is assessed based on the correspondence between the meaning of the query and the meaning of the result, but more importantly, based on the informational value of the result in relation to the query submitted by the user. Given that query formulations—and the corresponding needs for information—are typically highly heterogeneous, it is nearly impossible to link the documents stored in the archive to a fixed structure of cross-references that would infallibly enable users to retrieve the most relevant information as the need arises.[17]

However, as we have observed from the outset, the primary function of memory in archival systems is to organise information access. Since this organisation, by definition, cannot be based on arbitrary choices, it remains to be clarified how a machine can respond to user queries in a relevant manner—how, in other words, it can resolve an inherently unsolvable problem.

[16] Cf. Shannon and Weaver (1963, p. 3): "[The] semantic aspects of communication are irrelevant to the engineering problem". On the distinction between these two aspects, see Bar-Hillel (1955, esp. p. 92ff.).

[17] In this regard, Swanson (1977, p. 130) pointed out that "no index [...] has proved so through, no search method so effective, as to assure a high degree of success in this attempt".

5.3 Statistics Instead of Semantics

From the earliest experiments in automating indexing processes, scholars realised that the only way to address the semantic problem was to compensate for it through statistical computation.[18] As we have seen, the computer processes everything reducible to data and handles these data as if they were physical objects.[19] In an even more radical way than what occurred with the printing press, the computer deals with words as if they were things. What is a limitation on the one hand (the computer does not understand the meaning of its own operations) becomes an advantage insofar as the machine exploits its enormous computational power, far surpassing that of individual human minds.

In the 1950s, researchers began with very basic assumptions, such as the frequency of terms within a text, their position within sentences, and the proximity of the most frequent terms. The underlying hypothesis, also quite simple, was that frequency correlates directly with meaning, i.e., that the most frequent terms and the sentences containing them are also the most significant parts of a text. This enabled the machine to automatically extract an abstract without actually 'reading' the text. Stored documents could also be indexed to facilitate future access based on the words used as search terms.

Statistical computing provided an opportunity to experiment with different strategies in this context. Assuming that the real challenge of retrieval is the risk of excluding many relevant documents from search results, Melvin Maron and John Lary Kuhns (1960, p. 223ff.) suggested extending the search through a measure of proximity. The latter could apply to both index terms and retrieved documents, and could be defined in terms of either semantic or statistical relations.[20] The machine could thus create spaces of connected points and experiment with different heuristics (i.e., rules to move in the maze). Within the index space,

[18] See the pioneering research by Luhn (1957; 1958a; 1959). For Maron and Kuhns (1960, p. 217), the issue of selection depended on the closeness of meaning between index terms and documents content, and an approach to this semantical problem was via statistics. Luhn (1957, p. 317) was convinced that if the statistical approach were effective, "it would no longer be necessary to recognize the *meaning* of information for the purpose of encoding".

[19] See Sect. 4.2.

[20] A typical semantic relationship is synonymy. A statistical relationship is that linking the name 'Shannon' to the subject 'information theory'.

in particular, the machine could calculate the closeness and distance of several index terms, which in semantic indexing systems are typically connected through cross-indexing, using pointers such as 'see' and 'see also'. By assigning numerical weights to index terms and measuring proximity, the machine could automatically decide which index terms to 'see' and 'see also'.[21] In this way, as Maron and Kuhns argued, a probabilistic "association of ideas" could be *mechanized*.[22]

Many of these technical and statistical strategies are still employed by advanced information retrieval systems. However, with the advent of digital technology, computation techniques and ranking procedures have become significantly more sophisticated.[23] One of the most innovative contributions of Maron and Kuhns was the introduction of weighted index terms. The indexer was supposed to estimate the probability that a user interested in a given subject designated by the term would find the retrieved document relevant (Maron and Kuhns 1960, p. 220; cf. also Maron 2008, p. 971f.). In doing so, semantic noise was reframed as a problem of uncertainty, which could, in turn, be managed statistically and probabilistically.

Instead of relying on a binary yes/no classification, as is typical in semantic indexing, the pivotal idea was to assign each index term a relevance score and rank the retrieved documents accordingly.[24] Based on the assumption that users prioritise documents most likely to satisfy their information needs and are inclined to disregard those with low probabilities,[25] the experiments conducted by Maron and Kuhns demonstrated

[21] If a user wants to know whether a theory of information exists, she can enter the terms 'information' AND 'theory' in the query. The machine autonomously decides to see 'mathematical theory of communication' and to see also 'Shannon', even though the user has formulated none of these query terms.

[22] Maron and Kuhns (1960, p. 225). The same measure could then be performed on the set of retrieved documents. The machine could either extend the user's query or expand the set of retrieved documents. In other words, the machine could either act upon input or act upon output. In both cases, what changed was the output.

[23] Cf. Büttcher et al. (2010, p. 35ff.); Croft et al. (2015, p. 134ff. and 189). Google, for example, uses popularity as a proxy for relevance.

[24] Maron and Kuhns' (1960) pioneering research on probabilistic indexing was revisited and further developed by other researchers in the following years. Cf. Robertson (1977a; 1977b).

[25] Maron and Kuhns (1960, p. 238ff.) had set the threshold value at 0.5, i.e., documents with a probability higher than 50%.

that probabilistic indexing was significantly more selective, sparing users from reading approximately 30% more documents than binary indexing would have retrieved. In practice, relevance scores made it possible to filter out irrelevant material, thereby transforming uncertainty from a problem to be removed into a resource to be leveraged.

The main drawback of probabilistic indexing lay in its reliance on direct human intervention: the weights were determined by the indexer and then experimentally compared with user evaluations. Nevertheless, an intriguing aspect of probabilistic indexing was its potential to engage with user opacity.

For users, what matters is that the retrieved documents are relevant to their actual information needs. But the machine can retrieve documents based only on the users' query formulations. The problem is that the terms used in these formulations rarely align precisely with users' underlying information needs.[26] During their search, users may even discover information needs they had not considered when beginning the search. The probabilistic estimate of a document's relevance was thus conceived as a means of bridging the gap between query terms and information need without reducing retrieval to a rigid stimulus–response process. Moreover, probability left open the possibility of revising relevance scores, thereby transforming indexing into an open-ended and adaptive process.

With the introduction of probabilistic indexing, the notion that relevance is an intrinsic property of documents was abandoned. The measure of probability introduced the observer into the observed reality. In fact, estimating the probability that an event holds informational value is only possible if one knows the state of the observer. Even a simple choice between two possibilities carries different implications if it is known that, for the observing system, one option is significantly more probable than the other. As probability increases, the element of surprise decreases, thereby lowering the informational value compared to a scenario in which both possibilities have equal likelihood. Consequently, estimating informational value requires consideration of the structures of the observing system. However, since observers remain inaccessible to the machine, this estimation must once again rely on users' behaviour and their past interactions with the machine.

[26] Cf. Maron and Kuhns (1960, p. 233): "In a real library system N [i.e., a user's information need] will never be known, only its description R [i.e., the query formulation] in a rather artificial language, viz., a Boolean function whose variables are index terms".

A crucial consequence of these technical advances is that they render a *one-ranking-fits-all* approach obsolete. This principle is abandoned as soon as one accepts that the universe of knowledge cannot be organised from the outside, excluding observers from the observed reality, but only from the inside, incorporating observers into the process of sorting the results that the archive provides in response to their queries (Joachims and Radlinski 2007, p. 34). Taken to its logical extreme, this rejection of a single, observer-independent ranking implies that the 'correct' ranking does not exist (Lewandowski 2015, p. 89). Once sorting becomes primarily information-oriented rather than meaning-oriented, any project of knowledge organisation becomes obsolete.

The distinction between *static* and *dynamic* ranking essentially reflects this shift from observer-independent to observer-dependent knowledge organisation (Büttcher et al. 2010, p. 517). The difference between static and dynamic rankings, in other words, serves as a shorthand for a technical-evolutionary advancement that discards the notion of a fixed order of knowledge while still maintaining the possibility of bringing order to the knowledge. This advancement also profoundly transforms the meaning of mnemotechnique.

Whereas in rhetorical culture, the task was to 'find' something stored according to a predetermined order of commonplaces (*loci*), in performative memory based on automated indexing systems, the search takes the form of a 'conjecture' advancing through trial and error (Swanson 1977, p. 138ff.). Moreover, each result generated by the exploratory activity undertaken in collaboration with the machine can serve as a stimulus for further exploration.[27] Ultimately, there is no final result in the strict sense of the term. Here again, there is a striking difference from the exploratory activity within the rhetorical storehouse.

Orators wandering through the rooms of their mental storehouse sought active images to trigger meaning associations that would lead them to the thing to be remembered. Each image was an end point, as it could neither be replaced by other images nor relocated to different places. Reminiscence itself had to strictly follow pre-established meaning connections; otherwise, there was a risk of recalling the wrong thing or failing to remember anything at all.

[27] Swanson (1977, esp. p. 138f.) distinguished, in this respect, a *direct* from an *indirect* use of retrieved documents.

When users interact with an archive that operates mechanically, the activity of exploration instead aligns with their information needs. This implies that no content in the archive can be considered the ultimate *goal* of the search,[28] nor is there a fixed location where it can be found. Information is a relational product and is not located in any specific place. However, the user must also be spared the effort of testing all the possibilities that the archive theoretically offers. Exploration is thus open-ended but also highly constrained, stopping provisionally whenever users manage to satisfy their information needs.

The perception of archive's intransparency also changes correspondingly. For orators, the challenge was to orient themselves within a spatial framework and retrieve memorable content from the closets where images were stored.[29] For the user of a digital archive, by contrast, the challenge is to navigate the complete intransparency of the archive through search engines whose sorting rules (the algorithm) are themselves opaque.[30] The paradox of this interaction is that the archive's unlimited storage capacity coincides with its virtual transparency. In principle, everything stored is retrievable, provided one knows how to use search engines effectively and has the patience to carry out a thorough search. Yet, it is precisely this visibility—this public access to everything stored in the archive—that renders available knowledge rather opaque. Total transparency becomes an almost unmanageable form of intransparency.[31] This

[28] With the consequence that, once retrieved, the same content would determine the *end* of the search.

[29] See the famous account by Augustine of Hippo (*Conf*., X, VIII).

[30] This intransparency has raised many concerns. The problem arises when intransparency is interpreted as a deliberate form of manipulation. This debate was notably initiated by Introna and Nissenbaum (2000), yet their concerns were considerably downplayed a decade later. Cf., for instance, Granka (2010, p. 364ff.). Granka argued that full disclosure of indexing and ranking algorithms would not only be commercially unfeasible but would also provide users with the possibility of "gaming the system". Precisely transparency, therefore, would enable the adverse manipulation of Web ranking systems (p. 366).

[31] This paradox has always been the crucial problem of any 'universal library'. And the ideal of a universal repository of knowledge has always been a semantic correlate of communication technologies—first typography, later telematics, and more recently digital technologies. Projects such as Wells' (1938) 'world brain', Bush's (1945) Memex, and Davies' (1967) 'universal brain' share a common feature: the complete differentiation and autonomy of social memory from individual psychic memory, and the resulting internalisation of the criteria for discriminating between remembering and forgetting.

is not only because there is insufficient time to consult all available content, but also because numerous latent connections remain unnoticed, thereby failing to generate opportunities for further discoveries.

Swanson spoke of *undiscovered public knowledge*: the knowledge exists, yet it remains unretrievable—or only scarcely retrievable—through traditional indexing systems.[32] With regard to scientific knowledge, in particular, Swanson identified its increasing complexity as the main issue. The growing volume of scientific publications makes it impossible for any individual to assimilate all research findings. A typical strategy to reduce complexity is to differentiate knowledge domains and specialise disciplines. But even this does not fully resolve the problem; rather, it creates a new one. Much valuable information is embedded precisely in the interdependencies that discipline specialisation breaks down, effectively removing these interdependencies from subsequent research. If the number of elements increases arithmetically, the possible relationships between them grows geometrically (i.e., exponentially). It is precisely this vast network of possible relationships that remains largely unexplored, despite its potentially immense informational value for science.

The first experiments in automating indexing systems sought to address these problems.[33] The growth of knowledge is both unstoppable and desirable. This growth generates increasing complexity that demands appropriate selective mechanisms. Information retrieval systems are expected to perform this function effectively. However, the very interaction with such systems becomes an opportunity for conducting further research whose products are subsequently archived, made available, and used to generate new avenues of exploration. Thus, while the growth of knowledge poses a challenge for information retrieval systems, it is equally true that information retrieval systems are a prerequisite for the growth of knowledge. The solution therefore reproduces the problem that the solution is expected to resolve. The relationship between information retrieval and the growth of knowledge is inherently circular.

[32] Swanson (1986, p. 103ff. and 108ff.; 1993, esp. p. 611ff.); Swanson and Smalheiser (1996, p. 295ff.). It should be noted that the matter, here, is not private knowledge, that is, the content of individual consciences, but public knowledge, that is, the product of intellectual activity accessible through communication. While the former is by definition publicly inaccessible, the latter becomes so for other reasons.

[33] For an overview, see the contributions edited by Kochen (1967).

This circularity is a structural precondition of modern memory and has immediate consequences for how society remembers and forgets. Typically, a significant amount of forgetting occurs spontaneously, so to speak, through a filtering process that determines what is worth remembering. As Paul Weiss (1967, p. 215) pointed out, "graded in terms of relevance, not every observation is worth reporting; not every report is worth recording; not every record is worth publishing; not every publication is worth preserving for the eternity". However, even publications deemed worthy of preservation risk falling into oblivion as the number of accessible publications continuously increases. In this regard, Leibniz (1959, p. 165f.) had already express concern that the press might plunge society into a form of "scholarly barbarism". Faced with the relentless production of new publications, the modern library user is indeed left feeling lost, while even the most distinguished authors risk fading into "general oblivion".

One way to counteract this oblivion and mitigate the inevitable obsolescence of all publications is through citation. Yet, even research based on a citation index cannot guarantee memorability. Citations serve as a selective mechanism but must contend with the variety continuously reproduced by communication technologies.[34] Moreover, citation indexing fails to address another critical issue. The complexity of knowledge arises not only from the multiplication of information theoretically embedded in archived documents but also from the combinatorial explosion of unintended logical connections between them.[35] These connections are precisely what a standard subject-based indexing system fails to capture. However, since what does not appear in search results remains, for all practical purposes, non-existent, a significant portion of available knowledge risks remaining undiscovered.

The problem here, once again, is not archiving but indexing. What is not linked to the cross-reference system is effectively lost. Merely extending the list of cross-references, however, is insufficient. What is needed, first and foremost, is a fundamental shift in the search methodology and design. The evolutionary advance lies, therefore, not only in the information-processing potential of secondary memories but also in

[34] Cf. also Solla Price (1967) based on Garfield's research.

[35] Cf. Swanson and Smalheiser (1996, p. 295). Cf. also Swanson (1979, p. 3ff.; 1989, p. 356ff.; 1993, p. 616ff. and 619ff.); Swanson and Smalheiser (1997, p. 183ff.).

an epistemological transformation of the search itself. The latter resembles scientific conjecture and is, by definition, subject to continuous refinement.

When transitioning from knowledge to information, search becomes chronically uncertain.[36] For users, this means facing a sort of *second-order ignorance*: the issue is not only that they do not know (and know that they do not know), but also that they do not know that they do not know. This blind spot can be managed but not eliminated. After all, the appreciation of modern scholars for the combinatory potential of knowledge—loosened from the constraints of topical organisation and disaggregated into elementary units—was already a consequence of the fact that the information virtually contained in stored materials could only be fully exploited by enhancing the structure of cross-references. In this way, exploratory possibilities could be multiplied without requiring explorations to be pre-planned.

In search engines, this possibility is limited by the absence of semantic understanding. However, as we have seen, this absence is counterbalanced by the computational capacity of the machine, which processes data through highly sophisticated statistical operations. Swanson himself sought to address the human inability to discern connections between complementary but non-interactive subsets of scientific literature by designing an algorithm capable of generating rankings.[37] This algorithm was intended to overcome the limitations of classical databases by enabling the machine to index not merely *contents*, but also *relationships* between contents. For example, the algorithm could relate an article discussing the beneficial effects of fish oil on blood viscosity to another article examining blood viscosity in relation to Raynaud's syndrome—even though the former article never mentions this syndrome and the latter never mentions fish oil.

The remarkable aspect of this automated process of identifying relations with informational value lies in the fact that the machine (i.e., the algorithm) is not truly capable of recognising what escapes human attention—namely, the presence of interesting connections—but operates *as*

[36] For Swanson (1986, p. 114), "information retrieval [...] is necessarily *uncertain* and forever *open-ended*" (italics added).

[37] It was the so-called ARROWSMITH software. See Swanson and Smalheiser (1996, esp. p. 298; 1997, p. 203ff.).

if it were able to do so.[38] The machine, in other words, seems to be intelligent but is not—at least not in the way this faculty is typically attributed to humans or animals.[39] This, after all, is true of all machines operating through algorithms: they possess no capacity for abstraction, do not understand the meaning of their selections, and have no intrinsic awareness of what is genuinely relevant to a particular user. Yet, the results of their classifications are by no means arbitrary, and users often have the impression that the machine understands both its own operations and users' information needs better than they do themselves. In reality, the machine does not artificially replicate human intelligence but rather parasitically exploits the intelligence that users, so to speak, make available to it through their continuous generation of vast amounts of training data.[40]

The machine, ultimately, does nothing on its own. Even statistical computations can only be refined—if not truly informed—through continuous interaction with users. The discriminatory capacity of the machine's operations depends entirely on this interaction. This development definitively reframes the problem of knowledge retrieval from one of *content* to one of *procedures*. The issue is not about directly instructing the machine on which results are most relevant, nor about immediately determining what should be remembered or forgotten. Digital technologies preserve connections—that is, explorability—and in this sense, they function as a true forgetting technique.[41] The key question then becomes how to regulate this explorability, turning complexity from a challenge into a resource. In the next chapter, we will examine how this can be achieved by multiplying access points to the archive and diversifying exploratory paths within it—in other words, by increasing rather than reducing the complexity of indexing structures.

[38] "ARROWSMITH possesses no algorithm for recognizing 'interesting' relationships such as transitivity or complementary, but it *seems* to have such a capability" (Swanson and Smalheiser 1997, p. 198).

[39] Swanson and Smalheiser (1997, p. 198) spoke of *impression of intelligence* and *implanted intelligence*.

[40] As explained by Esposito (2017a, p. 356ff.; 2017b, p. 5f.; 2022).

[41] Esposito (2002, p. 339 and 356). Cf. also Locke (2000, esp. p. 31): "Forgetting is not a useful attribute for a storage system. [...] But forgetting *is* a useful attribute for an intelligent agent navigating such a system".

CHAPTER 6

The Memory of Tags

6.1 A Virtual Renaissance of Metadata

The automatic indexing procedures examined in the previous two chapters have not entirely eliminated direct human intervention. On the contrary, the technical developments of the past two decades have made it possible to re-engage human agents in the organisation of social memory, offering unprecedented opportunities for manual indexing that closely resemble the commonplace-book practices of early-modern learned readers.

These innovations are particularly evident in what is known as *social tagging*: users are given the ability to add 'tags' to archived resources, facilitating their retrieval when needed. Users can freely assign any tag to any resource—not only books or documents but also images or videos—according to their own perspective, preferences, or personal approach to categorisation. Tags function as genuine subject headings and can be used as index terms (Croft et al. 2015, p. 400ff.; Navarro Bullock et al. 2018, p. 313ff.). Taken together, these tags form a kind of supplementary register, albeit one with very distinctive properties, as we shall see in subsequent sections.

The fundamental problem remains unchanged: there is no direct access to the data stored in the archive (this would be akin to entering a library and leafing through every book on the shelves in search of the one most relevant to us). Access to data is only possible through metadata.

A. Cevolini, *Indexing Systems*
https://doi.org/10.1007/978-3-032-13813-2_6

This is why the organisation of information access plays such a crucial role. As a perfect system of organisation is inherently unattainable, it is not surprising that continuous efforts are made to refine methods and procedures for indexing archival resources as effectively as possible. When archives become digital, the opacity of their contents reaches an extreme, making the issue of metadata even more pressing. This has prompted a kind of "virtual renaissance" (Cukier 2010, p. 11) of metadata, resulting in the rather paradoxical situation where, in order to address the problem of information overload, it has been necessary to increase the amount of information available about what, within the archive, may hold informational value for each user.

The ability to freely tag resources is highly appealing, as it allows users to add metadata that should facilitate the efficient retrieval of relevant resources. These user-generated metadata complement those automatically generated by the machine and are subsequently integrated into the indexing and ranking mechanisms through which the system responds to user queries. Over the past two decades, extensive research has focused on social tagging and the so-called *folksonomy*—the categorisation structure emerging from the collective tagging of multiple users contributing to knowledge organisation.[1] Some scholars even regard this novelty as a true "revolution",[2] whose effects are generally assessed with optimism, despite the presence of several challenges. A widely held view is that tags not only enhance existing indexing methods but also introduce a fundamentally different approach. If the core function remains unchanged—namely, organising information access—it becomes essential to articulate how tags can improve this function. The literature on the subject identifies three main answers to this question.

The first answer draws on the distinction between *active* and *passive* users. In the initial phase of indexing automation, users were entirely

[1] The literature on the subject is extensive. Peters (2009) alone reviews approximately 700 articles and scholarly essays. An excellent summary of the main issues discussed in the realm of social tagging is provided by Benvenuti (2007). It is highly likely, however, that the body of literature has more than doubled in the past two decades. For updates, see Kipp and Campbell (2010); Yedid (2013); Silva (2017); Dimitrov et al. (2018). It is interesting to note that the tagging activity itself is referred to by various terms in the scientific literature, including *user-generated metadata*, *democratic indexing*, *social bookmarking*, and others.

[2] See Weinberger (2005, p. 29): "We are right at the beginning of the tagging revolution".

excluded from these processes, which were entrusted to machines operating through statistical techniques. In a later phase, however, automation sought to reintegrate users by enabling them to contribute to resource indexing through tagging. The primary advantage of automation lies in the machine's capacity to replace human agents (i.e., psychic systems) in performing complex and time-consuming information-processing operations. Yet, this advantage comes with a limitation: it excludes what only human agents can do—namely, understanding the meaning of these operations.

This limitation explains the enthusiasm surrounding the reintegration of users into indexing processes. From being passive consumers of entirely opaque indexing systems, users become active collaborators, benefiting not only from their own contributions but also from those of others engaged in the same activity. As a result, the asymmetry between machine and user is significantly reduced. Archive exploration is no longer exclusively mediated by search engines whose selection capacity is based on statistical operations and algorithms; it also incorporates the human ability to assign meaning to archived resources. In this sense, as Isabella Peters (2009, p. 153) argues, users themselves become indexers.

The second reason why tags might enhance access to the information virtually contained in archives lies in the fact that user-generated labels reflect *natural* language rather than adhering to the *artificial* language conventions typically employed by professional indexers. The advantage is evident: the average user is more likely to categorise an image with the word 'cat' rather than 'feline', or with 'orchid' rather than 'phalaenopsis', thereby increasing the likelihood of retrieving the image when searching for cats or orchids. The major drawback, however, is that this approach introduces a significant amount of semantic noise into the indexing system. Unlike professional indexers, users tend to overlook issues of synonymy and polysemy; in other words, they do not account for the fact that the same term might denote different objects, just as different terms might refer to the same object. More generally, users do not systematically or rigorously verify the terms they assign as labels to resources.[3]

The issue of semantic noise is rather complex. First and foremost, it is inherently difficult to adequately denote the subject matter of an item

[3] See Rolla (2009, esp. p. 175), which contains a comprehensive review of the literature.

using one or more index terms.[4] Secondly, users themselves face challenges in accurately formulating their information needs through one or more query terms. However, the core problem of semantic noise lies in the fact that, irrespective of the indexing term denoting a resource and regardless of the search term chosen by users to articulate their information need, retrieval only occurs when the two terms match. Functionally speaking, then, the problem of semantic noise exists in the relationship between users and the archive. And precisely this 'in-between' is what cannot be controlled.

When the match fails, the failure can be attributed either to the item being categorised incorrectly or to the user formulating an unsuitable term to retrieve it. A classic solution is to specialise the indexing system, tailored to a specific library,[5] and restrict users to predefined indexing terms. However, in an undifferentiated or deliberately unspecialised archive, this precondition no longer applies. In such cases, users compensate, so to speak, for the absence of constraints with an increase in semantic noise. On the other hand, every relationship between users and the archive is unstable, contingent, temporary, and unpredictable. It often depends on a context that the indexing system struggles to accommodate.[6] As the context itself varies both temporally and socially, the likelihood of a match between indexing terms and user query terms is very low.

The claim that tags are 'inherently noisy' should therefore be reconsidered in light of the fact that this is not a flaw intrinsic to tags themselves, but rather a consequence of the dynamics of the search process. Noise, in other words, is not an inherent property of tag. Otherwise, one could question what tags—except in highly codified and structured contexts such as scientific disciplines—would not be noisy. This does not imply that semantic noise cannot be reduced. For instance, avoiding a multiplicity of unnecessary terms or ensuring a closer correspondence between the chosen term and the most relevant term for the denoted object would be instrumental. However, the uncertainty surrounding retrieval remains a chronic problem that cannot be solved once and for all.

[4] As Hottinger already pointed out in the seventeenth century. See Sect. 3.3.

[5] Maron and Kuhns (1960, p. 218f.) speak of *ideoglossary*.

[6] For example, 'pig' was the term used to disparagingly refer to London police officers in the early nineteenth century and then again during the youth protests of the 1960s. Cf. Jacob (1993, p. 115).

This is, moreover, the crucial aspect of what is referred to as 'noise'. In communication systems, the issue concerns the uncertainty in retrieving information.[7] This uncertainty arises from the inherent complexity of meaning. If the meaning contained in a document is distilled into a subject matter, and the subject matter is denoted by one or more index terms, uncertainty would be eliminated if there were no alternative possibilities in the retrieval process. But complexity precisely implies an excess of possibilities compared to those that can be considered at any given time. Not only because a single document might encompass multiple subject matters simultaneously, but also because the same subject matter might be denoted by different subject headings, and the same subject heading could be formulated differently. Given this complexity, the likelihood of a perfect match between a search term and the category assigned to a resource becomes highly improbable.

The increased involvement of users in indexing processes and the adoption of more natural language in categorising resources stored in the archive result in a final distinction that explains the success of tags, while also raising significant concerns: the difference between *controlled* and *not-controlled* use of indexing terms. This distinction is rooted in a sort of asymmetry of social roles between professional indexers (the experts) and the user community (the non-experts). This asymmetry is often framed as a hierarchical distinction between *top-down* and *bottom-up* indexing. In the former, indexing is implemented by means of a pre-established classification meticulously controlled by experts, based on common rules and an authoritative language. In the latter, users are given the freedom to add indexing categories to resources, without the obligation to adhere to unchangeable schemes or predefined vocabularies (Navarro Bullock et al. 2018, p. 317).

This hierarchical difference, however, merely describes two different approaches and does not explain what their functional distinction consists of. The same difference has been the focus of extensive empirical research aimed at evaluating the effectiveness of tagging compared to the library-based approach.[8] Specifically, these studies investigated the extent to which tagging practices, carried out by amateur users, could approximate the coherence, quality, and completeness of the library approach

[7] Cf. Maron and Kuhns (1960, esp. p. 220). See also Sect. 5.3.

[8] Cf., for example, Heymann et al. (2010, p. 51ff.).

led by professionals. However, such an inquiry already implied a set of expectations that assumed the library approach as a normative standard against which the degree of deviation in the tagging approach was to be measured. As a result, the research implicitly suggested that tagging could only be truly effective if it aligned with the structural norms of cataloguing systems, thereby erasing the distinction between tagging and professional indexing.

Fairly quickly, however, it was recognised that the polarization of the debate between proponents of the library-based approach, which relies on pre-established and repetitive taxonomies, and supporters of the tagging approach, which produces new folksonomies, stemmed from a misunderstanding: the two approaches are, in fact, complementary. There is no opposition between the structured vocabulary of professional indexers and the seemingly chaotic vocabulary of users, and the limitations of both can be mitigated through their reciprocal integration (Smith 2008, p. 92). Subsequent research has consistently confirmed that controlled classification and user-generated categorisation are not rivals, but rather two distinct methods for achieving the same goal. The use of one does not preclude the use of the other, and both can enhance their effectiveness to the extent that they incorporate the opposite approach. In short, tags do not replace subject terms but complement them, while subject terms are more effective when paired with tags (Halpin et al. 2007; Stock 2007; Halpin et al. 2009; Kipp 2011; Gerolimos 2013).

In the scientific literature, it is widely acknowledged that tags are far more ambiguous than the categories used by indexers to classify archive resources. However, empirical research shows that this ambiguity ultimately benefits users, as it allows them to choose the level of specificity or generalization that best suits their needs (Kipp 2011, p. 258ff.). Nonetheless, this does not fully explain the operational meaning of this ambiguity and why it becomes an advantage when it comes to organising access to information. As we have seen, research has focused on specific dichotomies, such as controlled versus not-controlled vocabulary, natural versus artificial language, structured (closed) versus unstructured (open) indexing system. Similarly, the distinction between taxonomies and folksonomies has been investigated through oppositions like pre-designed versus ad-hoc category structures, expert professionals versus amateur users, unambiguous versus intrinsically ambiguous indexing systems. While these distinctions are undoubtedly significant, those who rely on them neglect alternative perspectives that could provide new insights into the practice of tagging, particularly within the broader context of the evolution of social memory. In the following sections, I propose three alternative viewpoints.

6.2 The Function of Tags

The first perspective concerns the *function* of tags. That their purpose is to organise information access is undisputable. Tags are primarily connected to the memory of communication rather than to the memory of individual minds, even though the latter do contribute of course to their assignment. In this sense, tagging is an individual act, but its effects are inherently social. Once a tag is assigned to a resource, it moves out of the opacity of individual consciousness into the visible realm of communication, which is entirely independent of psychic activity. The identity, timing, and motivations of the person who assigned the tag are entirely irrelevant when the user explores an archive to retrieve information. A tag functions effectively not *despite* the impossibility of tracing the real intentions of the person who chose it, but precisely *because* it is unnecessary to investigate those intentions. The communicative visibility of tags renders any speculation about the underlying psychic systems entirely superfluous.

From this perspective, tags perform the same function as commonplace headings in the notebooks and filing systems of early modern scholars. They act as access points to the archive's contents, increasing the ease of information retrieval.[9] Tags, therefore, perpetuate the modern trend of transferring to users the responsibility for determining the categories that can facilitate future retrieval of the past. Like all metadata, tags are also the result of a duplication process that ultimately serves the purpose of forgetting. The exact contents of an archive remain unknown until exploration begins, and similarly, no one would be so foolish as to memorise the tags assigned to its resources. It suffices for these tags to be visible within a communication system—such as when users access a library catalogue—to initiate search procedures. Memory thus shifts to the procedural level, relying on the interaction between users and secondary memory systems.

In modern semantic indexing, as we have seen, users relied on hierarchical reference structures expandable through extended branching. These structures ensured that everything had its place, and there was

[9] This definition is to be found in Silva (2017, § 4). See also Mathes (2004), whose article has inspired all subsequent research.

a place for everything. In this sense, they constituted true taxonomies, whose primary advantage lay in the repetitiveness of the overall order, which enhanced its memorability. The main drawback, however, was that reaching a specific node within the structure required not only an understanding of the general rules of classification but also the ability to navigate the entire hierarchy—from the initial unit to the desired point—by progressing through successive divisions. This meant that users needed pre-knowledge of the path to follow; in other words, they had to know in advance where the object of their search was located.

This rigidity was countered by the concurrent practice of commonplace-books, which granted individual readers the freedom to assign categories to each entry without being obliged to adhere to a specific order or reflecting any supposed structure of known reality. The trade-off for this freedom, as we have seen, was the need to address an inherently undecidable question: determining in the present under which category a previously archived content would be sought in the future.

Readers primarily relied on the personalisation of categories and their self-knowledge to recall how they had categorised their memories. However, this was insufficient to eliminate the uncertainty surrounding the future retrieval of relevant past. Rather than attempting to find the single correct reference, one solution was to multiply the available references, thereby increasing the internal complexity of external memory. In doing so, they anticipated a technique later employed by digital memory systems, as we will explore further.

Tags share with commonplace headings the ability to categorise without classification constraints (Jacob 1992, p. 73ff.; 2004, p. 527ff.). The primary difference lies in the binding nature of a pre-established structure for classification. While categorisation aligns with the user's stream of consciousness and capacity for abstraction, classification necessitates adapting information to a predetermined order of knowledge. Categorisation, therefore, is contingent and relatively unpredictable, whereas classification is stable and resistant to modification. In the former case, associations and connections between categorised items are 'discovered'; in the latter, they are 'found'—a distinction that significantly limits the informational potential of the archive's content.

One of the major advantages of categorisation is its adaptability to context, which makes it inherently provisional. What is categorised today as a 'piece of furniture' might tomorrow be re-categorised as 'junk', without necessitating a revolution in the order of knowledge, let alone in the order of things. Classification systems, by contrast, lack such flexibility. Although their divisions—even when dichotomous—retain a degree of arbitrariness, once a division is accepted as the basis for further divisions, the degrees of freedom in searching activity are drastically reduced. Moreover, in classification systems, each element can typically occupy a single, fixed position within the order of classification; within a categorical framework, by contrast, an element can belong to multiple classes simultaneously without disrupting the overall order (which, notably, does not exist).

Categorisation is a form of complexity reduction that operates within the medium of meaning. To categorise means to construct 'grouping' rules based on the distinction between inclusion and exclusion (Bruner 2009, esp. p. 69; Jacob 1993, p. 103; 2004, p. 518). Once a decision is made regarding which distinction determines inclusion or exclusion, reality can be categorised.[10] This decision-making process has no inherent limit, although Plato (*Phaedrus*, 265E1-3) advised following the example of the butcher, who carefully observes the natural divisions of the body when deciding where to cut in order to avoid separating the muscles incorrectly. This advice, however, presupposed an ontological understanding of reality, in which similarities and differences are seen as intrinsic to things and merely need replication in the realm of categories. From the perspective of socio-cultural evolution, by contrast, the ability to group based on perceived similarities is a cognitive skill acquired through the internalisation of communicative technologies. As such, it is more a construction of reality than a mere representation of it.[11]

When dealing with an element, an observer who has learned to categorise does not react to the element itself but first to the category to which the element has been assigned, and only through that category to the element in question. Indeed, any element would be unknowable if it were not first categorised (even if only as an 'unknown' element).

[10] The category of household appliances (which employs two distinctions) includes, for example, televisions and vacuum cleaners but excludes microphones and overhead projectors, even though these devices also operate on electricity.

[11] For Bruner (2009, p. 16ff. and 69), categorisation is not an act of 'discovery' but an act of 'invention'. On the hypothesis that this invention depends on internalised communication technologies and is, therefore, historically variable, see the classic study by Luria (1976).

Thus, one does not categorise something because it is recognised; rather, something is recognised because it can first be categorised.

To achieve this result operationally, redundancies within the variety of environmental events must be isolated. By doing so, the system can impose a certain order on its environment, avoiding the need to address an infinite multiplicity of unique and unrepeatable events (Jacob 1993, p. 103; 2004, p. 518). Research shows that cognitive systems manage redundancy by adhering to a principle of economy, aiming to maximise inference with the minimum number of available clues.[12] A corollary of this principle is the tendency to avoid excessive generalisation and excessive specification when assigning categories, as both prove highly costly. An intermediate level between these extremes appears to provide the greatest degree of adaptability with the least cognitive effort.[13] The transition between levels of abstraction is, however, highly dynamic and depends on the observer's technical skills and educational background. Experts and professionals are more likely to assign specific labels to objects that non-experts categorise using general terms (e.g., 'femur' instead of 'bone').[14] Experience, in other words, corresponds to the ability to introduce differences that make a difference, thereby increasing the amount of information that can be processed.

Based on these considerations, we can attempt to explain the relative success of tags compared to traditional classification and semantic indexing systems. Research has primarily focused on the ease with which users can assign tags to resources in digital archives (Peters 2009, p. 161ff.). However, this merely shifts the question to the actual meaning

[12] Clues, in this context, are the correlate of the system's interaction with its environment. On the possibility that certain elements might function as clues for categorising observed reality (the so-called *clue validity*), see Medin (1983). In every interaction with its environment, the system "prefers" (in the Latin sense of *praediligere*) certain elements, as Bruner (2009, p. 87) explains—that is, it "pre-selects" the attributes that best function as clues to a reality that can be categorically understood. Clues, of course, do not exist in nature. Rather, certain elements can serve as clues if they are capable of reactivating redundancies (schemas, models) that render the reality with which the system interacts 'recognisable'.

[13] In cognitive psychology, scholars speak of *basic level*. Cf. Rosch et al. (1976, p. 382ff.) and Rosch (1998, p. 254ff.).

[14] Research is extensive. Cf. only Tanaka and Taylor (1991, p. 458ff.); Taylor (2003, esp. p. 119ff.).

of this ease. What does it mean to say that tagging is easier, assuming it is? And what factors contribute to this ease in the tagging process?

Among the defining characteristics of folksonomies, as we have seen, is their ability to free users from the need to familiarise themselves with complicated hierarchical classification structures before assigning a category to a given resource. This feature alone saves a significant amount of time and cognitive efforts, allowing users to tailor categorisation to their own needs and preferences, rather than conforming to a classification system designed by others and based on principles that often remain obscure.

Added to this is the issue of anticipated concerns about memory. When selecting metadata to facilitate data retrieval, the primary question is whether metadata align with the access method that prospective users will employ to retrieve data they have since forgotten. There is no guarantee that the categories best representing a resource's content will also be the most efficient for this purpose (Sinha 2005). For example, a biography of Christopher Columbus may interest historians of navigation techniques, geographers, or those simply curious about the private life of a famous figure. Perspectives and areas of interest are not only multiple but also unpredictable, especially when considering prospective users who cannot be consulted. The same holds true for each single user over time: what is interesting today may lose relevance tomorrow, while something the user not even think about today may gain importance in the future. Meaning is complex not only socially and in terms of content but also temporally, as time enriches the connections that the same data can reactivate.

This is precisely where the primary limitation of taxonomy becomes evident: as the indexer must decide the appropriate place to assign a resource, the risk of making an incorrect decision is significantly high. Not so much because the assignment is inherently wrong, but rather because it may fail to align with what other users (or even the same user in the future) might consider relevant to their needs. The result, as often occurs, would be that the sought-after item is indeed contained in the archive but cannot be found, or is found only with great difficulty, making it effectively as though it were not there at all.

The problem can be partially managed, though not entirely resolved, by abandoning the principle that the indexer must assign a single category to a resource, or that the resource can be located in only one place within the archive. Singleness, in fact, leads to over-specification, thereby significantly increasing the risk of user frustration. Paradoxically, the certainty of taxonomic structures based on pre-established location ensures memorability if the overall organisation is already known. However, it greatly increases the uncertainty of future retrieval when the structure is unfamiliar, and user queries are highly diverse.

Tags circumvent the issue of resource location by allowing multiple categories to be assigned to a single resource. While the choice of a single location forces the indexer into the dilemma of whether it is the right or wrong one—often resulting in a 'paralysis' (Sinha 2005) of analysis regarding the terms that could facilitate future retrieval of archived content—the ability to assign multiple categories simultaneously liberates indexers from this dilemma, though it does not relieve them of the burden of making a decision.

The break with a comprehensive system of topics (*topica universalis*) occurred precisely at this juncture: while the system of topics relieved readers of the need to determine the proper place for assigning each element of knowledge, the Renaissance practice of commonplace-books shifted the burden of selecting headings onto the readers themselves. Readers relying on a comprehensive system of topics, in short, did not have to make any decisions, as the order of knowledge was already predetermined. This could be a relief on one hand but a limitation on the other, particularly as the body of knowledge with which learned readers engaged was continuously expanding.[15] The choice of headings, by contrast, required the readers to reflect on how best to categorise what they decided to archive. At the same time, however, it provided the opportunity to organise access to the archive according to their own preferences, thereby multiplying entry points and creating associative pathways as needed.

Tags, in a sense, represent an extreme form of this evolutionary advancement. A scholar delivering a lecture in Berlin on social memory at the Max Planck Institute for the History of Science might save the documents produced for this conference in a folder titled 'Berlin', knowing that memory operates associatively and that she is likely to recall the conference by associating it with the city where it took place. However, the same documents could just as easily be archived in a folder titled 'Max Planck', 'Social Memory', or another entirely different label. If the researcher organises files into folders with only a single heading, she risks

[15] This point is emphasised particularly by Yeo (2001, esp. p. 83 and 97).

failing to locate what she is looking for if she relies on the wrong association—one that is technically correct but proves ineffective in practice. By contrast, if she organises files into folders and attaches multiple tags, she could retrieve documents saved under 'Berlin' by searching with the tag 'Max Planck'—or vice versa, retrieve documents saved under 'Max Planck' by searching with the tag 'Berlin'.

The view that the relative simplicity of tagging procedures stems from the elimination of the need to make decisions should, at this point, be reconsidered. The absence of decisions would equate to the absence of tags and, consequently, to the impossibility of accessing the resources stored in the archive (unless traditional systems are employed). In reality, the opposite is true: users do not abandon decision-making; instead, they multiply their decisions. This, in turn, also increases the uncertainty they face (will I search for this resource under this term or that one?). The presence of tags functioning as index terms has a cumulative effect on the likelihood that retrievable resources will also be relevant. Paradoxically, by amplifying uncertainty at the moment of categorisation, tagging reduces the uncertainty surrounding the future ability to efficiently retrieve a relevant past (Cevolini 2019b, esp. p. 214f.).

6.3 Search by Associations

As knowledge becomes more complex, the order that once served as a solution transforms into a problem. This shift occurs for several reasons. Firstly, users who are not thoroughly familiar with the indexing system designed by professionals (which essentially includes the vast majority of the user community) often struggle to navigate. From their perspective, the rules of distinction may appear unclear and unjustified,[16] resulting in slow and frustrating retrieval processes. The assignment of a resource to a single precise location—this one and no other—within the intricate hierarchical stratification of a taxonomic structure ultimately undermines the very function it is meant to facilitate: the retrieval of archived content. In other words, the subject headings denoting topics (i.e., the index terms

[16] Indeed, even from the perspective of professional cataloguers. Cf. Wachtel (1953, p. 69), who honestly acknowledged that "the classification maker must make many *arbitrary decisions* as to which material he wishes to bring together and which he is willing to scatter" (italics added).

used in library catalogues) simultaneously enable and hinder access to information.

A second reason is the previously mentioned issue of *multiple storage*. From a historical perspective, it is worth noting that concerns about the inadequacy of classification systems in managing the complexity of knowledge through archives had already emerged in the early modern period and resurfaced in the first half of the twentieth century—long before the mechanisation and subsequent digitisation of archives. In the 1930s, several scholars lamented that, given the increasing complexity of knowledge, library classification systems were "obsolete and unsatisfactory".[17] One key reason for this dissatisfaction was that every classification system, like every method of categorisation,[18] imposes rigid rules of inclusion and exclusion. Faced with the complexity of meaning, classifiers must yet contend with the challenge of managing ideas that can be considered from multiple perspectives and cannot be neatly confined to "mutually-exclusive, all-inclusive classes".[19] This issues implies that the same resource could be placed in multiple locations, which directly contradicts the principle of classification requiring each element to occupy a single, fixed place. Assigning multiple locations would not only be misleading but would ultimately result in forgetting.

Perhaps the main reason why order becomes a problem lies in the fact that taxonomic structures are decided in advance and follow rigid rules that, while theoretically open to alternative formulations, become unchangeable once established. When dealing with a reality that remains constant over time, this preference for an unchanging system of distinctions can be highly effective. However, in the context of continuously expanding knowledge, such invariance becomes an obstacle.[20] Those who seek information and aim to contribute to the production of new

[17] Lund and Taube (1937, p. 373). Bush's (1945) critique of the "artificiality of systems of indexing" was therefore not without precedent. Cf. also Bush (1987, esp. p. 179); Rolla (2009, p. 175 and 182); Kipp and Campbell (2010, p. 239ff.).

[18] See above Sect. 6.2.

[19] Wachtel (1953, p. 69). Milk, for example, can be classified based on the distinctions liquid or solid, white or black, edible or non-edible. Each of these aspects requires the construction of its own classification system. However, a classification system encompassing all classification systems, without multiplying locations, is impossible.

[20] Cf. again Lund and Taube (1937, p. 373), for whom the issue was precisely the "permanence" of library classification systems and, consequently, "the absurdity of providing for all future knowledge by subdivisions or expansions of present systems".

knowledge, rather than being bound to reiteration, perceive excessive structure as a source of friction that should possibly be minimised. This is not, of course, about abandoning structure altogether but rather about transitioning from one type of structure to another.

One reason why users readily resort to tags is that they do not require consensus on the rules for their assignment, either before or after each tag is assigned (Spiteri 2006, p. 80; Navarro Bullock et al. 2018, p. 313). Such consensus presupposes the existence of a common world expected to be reflected in a common order of knowledge. However, it is precisely this shared framework that the practice of tagging disrupts. Instead of assuming that the storage of knowledge should align with a world common to all observers—whose order is independent of those observing it—the assignment of tags depends on observers' self-reference and expectations. Rather than adapting their worldview to a shared categorisation, users tailor their categorisation to the world that is relevant to them.[21]

Practically speaking, abandoning the need for preliminary consensus almost automatically resolves the issue of determining where to assign each resource within the archive. Each user can, in a sense, express his or her own perspective and place the resource where he or she considers it most appropriate.[22] What is striking about this practice is that it seems to overturn a classical precept of the theory of reminiscence: that the multiplication of mnemonic anchors leads to forgetfulness. Orators who constructed repositories filled with vivid images were aware that the only way to get rid of what they had painstakingly fixed through imagination was to multiply references. An excess of references would result in disorientation; the anchors would become misleading (milk is white like snow, so the season might also be winter), and, ultimately, orators would forget what it was they wanted to remember.

With tags, this rule is reversed. The multiplication of references facilitates retrieval by diversifying the access paths to the sought-after resources. Traditional classification systems also attempted to make retrieval easier by diversifying access points (by author, by subject) and incorporating cross-references, but the overreaching taxonomic structure

[21] Cf. also Weinberger (2005, p. 3): people abandon the "old dream of finding a single, universal comprehensive way of organising the world's knowledge".

[22] Cf. Smith (2008, p. 3 and 18); Weinberger (2007, p. 14): "Instead of everything having its place, [...] things can get assigned multiple places simultaneously".

imposed an insurmountable constraint. Tags circumvent this obstacle by encouraging an assignment process that, in principle, has no limits. They amplify the capacity to remember not so much because they oppose a pre-established order, but because they abandon the idea that such an order of knowledge exists in the first place.

On the other hand, the assumption that order provides an excellent solution to the problem of memory is perfectly reasonable—especially given that, under certain conditions, order does indeed functions effectively. For this reason, contradicting this assumption understandably raised significant doubts at the dawn of modernity. From an evolutionary perspective, this implied a departure from a perfectly plausible principle. In other words, it involved surpassing a certain threshold of improbability: how could the absence of order be a solution, rather than a problem, when it comes to organising information access? How can the best form of order be the lack of order?

Semantic indexing, while decoupling the order of the repository from the order of the register, did not entirely abandon the notion that each item has an appropriate place and that the indexer's role is to determine that place. With the advent of digital memory, however, both spatial constraints and taxonomic order have proven inadequate for managing the complexity of knowledge, leading to the adoption of more flexible and contingent solutions, such as the use of tags.[23]

Structurally speaking, however, the shift is not from order to disorder, but rather from one type of order to another.[24] At the operational level, it may appear as though one is dealing with the disorder of the categories used to retrieve stored resources. Without some form of structure, disorder would simply be unmanageable. Furthermore, disorder is conceivable only against the backdrop of a reference order, with which disorder (which may, in fact, be a different type of order) is compared.

Even with tags, order is structurally ensured by the network of references and connections without which a resource would remain unretrievable. The most evident consequence is that there is no pre-established order to which the search must conform; rather, order emerges as the

[23] Weinberger (2007, p. 5ff. and 17ff.) speaks of the "third order" of knowledge organisation.

[24] Exactly as in the case of *adversaria*. See Sect. 3.2.

very outcome of the search process.[25] Tags, in essence, allow order to be operationally derived from chaos. In this way, every order is inevitably provisional: everything can be composed and dismantled, only to be recomposed differently, depending on the preferences and interests of users.

The evolutionary novelty of this approach becomes particularly clear when considered from a temporal perspective. On one hand, tags represent a new form of indexing oriented toward an open future. Not being bound, in principle, by any specific classificatory rule, tags offer high flexibility and, consequently, exceptional adaptability to constantly changing contexts.[26] Flexibility is the natural correlate of an indexing process that is primarily future-oriented rather than past-oriented. Adaptability, in turn, poses a significant challenge, especially when the interaction between users and machine must accommodate highly heterogeneous requests. As we have seen, users have their own way of categorising the past, shaped by their unique perspectives and priorities. The variety of the environment that the social system must address is therefore substantial. Once tags are assigned to a digital resource, however, they become public and enter the recursive cycle of communication. In doing so, the social system equips itself with the variety necessary to cope with the variety of its environment, thereby maintaining its adaptability to ever-changing situations (previously assigned tags do not prevent the addition of new ones).[27]

Unlike taxonomic classification systems, which remain bound to the same principle underlying Platonic dialectics—namely, that one must always begin with an original unity and proceed through successive dichotomous divisions—the practice of tagging eliminates the need for a single entry point and transforms every tag into a node within a network that could be further articulated without limit. This variation in access points to archive contents accommodates the diversity of user queries and significantly reduces the dispersion of relevant results. In this sense, as Nicola Benvenuti (2007, p. 39) points out, the great abundance of

[25] Cf. Weinberger (2007, p. 124): "[The] ordering is postponed". Cf. also Shirky (2005): "The filtering is done post hoc".

[26] On this point, researchers are unanimous in their opinion. Cf. Wu et al. (2006, p. 111ff.); Spiteri (2007, p. 13ff.); Halpin et al. (2007, p. 211); Navarro Bullock et al. (2018, p. 317).

[27] On this function of variety, see Sect. 4.4.

available access points serves as a resource for users, rather than merely constituting a form of *meta noise*.

From this perspective, tags represent the digital adaptation of a strategy already tested in early mechanical experiments with indexing systems based on the association of ideas (Taube 1954a, esp. p. 72; 1954b, p. 81ff.; 1954c, p. 100ff.). The underlying rationale was to transform each idea into a "point of entry" for searching the archive while simultaneously enabling users to associate various ideas by coordinating them through logical operators (conjunction, negation, alternation).[28] This associative strategy preserved conventional classification systems, offering users the flexibility to explore the archive either through a search by indexing or through a search by association. The primary advantage of coordinating ideas lay in its ability to generate complexity through selections. The associations of ideas that could be explored were limited to those recorded in the machine, representing an actual subset of all potential associations of ideas derivable from the archive's contents.[29] Through coordinate indexing, users were provided with increased complexity of control, that is, a broader range of browsing possibilities.[30] The result was the discovery of unexpected combinations of ideas (Taube 1954a, p. 80), different for each user depending on their unique perspectives and information needs.

In digital archives that allow social tagging, the ability to manage far greater variety stems not only from the multiplication and diversification of access points but also from the concurrent proliferation of associative paths that users can follow. Compared to coordinate indexing, which was limited to a few logical operators, tags, in principle, fully implement the 'search by association' envisioned by Vannevar Bush.[31] Bush's idea was revisited and developed about twenty years later in projects aimed at constructing a 'semantic memory'. Here too, the guiding principle was to create a system composed of nodes and associative links between

[28] Cf. Wachtel (1953, p. 65ff.) and Taube and Wachtel (1953, p. 73ff.) on the well-known *coordinate indexing* and the corresponding use of *unit terms*.

[29] Cf. Taube (1954b, p. 81; 1954c, p. 104). The distinction between actual and potential already implies complexity by definition.

[30] On the notion of 'complexity of control', see Sect. 2.7.

[31] As suggested by Kipp (2011, p. 259). Cf. Bush (1987, p. 180; 1992, p. 1/49). See also Krippendorff (1975, esp. p. 28ff.).

nodes, much like a filing system.[32] This structure not only eliminated any hierarchy among the basic units of knowledge but also ensured highly diversified access to memory. Every node became a potential entry point into the network of associations and could be used to reactivate the memory structure. In such a system, it was practically impossible to predict which memory would be reactivated, as this depended on the interaction between users and the machine and on the possibility that each interaction could lead to the exploration of new associative paths.

When compared to subsequent technical developments, the term 'semantic memory' may appear misleading, if only because machines do not actually process meaning. For this reason, greater caution is warranted when making claims about tags in relation to *sensemaking* or their role as a foundation for building a semantic Web (Golder and Huberman 2006, p. 202ff.; Halpin 2012, p. 134ff.). Such statements often fail to clearly distinguish between the user (understood as an individual psychic system), the machine (which functions according to its design), and the reality emerging from their interaction—namely, communication.

The same applies when discussing 'collective intelligence'. This expression leaves undefined both the concept of intelligence and that of collectivity, merely hinting at the fact that the outcome of selection can be attributed neither to individual users nor to the machine. Instead, it arises from the feedback loop initiated whenever users and the machine interact.[33]

Among the structural properties of semantic memory is the fact that, with the continuous addition of new elements, the branching of associative links in the network expands disproportionately (Quillian 1966, esp. p. 47). As a result, the number of associative paths that could be followed becomes overwhelming. In other words, memory generates its own complexity. This also implies that it rapidly becomes opaque, as exploring all accessible paths is impossible. Furthermore, since every interaction contributes to the creation of new paths, making the network even more intricate and opaque, users ultimately interact with a machine that is always different precisely because it is the same machine they interacted with before. In other words, the machine is not only capable of learning

[32] Cf. Quillian (1966, esp. p. 13 and 20ff.). The comparison between the Web and the filing cabinet, based on the shared structure of nodes and links between nodes, is suggested by Berners-Lee (1999, p. 11).

[33] Cf., for example, Halpin et al. (2007, p. 213).

but also functions as a historical machine, tracking the outcomes of previous interactions and reacting to new inputs based on those outcomes (Bush 1987, p. 188; 1992, p. 1/51f.; Weston 1970, esp. p. 84).

Research has shown that when addressing the increasing complexity of memory operating through associations, the traditional hypothesis—that retrieval time for a memory lengthens as the number of elements increases—should be reversed.[34] This traditional hypothesis considers only the elements comprising the unit to be recalled, and in this sense, it is more a hypothesis about the complexification of memory than its actual complexity. However, if associative links are added, the hypothesis is inverted (referred to as the 'connectivity' hypothesis): as the number of elements progressively increases, the relationships connecting these elements grow exponentially, resulting in a proportional decrease in retrieval time.

When digital memory is equipped with tags and corresponding hyperlinks, it becomes possible to diversify the types of search pathways available. This functionality is known as *pivot browsing*: users interacting with the results of their queries can choose to explore the different tags assigned to a retrieved resource, discover which other users have used the same tag and what else they have consulted, or follow resources tagged in the same way. This diversification of search possibilities is not intended to reach a final result through alternative routes, but rather to encourage the continuation of the search—a form of selections reproducing selections.[35] In other words, pivot browsing does not ensure a comprehensive exploration of the archive. Instead, it promotes its never-ending explorability.

The unexpected consequence is that memory, in this way, is deliberately structured to produce 'chances', that is, opportunities for surprise.[36]

[34] This is the hypothesis of the so-called *fan effect*, which has been countered by the hypothesis of the *inverted fan effect*. On this topic, see the important experimental study by Kroll and Klimesch (1992, p. 192ff.).

[35] Cf. Smith (2008, p. 106): "The goal of the pivot is not to guide people to specific content, but merely to give them many paths to discover information". The combination of selection and randomness is highly valued in research, which refers to it as *serendipity*. Cf. Auray (2007, p. 74ff.); Sinclair and Cardew-Hall (2008, p. 23); Navarro Bullock et al. (2018, p. 317).

[36] This structure is already embedded in the filing system organised into loose entries, following Luhmann (1992c, p. 54 and 60), who speaks of the "generation of chances with sufficiently condensed opportunities for [making a] selection".

Interaction with the machine is not solely about finding an answer to a specific question but also about suggesting questions the user might never have otherwise formulated. The essence of exploratory capability lies precisely in this: there is no single 'correct' path within the archive, but rather an infinite number of possible paths that can unfold—even randomly—during exploration, starting from the provisional results already achieved. However, chance cannot be generated by chance. It must be technically facilitated through the multiplication of nodes and, most importantly, the connections between those nodes.

In this way, chance is paired with the possibility of selection: every time users interact with a resource tagged in multiple ways, they can decide which tag to follow and let themselves be surprised by the results of their choice. External memory is designed so that each interaction with it can, in some way, be engaging for the user. Selection reduces complexity, as the user, out of all the available tags, chooses just one at any given moment. At the same time, it reproduces complexity, as each choice opens up a space of alternative possibilities that exceed the users' actual capacity to process information, compelling them to make further selections. This dynamic has very concrete implications that deserve deeper exploration.

6.4 Provisional Categorisation

The technical development of indexing systems necessitates embracing a seemingly counterintuitive notion of memory. The ways in which users interact with machines functioning as succedaneous memories suggest that the primary function of memory is not to retrieve the past but to respond to future questions. Since both the formulation of these questions and the underlying information needs are unknown, the machine must be designed to make conjectures. As a result, the inferential performance of memory assumes greater significance than the simple retrieval of something that is 'given'.[37] This shift, as always, should be understood not merely as a result of technological development but as a consequence of socio-cultural evolution.

[37] See the seminal contribution of Foerster (1969). This does not mean that the reference to the past is eliminated. Inference itself would not be possible without such a reference. Cf. Quillian (1966, p. 42ff.), who distinguishes between memory as a *retriever of information* and memory as an *inference maker*.

When examined from a functional perspective, the practice of tagging bears a certain resemblance to the Category Index conceived by Emanuele Tesauro. Whether intended as a serious endeavour or merely as an erudite pastime, the Category Index was designed to explore, through associations, the semantic potential embedded in ideas.[38] When ideas are connected through rigid, pre-established structures, this potential remains untapped. Such structures freeze, as it were, the connections and enforce reiteration. In other words, they technically reduce the complexity of meaning, and this technical reduction inhibits the exploration of what remains unknown. The Category Index sought to liberate ideas from these constraints, creating a potentially infinite space of associations that users could explore at will, without, however, the exploration itself going in blind.

In digital archives, users can freely categorise resources. In doing so, they create complex networks of relationships that can lead to unexpected outcomes. Through tags, elements can be continuously contextualised and recontextualised, suggesting perspectives that may appear novel to many users and that a pre-established order of relationships would have inevitably sacrificed. This is, among other reasons, why disorder is sometimes preferable to order: as early-modern learned readers already recognised, if the goal is to foster the production of information, one must abandon the reiteration of hierarchical structures or branched frameworks designed to technically organise knowledge retrieval. Only by keeping a combinatory space open can opportunities for surprising discoveries be generated.[39]

Since information cannot be stored, it is essential for memory systems to be designed to continuously accommodate new inputs. The system's redundancy is constantly updated to maintain its sensitivity to variations. The relationship between redundancy and variation within the system is therefore recursive. Temporally, this recursion is facilitated by the ability to continuously add new tags to already stored resources. The assignment of index terms, in fact, is an ongoing operation: users do not need to guess the correct tag and—unlike professional indexers—are not restricted in

[38] The Index was to be used, according to Tesauro (1669, p. 83), to "penetrate objects subtly hidden under various Categories, and compare them with one another". See also Eco (2007, esp. p. 45ff.).

[39] Cf. Weinberger (2007, p. 7): information "wants to be *miscellaneous*" (the German translation has *ungeordnet*; cf. Weinberger 2008, p. 8).

their assignment of index terms because they are not bound by a pre-established taxonomy. Tagging, in this sense, is an open-ended practice (Smith 2008, p. 5 and 24; Spiteri 2007, p. 13f.; Wu et al. 2006, p. 111).

The fact that tagging-oriented indexing addresses an open future also implies a proper relationship with the past. As we have seen, this was the fundamental challenge faced by early modern scholars who were among the first to contend with the increasing complexity of knowledge. If an 'open future' is understood as the unpredictability of what might be stored—and, consequently, the unpredictability of what might require a connection to the network of references constituting the indexing system—then, in the face of such a future, adaptability can only be preserved by ensuring that past decisions do not constrain what might need to be done in the future.

The principle remains that only a loose past can unlock the present and keep the future open.[40] This principle applies more to indexing than to archiving. What changes is not only the available past—new resources (books, documents, etc.) can continually be added to the archive, transforming the content users can explore. More importantly, what changes is access to the available past, that is, the criteria that enable users to distinguish between what they want to remember and what can be forgotten. This is where indexing techniques make a difference and must be appropriately structured. The relationship between data and metadata is the systemic correlate of this restructuring.

In the scientific system, this need has driven efforts to address a problem commonly referred to as 'scientific friction'. This issue arises when different disciplines, or even research groups within the same discipline, index the same data (or data that could be useful to both) in different ways, making these data mutually inaccessible. One proposed solution is to treat metadata not as a finished and enduring 'product' but as an ephemeral and always provisional 'process' capable of adapting to needs that were unforeseen at the time the data were produced (Edwards et al. 2011, p. 667ff.). While metadata conceived as a product aim to be complete and immutable, metadata conceived as a process are, by definition, chronically incomplete and replaceable. In the former case, the indexing system is structured in a 'tight' manner, whereas in the latter, it is structured in a 'loose' manner (Edwards et al. 2011, esp. p. 684).

[40] See Sect. 3.4.

Regardless of the question concerning the most effective way to operationalise the production of ephemeral metadata, the noteworthy aspect of this proposal is that it recognises the transitory and improvable nature of organising information access as an advantage to be leveraged. The creation of these metadata does not, in principle, replace pre-structured indexing systems but rather complements them, compensating to some extent for the alternative possibilities that any indexing decision inevitably excludes when opting for a particular choice. In this way, it becomes possible to combine a static and definitive system with a dynamic and provisional one, thereby fostering interdisciplinary communication and facilitating the discovery of surprising relationships that would otherwise have remained latent in the available data.

This proposal makes the coupling between past and future contingent. Like all mnemonic techniques, metadata serve to operationalise latency. However, when metadata shift from being a 'product' to becoming a 'process', this operationalisation comes to depend on the ever-provisional needs of the present, the evolving research interests of scientists, and the perspectives of individual disciplines, all of which are subject to change. In this way, the present gains the freedom to reconstruct the past differently, even when the past itself remains unchanged. The abandonment of a taxonomic order, often described as a preference for disorder, should be reconsidered in light of this preference for contingency—that is, for what is structurally unstable and transitory. Compared to comprehensive systems of topics, tags represent a shift from a "cosmology of essences" to a "cosmology of contingency".[41]

The practice of tagging in the management of digital memory content has perhaps been embraced with such enthusiasm precisely for this reason. The free assignment of labels to resources stored in these memories creates a "loose categorisation system" (Cattuto et al. 2007, p. 1461) that preserves the possibility of adding new labels to reorganise access to the information potentially stored in the archive. Users simply express preferences that are always only provisionally binding: what is categorised one way today may be categorised differently tomorrow, without the user ever needing to decide, *once and for all*, which of the various categorisations is correct. When perfectibility replaces perfection, the preference for variability supplants the preference for invariance.

[41] This formulation is drawn from Luhmann (2005d, p. 39).

6.5 Tagging as a Second-Order Observation

When users and machines interact through the personalisation of indexing term selection, it may seem that their relationship becomes transparent. However, tags do not render either the machine or the user fully transparent. Instead, they create a relative transparency by associating resources with categories that hold meaning for the user. Additionally, users can observe what has already been done by others who have contributed to the categorisation process. Nonetheless, this concept of 'collaboration' requires reconsideration in a more nuanced manner.

In strictly operational terms, there is no collaboration among users if, by 'collaboration', we mean contributions based on decisions made through intersubjective consensus. Each user observes what other users have already done without their consent and without seeking assistance. Similarly, each user assigns tags independently, without requesting the consent or help of others. With tags, what is enacted is not a collective form of indexing but rather a specific form of *second-order observation*.

Those interacting with tags associated with a resource do not immediately access the content of the resource itself but instead see how other users (or professional indexers) have categorised it. Tags, therefore, do not directly provide information about the content of archived resources; rather, they reflect what users believe the content to be. What remains unnoticed—at least until actively considered—is the resource itself. In this sense, users do not directly engage with the reality they are exploring through the indexing system. Instead, they deal with other observers and with their way of dealing with reality.

This form of second-order observation also applies to 'popularity', often graphically represented by the size of tags within the cloud where they are displayed. Here, too, the size is not a judgement on the resource itself but a reflection of the users who have interacted with the resource and expressed their opinion on the most effective way to represent its content. This particular observation of observers constitutes one of the most intriguing innovations of social tagging.

Traditional semantic indexing neutralised the issue of consensus by assuming that the world being observed is the same for everyone. It was natural to hesitate when confronted with the challenge of designing an indexing system that was both complete and consistent. However, there was no reason to question the existence of a single adequate category to represent each element of reality that could be known by means of categories. This approach, however, presumed that the world could be observed independently of the observer. The distinction between *top-down* and *bottom-up* categorisation, which we have already encountered, should be reconsidered in light of these premises.

The hierarchical distinction between indexing procedures carried out by professionals and those performed by amateurs conceals a more fundamental difference: that between categorisation dependent on the observer and categorisation independent of the observer. In the first case, observers, so to speak, re-enter the observed reality and appear alongside their categorisation choices. While the classic 'subject index' in libraries neutralised the presence of the observer by standardising the rules for assigning indexing terms, the practice of tagging foregrounds the observer precisely because it assumes that the assignment process is a personal matter. Free from the constraints of pre-established rules, observers can focus entirely on themselves and their own preferences each time they assign a tag to a resource.

The second-order observation enabled through tags operates via communication. Users interacting with tags are engaging with the outcomes of actions taken by other users who have interacted with the resources in the archive and made indexing decisions. Since each user can take a position in response to these outcomes, users interacting with tags are ultimately engaging with social memory and, via this engagement, reflecting on themselves.

6.6 Remembering and Forgetting Tags

The relationship between tags and social memory is twofold. On the one hand, tags organise access to the content stored in an archive, enabling the recall of what has been selected as memorable. On the other hand, tags signify what society retains as a collection of ideas deemed worthy of attention. Like the themes of communication, tags selectively delimit the categorical space that gains communicative visibility, thereby temporarily saturating the information-processing potential of concrete operations. Everything discarded remains unseen—it effectively falls into oblivion. In other words, all alternative possibilities excluded by tags constitute the unmarked space of social memory based on collaborative indexing systems.

Oblivion, as such, cannot be operationalised. Every tag leaves unspecified which side of the distinction remains unmarked—the label 'sociology' assigned to a book does not clarify whether the distinction is between sociology and psychology, sociology and philosophy, or general sociology and the sociology of knowledge, and so forth. Much semantic noise could be resolved if, instead of adding tags as isolated units, tags were added in the form of distinctions. A distinction would require specifying which side is indicated and which side is distinguished by the distinction.

This would also clarify the structure of the tag as the unity of the difference between an external reference and an internal reference. Every tag always indicates something else (for example, 'salt' or 'sugar' on kitchen jars) while simultaneously distinguishing that something else from everything else, including the tag itself (the tag is not what it indicates, even when the items in the box are tags). The distinction between indication and distinction thus provides the unity with a concomitant self-referentiality, preventing the conflation of the reference to reality with the reality being referred to.

If what is indicated were clearly distinguished from the other side of the distinction—if what is indicated also specified the opposite side of the distinction—the retrieval of memorable content could become more precise. Ashby pointed out, in this regard, that the great evolutionary advantage of dichotomies lies in their cognitive efficiency, particularly when dealing with exponentially increasing variety. For example, searching for an atom in the universe, even with a computer capable of examining a million elements per second, would require an unmanageable number of centuries. However, if instead of proceeding by units (is the atom located at this exact point in the universe?), the search proceeded through distinctions—such as above/below, or right/left—the search time would decrease dramatically. Once it is determined that the atom is in one half of the universe rather than the other, and similar steps are repeated, the atom could be located in just four minutes (Ashby 1956, § 13/20, p. 260f.).

If the unmarked *side* of the distinction can somehow be managed operationally, the unmarked *space* remains unreachable. Observers examining how others have categorised available resources may, of course, wonder whether something else has been excluded. However, this always occurs within the context of tagging practices—that is, through the addition of other marked sides—and not from a perspective external to the social system that implements this form of indexing. There is no way to observe social memory from outside society. The discrimination between what can be remembered and what can be forgotten always takes place within the system, contributing to structure its approach to processing information.

The practice of tagging clarifies only the self-referential nature of social memory; it does not resolve the issue of which criteria to adopt to determine what is memorable and what is not. From this, two characteristics of tags become apparent: their redundancy and their relative stability.

Empirical research has shown that the variety of tags is much more limited than one might expect. Although, in principle, there are no specific thresholds for adding new tags that reflect the heterogeneity of users' perspectives, what is observed in practice is that a certain degree of repetition quickly emerges. From an evolutionary perspective, this result should not be surprising. Semantic evolution, too, never explores all the possibilities that could theoretically be realised but stops provisionally when it finds those that ensure the continuity of operations within the system and maintain adaptation to the environment.[42] In the case of tags, what matters is that access to information functions effectively and that users can understand what tags indicate.

In the literature, as we have seen, frequent reference is made to 'collective intelligence' and 'consensus-based indexing'.[43] These approaches require the active participation of a critical mass of users and the achievement of consensus on the most relevant tags. This consensus is understood to be observable by identifying the tags assigned most frequently, either to the same resource or to resources stored in a particular archive. Consensus, therefore, is not the result of mutual agreement on the meaning of tags but rather the statistical correlate of frequency in the tagging process. The final outcome is often described as a form of order emerging from chaos.

When users can add their own tags to the same resource, it becomes possible to compare user behaviour and determine which tags have been most frequently used to categorise the resource in question. Conversely, when a tag can only be assigned once, frequency verification makes sense only at the level of the entire database—that is, across the set of resources contained in the archive.[44] The combination of these two frequencies enables the calculation of tag distribution. Empirical research has unequivocally demonstrated that this distribution follows a pattern resembling the

[42] On the principle of limited possibilities, see Goldenweiser (1913).

[43] See above Sect. 6.3. Cf. also Peters (2009, p. 166ff.), with extensive literature.

[44] Cf. Peters (2009, p. 164ff.) on the so-called *broad folksonomies* and *narrow folksonomies*.

'power law': a few tags are assigned very frequently, while many tags are assigned only rarely, forming the so-called 'long tail' of the distribution curve.[45]

Generalising the research findings, it appears that, over time, the distribution of tags achieves a certain stability. Consensus ultimately correlates with the point at which users stop experimenting with variation. When users stop adding different tags, they probably accept the already assigned tags as valid categories for denoting the archived resources. In short, consensus can be understood as another way of indicating that users cease to seek alternatives.

The reasons why this occurs are relatively inconsequential. Explanations have included 'imitation', suggesting that users may be inclined to adopt categories already used by others, which have thus become popular—following the principle that success breeds success. Alternatively, it has been suggested that users share the same basic knowledge and, therefore, the same categories. Another explanation points to the inherent constraints of language, which leave little room for variation (Golder and Huberman 2006, esp. p. 207; Wagner 2014, p. 735ff.). All these factors theoretically encourage a certain 'preference' for already-used tags, whether directly (by observing what others have chosen) or indirectly (by accepting suggestions generated by the search engine).[46]

These explanations are all undoubtedly plausible. However, they do not clarify the social significance of the supposed 'consensus' on tagging, independent of the contributions individual users might make. The visibility of tags exposes them to observation—this is the only empirically certain fact. It is therefore empirically relevant to examine what occurs when users tag resources without knowing which tags other users have chosen, compared to when they can consider others' preferences during the tagging process.[47] Temporally, this comparison also generates an obsolescence effect: recently added tags tend to attract more attention

[45] The scientific literature on this topic is extensive. Cf. Mathes (2004); Halpin et al. (2007, p. 214ff. and 220; 2009, p. 12ff.); Peters (2009, p. 171ff. and 174ff.); Halpin (2012, p. 109ff. and 112ff.).

[46] In this regard, scholars speak of *preferential attachment*. Cf. Navarro Bullock et al. (2018, p. 324f.).

[47] Cf. Cattuto et al. (2007, p. 1461ff.). Sinclair and Cardew-Hall (2008, p. 16) speak of a "mechanism of feedback".

and reinforcement, while older tags gradually fade and are eventually forgotten.

This preference for more recent tags suggests that tags follow the same mechanisms underlying socio-cultural evolution. Ideas circulating within communication systems are always the result of selective retention, drawn from the variety originating within the medium of meaning. As long as ideas structure the process of communication reproduction, they are remembered. The system becomes 'saturated', as memory theory describes, and this saturation limits its ability to process new information. A saturated system cannot accommodate new values, at least not until the previous ones are discarded to make room for new possibilities. In social systems, this highly selective process of saturation is particularly evident in the choice of themes that are addressed communicatively. The same applies to the categories used for indexing purposes.

In the practice of tagging, the selective retention of categories is graphically represented in the form of a *tag cloud*—a collection of categories most frequently associated by users either with a specific resource or with the set of resources stored in the database (Peters 2009, p. 314ff.; Gerolimos 2013, p. 36ff.; Croft et al. 2015, p. 406ff.). This selectivity is visually expressed through colours, but more prominently through the size of the tags: the more popular tags appear larger, while less popular ones are smaller. This creates a feedback effect: what is preferred attracts more attention, while what plays a marginal role is typically overlooked. In this way, socio-cultural memory mediated through search engines takes on a 'visible' form. It is not only visualised through the cloud of categories but can also be comprehended at a glance.

In semantic indexing processes based on user collaboration, what is particularly interesting is that one does not observe what might be expected: the permanent variation of tags. Empirically, the opposite is true: a few categories are repeatedly assigned, many are used sporadically, and many others are not used at all. But this is precisely the purpose of memory: it retains the small portion deemed worth remembering and forgets everything else. Tagging shifts this function to the level of information access but does not alter the function itself. Permanent variation would only mislead users, who would see the tag cloud constantly changing without sufficient time to adapt.[48] Permanent variation, in essence, would amount to a permanent form of forgetting.

One might argue that resources do not change over time (a book remains the same book, even if it is read by different users at different times for different reasons) and, therefore, that a relevant categorisation has a good chance of enduring. However, the practice of tagging begins with the premise that there is no correct categorisation capable of achieving universal agreement based on objective criteria independent of the observer. The selectivity of what is accepted and retained as an indexing term must, therefore, be explained differently.

If we consider that the categories used to index archive resources are not correlates of mental states but structures of communication, it becomes evident that structural variation in this context results from an evolutionary process involving the social semantic repertoire, rather than merely reflecting individual user preferences. These preferences, moreover, are already mediated by the semantic repertoire, as consciousness can formulate its thoughts only through the language that society provides by reproducing communication.

The agreement that users reach on indexing terms should be understood less as the result of a psychic consensus among individual users about the correct categories to assign to archive resources and more as a correlate of the challenges communication typically faces when it must surpass a certain threshold of plausibility. The potential variation of countless categories that could be used acceptably necessitates a corresponding selection. When this selection is reinforced through subsequent use, abandoning the trial-and-error exploration of other possibilities, a relatively stable set of categories emerges. What stabilises over time, therefore, is not consensus but social memory. Rather than consensus-based indexing, it would be more appropriate to describe this process as *evolutionary indexing*.

Interestingly, research has also investigated the possibility of uncovering a structure within the apparent chaos of tags attached by users.[49]

[48] A separate discussion should be made for the tags used to categorise news on online newspapers, as this depends on the memory structures of public opinion. See Luhmann (2009).

[49] Halpin et al. (2007, p. 211ff.) speak of "coherent categorisation schemes". Cf. also Halpin (2012, p. 107ff.). Benz et al. (2010), on the other hand, speak of "self-emerging ontologies" from collaborative tagging systems.

If this were the case, tags would resemble the taxonomy from which tagging practices originally sought to diverge. To uncover latent structures within the variety of tags, sophisticated *clustering* techniques have been employed. These techniques aim not only to identify the concurrent presence of different tags but also to determine whether this co-occurrence is, to some extent, meaningful—that is, whether it reveals surprising connections.[50]

What these techniques actually do, however, is use statistical measures as a surrogate for meaning. The presence of structures, therefore, is largely an assumption based on frequency. For instance, a graph generated through clustering procedures might relate the categories 'chaos', 'evolution', and 'complexity', but how this relationship should be interpreted remains unspecified.[51] Only users can assign meaning to this structure, and they do so in their own way.

Visualisation techniques primarily focus on highlighting those tags that, over time, have permeated the system and are reused to access the archive's resources. These tags represent a form of restabilisation that does not preclude the exploration of further variations but maintains its own invariance, at least as long as the resources remain relevant for communication and are accessed through categories that retain their plausibility and coherence within the context of the social semantic repertoire. The fading of tags, therefore, is primarily a consequence of the irrelevance of the resources, which, in turn, stems from the variability of the themes through which society structures its communication. As themes are forgotten, the categories that once served to recall those themes are gradually forgotten as well. Ultimately, the ontologies emerging from the chaos of tags are nothing more than an index of social memory, continuously subject to the mechanisms of variation, selection, and restabilisation governing socio-cultural evolution.

[50] On the techniques used to perform these measurements, see Halpin et al. (2007, p. 217ff.); Cattuto et al. (2008, p. 616ff.); Halpin et al. (2009, p. 15ff.).

[51] Cattuto et al. (2008, p. 617) rather bluntly observe that "no systematic characterization of tag relatedness in folksonomies is available in the literature".

CHAPTER 7

De-Indexing

7.1 Ecology of Forgetting

An intriguing consequence of the evolution of social memory is the shifting perception of forgetfulness. Over time, forgetfulness has come to be understood not merely as a natural phenomenon but increasingly as an artificial one. Communication technologies play a significant role in driving this evolutionary shift. Typography, for instance, had already overcome a certain threshold of improbability, leading to a corresponding transformation in the semantic distinction between natural and artificial memory.[1] In rhetorical culture, the difference between nature and technique marked the boundary between what self-reproduces itself and what is produced by something else.[2] Techniques can either enact or inhibit natural processes (consciousness tends to forget, rhetorical techniques counteract this tendency), thus offering a counter-concept to the notion of nature as a concept of externalisation.

The evolutionary success of succedaneous memories in early modern Europe reframed the issue of forgetting, shifting it from a natural phenomenon concerning consciousness to a technical challenge primarily related to archives. As individuals became accustomed to the idea that

[1] See Sect. 2.7.

[2] That is, between autopoiesis and heteropoiesis, according to the terminology introduced by Maturana and Varela (1999).

A. Cevolini, *Indexing Systems*
https://doi.org/10.1007/978-3-032-13813-2_7

knowledge can be retrieved from an external memory and that there are virtually no limits to storing expansions of the past, forgetfulness was increasingly perceived as a technical issue primarily related to indexing systems. Consequently, both the problem and the solution to the problem were internalised.

A general outcome of this evolutionary improbability is the *de-anthropologisation* of forgetting. When society entrusts knowledge to archiving systems, loss can no longer be attributed to the poor training of individual consciousness. Instead, it must be ascribed to the structural prerequisites that regulate users' interaction with archives—and, by extension, society's relationship with itself. This necessitates the permanent maintenance of archives. Such maintenance involves both storage and retrieval, that is, both archiving (pertaining to the environment) and indexing (pertaining to the system). In this section, I examine some challenges arising from the environmental side. In the next section, I will instead address issues emerging from the systemic side.

In social memory, the distinction between system and environment reappears in the form of a distinction between information and the vehicle of information.[3] Just as the environment is an indispensable prerequisite for the self-reproduction of systemic operations, so too is the vehicle an essential requirement for the self-reproduction of information in non-interactive communication systems. Therefore, society must take care of the vehicle before communication based on it can take place. Caring for the vehicle presents specific challenges, particularly those related to storage and preservation.[4] The archive was created primarily to address these issues.

When writing became a medium of communication and was used to produce not only accounting and administrative records but also legal and religious texts, physical objects began to accumulate in society's environment, necessitating their preservation. Designated places, such as rooms or storage facilities, were established and managed by specialised personnel responsible for organising these objects (e.g., clay tablets) according to relatively simple and context-based criteria. While

[3] This distinction has been extensively discussed in Sect. 4.2.

[4] When communication begins, however, what is forgotten is precisely the vehicle, at least as long as it ensures the continuation of the communicative process. Communication, thus, has its own *autonomy* while remaining *dependent* on the environment. Cf. Luhmann (2011, esp. p. 159f.).

these places may not strictly be termed ‘archives’,[5] their primary function was to safeguard physical media from the threat of loss.

Until the invention of printing, loss was one of the primary concerns of educated readers. The typical solution to this problem was redundancy. The methodical copying carried out in scriptoriums served to prevent the disappearance of a text in case the only available manuscript copy was accidentally destroyed. The production of redundancy was precisely aimed at safeguarding texts from the risk of irreversible loss. The function of the archive was thus primarily *hypomnestic* (Derrida 1996, p. 19): it was not merely about preventing texts from being forgotten but, above all, about saving the mnemonic supports of those texts from destruction.

The printing industry relieved scholars of this concern precisely because it could reproduce redundancy mechanically. However, this did not remove the underlying problem inherent in the distinction between vehicle and information. On the contrary, the increasing technologisation of communication made it even more evident that the more communication depends on technical systems, the more crucial their maintenance becomes to ensure the social adaptation indispensable for the proper functioning of social memory. This maintenance, however, can only be addressed if the environment is thematised within society.

In very abstract terms, this is possible if the distinction between system and environment is used within the system to generate observations. Observation, being a social operation, occurs within the system and connects to the network of operations recursively reproduced by the system. Consequently, the environment is both inside and outside the system. It exists outside society as a technical system installed for communicative purposes. However, it is simultaneously inside as a theme of communication. The re-entry of the distinction between system and environment into the system that originally generated it enables this duplication and unfolds the apparent paradox of a distinction that is no

[5] The notion of ‘cuneiform archives’ is questionable, not least because we do not even know whether the earliest forms of writing included a term corresponding to what is now properly called an ‘archive’ (Pelio Fronzaroli, personal communication about the Eblaite language, 7 February 2017). On cuneiform archives, see Matthiae (2008). Similar concerns have been raised by Georgoudi (1988, p. 221ff.) regarding ‘State archives’ in Greece during the fifth-fourth centuries BC. Cf. also Posner (1972, p. 4f. and 91ff.), who considers ancient archives to have been mere repositories for the preservation of material objects of public or private interest.

longer identical to itself when it re-enters into itself, while still being the same distinction.[6]

Based on these premises, one can speak of an *ecology of forgetting* whenever society produces communication about the environmental conditions that enable the implementation of social memory and uses this communication to encourage structural changes in social systems.[7] As with all forms of ecological communication, society does not react directly to factual events but rather to their observation. And since the environment cannot communicate, society reacts to itself through its own operations (Luhmann 1989a, p. 18; 1995b, p. 39f.; 2008, p. 31 and 41ff.). Due to this operational closure, the environment becomes socially significant—that is, it generates resonance within communication systems—only when it is thematised. In the case of social memory, this thematisation manifests in discussions about 'preservation'—a long-standing concern for libraries and archives that digital technologies have once again made crucial. In the digital realm, however, the problem of preservation presents distinct challenges that should not be overlooked.

In libraries, the primary challenge was typically the protection of books from moisture and rodents. In digital archives, instead, the issue lies in managing technical systems that enormously expand data storage capacity but also constantly generate far more data than ever before. Digital technologies produce a medium that only digital technologies can preserve, thereby triggering a potentially never-ending circular process. However, since not all knowledge originates from the digital age, preservation requires decisions about what to digitise and what to leave out. This decision is a social issue, even though it relates to environmental preconditions, and is discriminatory in terms of social memory, as it determines the accessibility of content. It is with respect to this accessibility that decisions must be made about what to retain and what to discard.

The ecological dimension of forgetting becomes evident when one considers that what is unavailable is, by definition, inaccessible, even though availability itself does not guarantee concrete access to stored

[6] Luhmann (2011, p. 462). The concept of 're-entry' is drawn from Spencer Brown (1979).

[7] For a definition of 'ecological communication', see Luhmann (2008, esp. p. 41).

resources.[8] Forgetfulness, in this sense, becomes a matter of decision-making. Content may be discarded based on an initial assessment of whether it is worth preserving, yet even something previously deemed worthy of preservation may later be disposed of.[9] In any case, by acting upon the environment, society creates both possibilities and impossibilities for systemic operations, without necessarily having to retain memory of these decisions. The environment becomes noticeable again only in cases of malfunction, and only when such malfunctioning re-emerges as a topic of communication.

Technological progress complicates the issue of accessibility by preserving technical supports (the vehicles) while rendering them unusable. Computers capable of accessing data stored on a floppy disk are now virtually unobtainable. This technical problem can only be resolved through technical tools. However, innovation introduces an additional challenge—obsolescence. Despite being conceptually opposed, innovation and obsolescence are intrinsically linked and tend to increase simultaneously. One cannot innovate without rendering previous technical products obsolete, just as obsolescence would not occur without continuous innovation. Avoiding the problem of aging technical equipment would require reframing from developing new devices. Yet, in a society structurally oriented toward the future—and thus toward the relentless enhancement of its performance—such a claim would be unacceptable.

Technical obsolescence generates a particular form of forgetting. As in ancient techniques of reminiscence, the content is not destroyed but remains latent somewhere. However, unlike reminiscence, where technical devices were specifically designed to bring out the content from the latency in which it lay, technical obsolescence turns the medium into an impediment that makes it difficult or even impossible to retrieve something that exists but cannot be actualised (Ridolfi 1994, p. 247ff.; Duguid 1996, p. 71ff.; Rothenberg 1995, p. 42ff.). The vehicle is preserved,

[8] Many books stored in a library are not read, and much of what is stored in digital memories is not actually retrieved through search engines.

[9] On discarding and disposal, see Lübbe (1994, p. 167ff. and 208f.). The dynamics of disposal also encompass the temptation to burn books. A different case, however, arises when the material support remains intact, yet the text it preserves is altered, as in the medieval practice of the palimpsest or in the continuous rewriting of the past dystopically envisioned by Orwell in *1984*.

yet access to the data it contains is hindered by the absence of suitable technical tools.

The problem is shifted, but not resolved, as contents stored on obsolete media, such as floppy disks, can be transferred to newer vehicles. This technical possibility unfolds a new fork between what is worth transferring and what can be neglected. This distinction replicates the fundamental choice between retention and discarding, once again requiring a decision.

Replacing storage media can solve many problems, but it also creates new ones. Digital technologies are expensive, require continuous maintenance, and are vulnerable to various risks. Their use also depends on prerequisites, such as the availability of electrical power, which must be ensured. The possibility of making a paper copy of digital documents is neither reasonable nor practical. But even transferring documents from one technical format to a more advanced one is not as straightforward as it may seem. When it comes to large public archives, the costs of such transfers can be prohibitively high and are not always economically sustainable. The production and destruction of redundancy must therefore be carefully assessed, and like all decisions, they can be planned.

When society addresses the challenge of knowledge management, the planning of forgetting becomes a social issue, even though it primarily concerns environmental maintenance. In this ecology of forgetting, as Pierluigi Ridolfi (1994, p. 254) rightly points out, the crucial issue is no longer the past but rather the future. An excess of memory can be problematic not only in economic terms but also in cognitive terms, as it hinders the selection of what truly holds informational value. It is therefore necessary to explore in advance what past the future might require and, at the same time, how to ensure future access to a past that remains technically retrievable despite the rapid obsolescence of storage devices.

In this regard, moral philosophy offers rather vague and dismissive advice. According to Luciano Floridi (2012, p. 437), for example, if the issue is determining which data to delete to make room for updated data, then it would suffice to know which data are truly indispensable. However, this perspective treats data as if they were mere objects. Moreover, one should ask: who decides what is indispensable and what is not? If data are conflated with information, one risks overlooking the fact that information always depends on the observing system, and this is precisely the problem that the organisation of information access must address. Jacques Derrida (1996, p. 47) is correct in stating that "the question of the archive is not […] a question regarding the past" but rather "a question regarding the future". Yet, this raises another fundamental question: does this merely amount to a "responsibility for tomorrow" that a society committed to remembering its own history must assume?

In a modern society functionally differentiated into subsystems, each subsystem addresses issues related to environmental maintenance through its own structures. This also applies to the ecology of forgetting. The economy, for instance, must assess to what extent it is profitable to preserve an obsolete technique or to transfer knowledge from outdated devices to more advanced ones.[10] Science, in turn, may engage in structural coupling with the economy by carrying on funded research on the benefits of innovative knowledge management techniques, as is currently happening in the rapidly evolving field of digital humanities. Law, on the other hand, can only determine whether and for whom the right to be forgotten applies, linking this decision to broader legal frameworks that establish what is legitimate and what is not.

However, none of these reactions can be centrally coordinated, as a functionally differentiated society lacks a central authority capable of making suitable and applicable decisions for the entire society.[11] Even though the issue at stake concerns social rather than individual memory, there is no 'central address' within society to turn to for this type of memory. The crucial question, therefore, is the extent to which society will be able to technically regulate its structural coupling with the environment, knowing that both its capacity to remember and its need to forget do depend on this regulation.

[10] Bell and Gemmel (2007, esp. p. 65) predicted that, to tackle the problem of technical obsolescence in archives, a 'small industry' would emerge aimed at preserving access to data contained on old computer media (using 'emulators' of old machines, for example), or transferring these data onto new media. However, they did not take into account the costs involved. According to Blanchette (2011, p. 32), data will require a "continuous process of re-instantiation into (newer) formats".

[11] In this regard, Luhmann (1989b, p. 36f.) speaks of a "decentralised" management of ecological issues.

7.2 Organising the Inaccessibility of Information

From a systemic perspective, the issue of forgetting takes on different connotations. Not only can a deficiency in indexing pose a challenge, but an excess of indexing can also turn into a (both technical and social) problem. Search engines may retain virtual information that users would rather forget. Moreover, there has long been a particular form of information asymmetry between users and the Web: the Web knows far more about its users than the users know about themselves (Mayer-Schönberger 2009, 1ff.; cf. also Brunton and Nissenbaum 2016). And as with all information asymmetries, users have little to no ability to act upon this disparity of information, even though, paradoxically, the excess information is provided to the Web by the users themselves. This has led to a growing appreciation for the possibility of sabotaging the very function for which search engines have been originally designed, namely, ensuring the retrieval of relevant information.

An illustrative case is the 'right to be forgotten', whereby some users claim that the Web should forget certain aspects of their personal history.[12] The right to be forgotten did not originate with search engines. It predates the advent of the Web and was originally intended to guarantee individuals who had, for various reasons, gained public notoriety the right not to be remembered in the court of public opinion for events dating back to the past. Before the widespread use of the Web, however, refreshing social memory typically required the dissemination of new publications (such as printing a newspaper article about a past event). With the internet, by contrast, it suffices for content to be published once and stored somewhere to be permanently retrievable via a search engine. The issue, therefore, is no longer publication but accessibility. It is not about republishing but about accessing what has already been published.

[12] The reference book on this topic is Mayer-Schönberger (2009). The debate arose following the landmark 'Google Spain' case, namely, the 2014 judgment of the Court of Justice of the European Union (C-131/12), which upheld a Spanish citizen's appeal against Google's indexing of two articles published by a widely circulated newspaper. These articles reported on the seizure of some of his real estate assets for the compulsory collection of social security debts. A considerable body of literature, particularly in the legal field, has since been produced on the 'Google Spain' case. See Salarelli (2014, p. 1ff.; 2015, p. 147ff.); Martinelli (2017a, p. 571ff.; 2017b, p. 156ff. and 163ff.).

Of course, newspapers were archived and indexed long before the advent of the Web. However, the technical limitations of traditional cataloguing systems, along with the time and cognitive energies required for consultation, acted as a sort of natural barrier to accessing information. In other words, the world of print provided a form of "institutional forgetfulness" (Blanchette and Johnson 2002, p. 34), which significantly reduced the risk of embarrassing facts being remembered. Search engines introduce a relatively new problem as they beget a certain hypertrophy of indexing systems. Not only do they remember more, but they also remember better, and above all, they remember permanently. The problem, therefore, is not just the archiving of content on the Web but its permanent accessibility (Finocchiaro 2010, p. 397).

Google's defence in the landmark 'Google Spain' case was based precisely on this point. While users store content in the archive, Google merely indexes what has been archived in the most efficient way possible. Its responsibility, therefore, is limited to maintaining and optimising the technical procedures used to organise information access and does not extend to the data stored in the archive. Functioning merely as a 'card catalogue', Google claimed that it does not create information but only makes it accessible.[13]

The legal system has acknowledged this technical peculiarity and has reinterpreted the 'right to be forgotten' as the 'right to be delinked', that is, the right to be detached from the indexing system that enables the retrieval of content stored in the archive.[14] What is eventually deleted is not the *record* itself but the *link*. For this reason, the right to be forgotten is not a modern form of *damnatio memoriae*. For strictly technical reasons, completely erasing data stored in digital memories is highly challenging. The only truly effective solution would be to intervene on the physical vehicle by destroying it. What can be done, instead, is to interfere with indexing procedures, selectively removing unwanted links in a targeted and intentional manner.[15]

The underlying idea is straightforward: if books in a library cannot be destroyed, one can destroy the library catalogue, making the books

[13] An argument of Kent Walker cited by Toobin (2014).

[14] Cf. Floridi (2015, p. 32ff.). On delinking systems, see also Jones and Ausloos (2013, p. 1ff.); Sica and D'Antonio (2014, p. 147ff.).

[15] On this important distinction between 'erasure' and 'removal', see Ziccardi (2019, p. 237ff.).

unfindable. Destroying the map, in a sense, also erases the territory it represents (Floridi 2015, p. 34f.; Esposito 2017b, p. 7; Vavra 2018, p. 108). Inaccessibility becomes a functional substitute for unavailability. Paraphrasing a well-known statement by Tim Berners-Lee, the issue is not so much that if something is not on the Web, then it does not exist, but rather that if something is on the Web but not indexed, then it does not exist.[16]

Since even deleting links is technically complex, the right to be forgotten has been implemented as a 'right not to be easily found' (Sica and D'Antonio 2014, esp. p. 153f.). By acting on the links, the goal is to drastically reduce the 'online visibility' of an individual whose name is known. If content associated to that name is moved to the bottom of the list, and the list consists of tens of thousands of results, it effectively disappears (Toobin 2014). However, the internet has reacted to these attempts at sabotage using the only means at its disposal, i.e., further indexing. Lists of what had been removed from the lists have been created, producing a kind of 'index of what had been de-indexed'. The aim was not to reinstate what had been removed, but rather to make visible the fact that something had been hidden—a paradoxical form of the presence of absence.[17]

In response to these developments, users have, in turn, implemented 'obfuscation' strategies (Brunton and Nissenbaum 2013, p. 164ff.; Brunton and Nissenbaum 2016, esp. p. 71ff.). Underlying these strategies is an old idea from *ars oblivionalis*, according to which forgetting can be achieved by multiplying memories rather than erasing them.[18] In rhetorical culture, scholars were aware that an excess of references generates confusion, and that confusion is as synonymous with forgetting as order is with remembering. The guiding principle was "ubi multitudo, ibi confuxio", that is, "where things are piled up [without any particular order], confusion arises" (Battisti and Saccaro Battisti 1984, p. 155; cf. also Bolzoni 1995, p. 146f.).

[16] Berners-Lee (1999, p. 176). Cf. also Introna and Nissenbaum (2000, p. 171): "Without much exaggeration one could say that to exist is to be indexed by a search engine". According to Floridi (2015, p. 36), "not being indexed by a search engine simply means 'not being', full stop".

[17] In this respect, Binns (2016) speaks of a "second-order principle of openness".

[18] Cf. Esposito (2017b, esp. p. 6f.), with reference to Eco (1988, p. 259f.).

The internet has mechanically reproduced what rhetoric once designed semantically. The purpose of obfuscation techniques like TrackMeNot is ultimately to conceal relevant information by simultaneously producing a mass of misleading data. These techniques exploit the fact that no user has the time and attention span necessary to discern relevant information from irrelevant noise. In this way, the paradox of *ars oblivionalis* does not even need to be resolved: the 'correct' information remains somewhere, but it is indistinguishable from everything else (Esposito 2017b, p. 7).

Mechanisms for organising information inaccessibility, such as delinking procedures or obfuscation techniques, are evidence that social systems not only remember selectively but also forget selectively (Luhmann 2011, p. 160ff.; cf. also Bowker and Star 1999, esp. p. 257). This occurs whenever communication 'intentionally' omits topics that individual consciousnesses may still remember.[19] Such voluntary forgetting avoids the paradox of a memory that remembers precisely what it would like to forget, provided that the operations of consciousness (i.e., psychic systems) are kept separate from the operations of communication (i.e., social systems).[20] On the other hand, communication remembers both much more and much less than individual consciousness. It is precisely this autonomy that allows communication to decide, relatively independently, what should be forgotten.

Underlying this decision is the assumption that forgetting is not always a problem but can also be a solution—that forgetting, in other words, is not merely a flaw but can also be a virtue.[21] On one hand, this has always been acknowledged.[22] What is novel about the ways voluntary forgetting is implemented in digital memories lies in their relationship with the temporal structures of modernity.

[19] Illustrative cases include amnesty (which etymologically refers to the will not to remember) and forgiveness.

[20] For the same reason, forgetfulness can be a 'goal-oriented' activity without implying contradiction. Cf. Krämer (2000, esp. p. 253).

[21] Cf. Connerton (2008, p. 59ff.). I do not deal with the historical and socio-political appreciation of forgetfulness, as this would require a separate examination. See, however, with what courage Rieff (2019) addresses this issue.

[22] If one is to believe Cicero, to the scholar who wanted to teach him the art of reminiscence, Themistocles replied that he would have preferred to be taught a technique for voluntary forgetting. Cf. Cicero (*De oratore*, II, 74, 299–300). On this anecdote, see Weinrich (2004, p. 12f.).

Nietzsche (1874, § 1, p. 7) had already argued that modern man should not hang on to the past but rather learn to forget. Those who live *unhistorically* do not squander their energies brooding over what has been; instead, they project themselves onto a future that is, in principle, open to any possibility. The crucial point is that this freedom affects not only imagination but also individual action (Nietzsche 1874, § 1, p. 10). If the past clutters the present, there is no room left to envision the future and act accordingly. There is no venture without the removal of history. Only in a present that has forgotten the past can the future take root (Nietzsche 1874, § 7, p. 64f.).

The right to be forgotten is a legal instantiation of this temporal structure. The 'Google Spain' ruling does not concern all searches on the web but only those using an individual's name as a search term. The primary issue addressed by the ruling is reputation, which, more generally, pertains to the social relevance of information concerning personal matters.[23] Reputation both precedes and follows the social career of individuals, influencing their access to the benefits of social systems. Obscuring search results linked to their name that could harm their reputation serves precisely to preserve the possibility of 'adjusting' their self-representation in a way that generates more opportunities than constraints. In other words, it is about safeguarding the ability to 'reinvent' oneself and take advantage of a 'fresh start'.[24]

The modern structures of social inclusion and exclusion provide many examples in this regard. A past bankruptcy may hinder one's ability to obtain credit from a bank again. An old juvenile offence can affect the chances of being admitted to university or securing employment. A history of delayed bill payments may jeopardize one's eligibility for insurance. In all these cases, forgetting functions as both a destructive and constructive force simultaneously (Krämer 2000, esp. p. 262ff.). Those who erase the past have an entire future to envision—they have, as Nietzsche (1874, § 9, p. 98) put it, an "infinite horizon" to explore.

[23] In legal terms, reputation concerns the "social projection of personal identity" (Finocchiaro 2010, esp. p. 398ff.). Building on this assumption, legal scholars have tried to place the 'right to be forgotten' within the context of personality rights but have failed to define it precisely. See, for example, Martinelli (2017b, p. 39ff.).

[24] Cf. Rosen (2010). In this regard, Ausloos (2012, p. 143ff.) speaks of a kind of "bankruptcy of reputation". Cf. also Salarelli (2014, p. 7ff.). The alternative would be a form of "permanent stigmatisation" of individuals who would be deprived of the chance to start over again. Cf. Blanchette and Johnson (2002, esp. p. 35ff.).

The legal significance of deindexing procedures, however, should not be interpreted as a functional contradiction of digital memory. The purpose of these procedures is not to dismantle indexing systems as such, but rather to render certain data irretrievable or difficult to retrieve. The issue at stake, therefore, is not the disorganisation of access to information, but rather the organisation of its inaccessibility.

Setting aside concerns related to reputation, the true advantage of forgetting should be understood in relation to the role of memory in dealing with complexity. Cognitive psychology has demonstrated that when complexity increases, forgetting can serve as a solution by facilitating information processing. This is particularly beneficial in the context of learning. Indeed, only by discarding obsolete or even contradictory information can one preserve adaptation in a rapidly changing environment. One does not learn in order to adapt; rather, one maintains adaptation through learning. This is why it is essential to eliminate everything that is unnecessary. As paradoxical as it may seem, "learning must imply the ability to forget".[25]

These findings of cognitive psychology can be generalised if the systemic reference is shifted from individual psychic systems to social systems. This shift is also essential for understanding the dynamics of a memory that depends on communication technologies. In search engines, as we have seen, forgetting is mechanised. The performance of search engines does not improve by increasing the quantity of information they can retrieve, but rather by increasing the selectivity of retained information while discarding everything else.

To implement this selectivity, search engines must be designed as machines capable of learning. This occurs, for example, when search engines push less relevant or obsolete pages further down the list of results, thereby reducing interferences that would otherwise be redundant and distracting for users. But it also happens every time the indexing system leverages behavioural data to adapt its performance to provisional and contingent information needs.

The widespread use of digital technologies and the continuous production of data from which information can be extracted increase the need for learning and compel social memory to establish a form of dynamic

[25] Parlangeli et al. (2003, p. 32). Cf. also Bagnara and Parlangeli (2000, p. 461ff.); Rizzo et al. (2003, p. 83ff.). Of course, one must forget what has been forgotten without yet forgetting to forget.

stability. The problem is not simply which past deserves to be remembered in the future—this will be decided by an unpredictable future present. Rather, the question is how we can preserve our capacity to forget in response to the complexity reached by the social system. It is likely that the solution to this problem will, for a long time to come, depend on the interplay between archiving techniques and indexing systems, and on how the latter manage to combine order and disorder of knowledge.

CHAPTER 8

Conclusion

Although the literature on search engines is very extensive, scholars rarely emphasise that these tools cannot be investigated “without reference to a larger social context, and to evolutionary social and cultural change” (Halavais 2009, p. 5). By adopting a socio-evolutionary approach, it is indeed possible to discern certain aspects of search engines that usually go unnoticed. Focusing on these aspects may not necessarily solve problems but can help uncover them and further explore their implications. This was the intention of the research presented in this book. Now, we can proceed to draw some conclusions.

Like all communication technologies, the Web has elicited mixed reactions from society. In a famous article published almost twenty years ago, Nicholas Carr (2008, p. 57) argued, for example, that Google was changing our minds. But this is a characteristic shared by all communication technologies. Since communication cannot occur without the cooperation of consciousness, every new communication technology is also a technology of the intellect (Goody 1989, p. 71ff. and 219ff.). An external symbolic system provides an opportunity to re-organise internal cognitive operations, with the result that the technology used for communication restructures our thought (Ong 1986b).

During evolutionary transitions, it is normal for this restructuring to generate some confusion and concern. Communication technologies liberate access to information from the constraints imposed by the physical

A. Cevolini, *Indexing Systems*
https://doi.org/10.1007/978-3-032-13813-2_8

presence of those participating in communication. Access then becomes a matter of choice, with consequences that are entirely unpredictable for those who have made the information accessible.[1] The same principle applies to archives, which function as external memories. They store knowledge that, at least in principle, remains accessible at any time and at will.[2] This corresponds to a clearer differentiation between communication and consciousness, as well as an increased autonomy of social memory from individual psychic memory.

This autonomy is closely intertwined with profound changes in how society remembers and forgets. Research on digital archives has pointed out that one of the less intuitive consequences of metadata is the possibility for users to explore, through these metadata, the dataset for purposes not initially envisaged (Edwards et al. 2011, p. 684). This potential for recombination, as we have seen, is directly correlated with the detachment of knowledge from pre-established organisation and facilitates the discovery of unexpected facts, that is, the production of information.[3]

However, familiarity with the use of external memories encourages a different approach to retaining and discarding relevant knowledge, leading to a different method of information processing. It has been observed that the Web prompts users to remember *where* to find information rather than the *information* itself (Sparrow et al. 2011, p. 777). Yet, as early as the late seventeenth century, scholars suggested that those who read extensively need not burden themselves with retaining everything they wish to remember, as it suffices to know where to find what they need (Sturm 1581, p. 51). External memory relieves individual memory of the burden of retention and, precisely for this reason, facilitates an information processing system that underpins the expectation of a never-ending growth of knowledge.

This relief implies a different allocation of attention. Carr (2008, p. 57) observed that the Web's structures for retrieving information cause, as a side-effect, a "drift of concentration", which impacts our reading habits. In particular, deep reading becomes a struggle. Consecutive and hierarchical reading would be replaced by a reading attitude that increasingly resembles skimming activity (Carr 2008, p. 58). However, even this

[1] This is pointed out by Luhmann (1993, p. 245), writing about writing.

[2] Sparrow et al. (2011, p. 776) about the Web.

[3] See Sect. 3.4.

change is not new. As early as the mid-sixteenth century, as we have seen,[4] scholars noted that indexes made browsing through books appealing, particularly when readers were searching for information. Therefore, the fact that some people used them to evade the effort of reading should not warrant their abolition. The problem, in other words, was not indexing systems per se but how readers used them.

Digital technologies have enhanced the browsing capabilities already established by complex early-modern indexing systems. Through structures such as hypertext links, the Web has given further impetus to the open-ended exploration of knowledge, which is both a prerequisite and a consequence of that preference for novelty that modernity has (positively) reassessed in terms of 'curiosity'. The question, therefore, is not whether digital archives limit or expand the human mind's capacity to process information, because they achieve both simultaneously.[5]

Carr (2008, p. 63) acknowledged that critiques of the Web are similar to those directed at other communication technologies, echoing Plato's criticism of writing or the reservations voiced by some early-modern scholars regarding the printing press. From a socio-evolutionary standpoint, the reiteration of such criticisms demonstrates that evolution is capable of self-observation, even if this self-observation cannot coordinate the mechanisms of evolution in order to achieve a specific goal. Being an observer observing observers, Carr also observes himself, thereby situating his insights within the broader context of a society grappling with the social consequences of its communication technologies.

While predicting the precise trajectory of evolution is impossible, it is reasonably certain that evolution relies heavily on its own advancements. Consequently, society finds it challenging to relinquish the possibility of archiving. However, every increase in storage capacity complicates the retrieval of what has been archived. Society archives more knowledge than it can effectively index,[6] exacerbating the challenges faced by the designers of indexing systems. The organisation of information access

[4] See Sect. 2.8.

[5] Cf. Kassirer (2011) and, in response to the latter, Lilford and Chilton (2011).

[6] Cf. Edwards et al. (2011) on scientific discoveries already available but not retrievable, or hardly retrievable, in archives. On the indexable Web and how to measure it, see Büttcher et al. (2010, p. 511ff.). On the other hand, as Halavais (2009, p. 182ff.) points out, precisely when everything is searchable, the structure of search becomes a challenge (p. 184).

becomes paramount, as it determines what information, if any, is accessible to potential users. This is why those who decide on metadata are not merely deciding on the past but also shaping the future.

The evolutionary approach suggests that a crucial problem lies in complexity. The growth of knowledge increases the complexity users must cope with, as the proliferation of data leads to an exponential increase in potential relationships between data. Indeed, information arises from the relationships between data rather than the data themselves. The function of search engines should be precisely to manage this growing complexity, drawing on the well-known cybernetic principle that only complexity can effectively bring down complexity.[7] Implementing this function undoubtedly poses technical challenges. However, many argue that this implementation raises moral issues as well.

In this regard, people speak of 'ethics of information'.[8] This ethics addresses several issues related to information access, drawing distinctions such as right versus distorted, or complete versus incomplete (picture of reality).[9] These concerns, grounded in moral arguments, are of course legitimate. However, this perspective fails to adequately reflect its own assumptions. Any access to information is inherently incomplete because every selection entails the exclusion of something else. And it is precisely from the vantage point of what has been discarded that doubts may arise about the truthfulness and reliability of the resulting picture of reality. Ultimately, the question arises as to whether moral scrutiny is the most effective approach for evaluating search engines and, more broadly, indexing systems.

The printing industry had raised similar concerns in early-modern Europe. The dissemination of books as consumer goods coincided with a decentralised and non-hierarchical circulation of information. Printing, even more so than writing, compelled authors to relinquish control over the situation (Luhmann 1990, p. 157; 1997a, p. 314). The social reaction, as is well-known, was censorship, that is, a pre-selection of the

[7] See Sect. 4.4.

[8] Floridi (2013, p. 22): the ethics of information is the study of "moral issues arising from availability, accessibility, and accuracy of informational resources". Search engines deal with all of these three issues.

[9] Hinman (2005, p. 19ff.). See further above Sects. 5.1 and 5.3.

information to be circulated.[10] However, this did not diminish the benefits of printing technology, namely, access to information at any time and in any place. Censorship itself had to be disseminated and circulated to be effective, leading to paradoxical effects.

The ethics of information does not specify who should undertake the selection process or how it should be carried out. Furthermore, even moral principles are subject to scrutiny, exposing themselves to the same logic of suspicion applied to information selection. Ultimately, conflicting yet equally legitimate claims emerge which are not easy to reconcile. For instance, the Universal Declaration of Human Rights acknowledges the collective interest in the unrestricted dissemination of ideas and information (Article 19).[11] This implies that everyone has the right to inform and be informed, while also underscoring society's responsibility in preserving memories that may have historical value.

These rights, however, inevitably clash with the principle underlying the right to be forgotten, namely, the interest in safeguarding one's personal reputation and the desire to erase the traces of a troubling past that might impede social rehabilitation. Even legal experts concede that it is difficult, if not impossible, to balance these competing interests.[12]

On the other hand, the main challenge for search engines lies not in retrieving the correct information but in discarding superfluous information.[13] To perform this function effectively, as we have seen, search engines require continuous training based on data generated by users' behaviour. However, this process directly conflicts with the right to privacy and the growing reluctance of users to share the data needed for machine learning. Consequently, there is a significant risk that machines may undergo insufficient training—or none at all.

If we reconsider storage and indexing systems from an evolutionary perspective, it becomes evident that they do not originate from deliberate planning. The very fact that evolutionary advancements take advantage

[10] The best-known case is Possevino's *Bibliotheca selecta*. Cf. Balsamo (2006).

[11] Literally, the right is to "seek, receive and impart information and ideas through any media".

[12] Cf. Werro (2009, esp. p. 290ff.). Even a seemingly naive question such as "When is personal information relevant to the public good?" (Floridi 2015, p. 42) does not allow for an unambiguous and definitive answer.

[13] This is generally true of everyday life. Cf. Connerton (2008, p. 66). See also, with reference to the Web, Simon (1997, esp. p. 8).

of structures initially designed for other purposes demonstrates that any attempt at planning leads to outcomes unforeseen in the original design. Evolution, therefore, does not strive for perfection. Without planning, there cannot even be a completed project.[14]

Rather than framing the problem in terms of planning or pursuing perfection, socio-evolutionary theory suggests addressing it in terms of complexity. From this perspective, the problem of adaptation takes on a different connotation. Given that memory can only be organised from within, the challenge of adaptation is no longer about society adapting to its external environment but about society adapting to itself. This occurs through the structures of social memory. In this regard, the only reasonable prediction that can be made is that adaptation must be maintained. This maintenance will depend, as always, on the complexity achieved and the functional equivalents that offer the greatest benefit relative to that complexity.

[14] Cf. Jacob (1977, esp. p. 1163), with reference to Darwin.

References

Abbamonte, Giancarlo and Kallendorf, Craig (2023): On Indexing: The Birth and Early Development of an Idea. *Journal of the History of Ideas*, 84(3), pp. 465–486.

Albertus Magnus (1519): *De animalibus libri XXVI*. Venetiis: Impensa heredum Octaviani Scoti.

Alsted, Johann Heinrich (1610): *Consiliarius academicus, id est, methodus formandorum studiorum*. Argentorati: Sumptibus Haeredum Lazari Zetzneri.

Amitay, Einat et al. (2005): Queries as Anchors: Selection by Association. In: *Proceedings of the 16th ACM Conference on Hypertext and Hypermedia*. New York: Association for Computing Machinery, pp. 193–201.

Ashby, William Ross (1956): *An Introduction to Cybernetics*. New York: John Wiley & Sons.

Ashby, William Ross (1958): Requisite Variety and its Implications for the Control of Complex Systems. *Cybernetica*, 1(2), pp. 83–99.

Ashby, William Ross (1962): Principles of Self-Organizing Systems. In: Heinz von Foerster and George Zopf (Eds.): *Principles of Self-Organization*. London: Pergamon Press, pp. 255–278.

Assmann, Aleida (2003): *Erinnerungsräume. Formen und Wandlungen des kulturellen Gedächtnisses*. München: C. H. Beck.

Atlan, Henri (1972): *L'organisation biologique et la théorie de l'information*. Paris: Éditions du Seuil.

Augustine of Hippo (1467): *De arte predicandi*. Mainz: Johann Fust/Peter Schoeffer.

Auray, Nicolas (2007): Folksonomy: The New Way to Serendipity. *Communications & Strategies*, 65, pp. 67–89.

A. Cevolini, *Indexing Systems*
https://doi.org/10.1007/978-3-032-13813-2

Ausloos, Jef (2012): The 'Right to Be Forgotten'—Worth Remembering? *Computer Law and Security Review*, 28(2), pp. 143–152.
Bacon, Francis (1876): *The Advancement of Learning*. Ed. by William Aldis Wright. Oxford: Clarendon Press.
Bacon, Francis (2002): *La grande instaurazione. Parte seconda. Nuovo organo* [orig. ed. 1620]. Ed. by Michele Marchetto. Milano: Bompiani.
Bagnara, Sebastiano and Parlangeli, Oronzo (2000): Dimenticare per imparare: la pianificazione dell'oblio nell'apprendimento. *Sistemi intelligenti*, 12(3), pp. 461–470.
Balsamo, Luigi (2000): *La bibliografia. Storia di una tradizione*. Milano: Sansoni.
Balsamo, Luigi (2006): *Antonio Possevino S.I. bibliografo della Controriforma e diffusione della sua opera in area anglicana*. Firenze: Leo S. Olschki.
Barbieri, Edoardo (2016): La *contractio* del piombo. Note su abbreviazioni e tipografia nel Rinascimento italiano. In: Alessandro Tedesco (Ed.): *Scriver veloce. Sistemi tachigrafici dall'antichità a Twitter*. Firenze: Leo S. Olschki, pp. 95–130.
Bar-Hillel, Yehoshua (1955): An Examination of Information Theory. *Philosophy of Science*, 22(2), pp. 86–105.
Bartoli, Daniello (1844): *Dell'ortografia italiana* [orig. ed. 1670]. Torino: Marietti.
Bartoli, Daniello (1845): *L'uomo di lettere* [orig. ed. 1645]. Venezia: Girolamo Tasso.
Bateson, Gregory (2000): Forma, sostanza e differenza. In: Gregory Bateson: *Verso un'ecologia della mente*. Milano: Adelphi, pp. 488–508.
Battisti, Eugenio and Saccaro Battisti, Giuseppa (1984): *Le macchine cifrate di Giovanni Fontana*. Milano: Arcadia Edizioni.
Beal, Peter (1993): Notions in Garrison: The Seventeenth-Century Commonplace Book. In: William Speed Hill (Ed.): *New Ways of Looking at Old Texts*. Binghamton: Renaissance English Text Society, pp. 131–147.
Bell, Gordon and Gemmel, Jim (2007): A Digital Life. *Scientific American*, 296(3), pp. 58–65.
Benvenuti, Nicola (2007): Social tagging e biblioteche. Implicazioni e suggestioni di una 'classificazione generata dagli utenti che emerge attraverso un consenso dal basso'. *Biblioteche oggi*, 25(3), pp. 35–42.
Benz, Dominik et al. (2010): Semantics Made by You and Me: Self-Emerging Ontologies Can Capture the Diversity of Shared Knowledge. In: *Proceedings of the 2nd Web Science Conference*. Raleigh: Web Science Trust, pp. 1–8.
Berners-Lee, Tim (1999): *Weaving the Web. The Past, Present and Future of the World Wide Web by its Inventor*. London: Orion Business Books.

Berners-Lee, Tim and Hendler, Jim (2010): From the Semantic Web to Social Machines: A Research Challenge for AI on the World Wide Web. *Artificial Intelligence*, 174, pp. 156–161.

Berners-Lee, Tim et al. (2001): The Semantic Web. *Scientific American*, 284(5), pp. 34–43.

Berns, Jörg (1993): Umrüstung der Mnemotechnik im Kontext von Reformation und Gutenbergs Erfindung. In: Jörg Berns and Wolfgang Neuber (Eds.): *Ars memorativa. Zur kulturgeschichtlichen Bedeutung der Gedächtniskunst 1400–1750*. Tübingen: Niemeyer, pp. 35–72.

Binns, Reuben (2016): How to Be Open About Being Closed. *Limn*, 6. Retrieved from https://limn.it/articles/how-to-be-open-about-being-closed/

Bizer, Christian et al. (2009): Linked Data—The Story So Far. *International Journal on Semantic Web and Information Systems*, 5(3), pp. 1–22.

Blair, Ann (2000): Annotating and Indexing Natural Philosophy. In: Marina Frasca-Spada and Nick Jardine (Eds.): *Books and the Sciences in History*. Cambridge: Cambridge University Press, pp. 69–89.

Blair, Ann (2010): *Too Much to Know. Managing Scholarly Information before the Modern Age*. New Haven/London: Yale University Press.

Blanchette, Jean-François (2011): The Noise in the Archive: Oblivion in the Age of Total Recall. In: Serge Gutwirth (Ed.): *Computers, Privacy and Data Protection: An Element of Choice*. Heidelberg: Springer, pp. 25–38.

Blanchette, Jean-François and Johnson, Deborah (2002): Data Retention and the Panoptic Society: The Social Benefits of Forgetfulness. *The Information Society*, 18(1), pp. 33–45.

Blum, Rudolf (1980): *Bibliographia. An Inquiry into its Definition and Designations*. Folkeston: American Library Association.

Bock, Walter (1959): Preadaptation and Multiple Evolutionary Pathways. *Evolution*, 13(2), pp. 194–211.

Bolzoni, Lina (1995): *La stanza della memoria. Modelli letterari e iconografici nell'età della stampa*. Torino: Einaudi.

Bonifacio, Baldassarre (1632): *De archivis liber singularis*. Venetiis: Apud Io. Petrum Pinellum.

Bowker, Geoffrey (2005): *Memory Practices in the Sciences*. Cambridge: The MIT Press.

Bowker, Geoffrey and Star, Susan (1999): *Sorting Things Out. Classification and its Consequences*. Cambridge: The MIT Press.

Boyle, Robert (1772): The Excellency of Theology, Compared with Natural Philosophy [orig. ed. 1674]. In: *The Works of the Honourable Robert Boyle*. London: Printed for W. Johnston et al., vol. 4, pp. 6–66.

Brewer, Eric (2001): When Everything is Searchable. *Communications of the ACM*, 44(3), pp. 53–55.

Brin, Sergey and Page, Lawrence (1998): The Anatomy of a Large-Scale Hypertextual Web Search Engine. In: *Proceedings of the 17th International World-Wide Web Conference*. Brisbane/Amsterdam: Elsevier Science Publishers, pp. 107–117.

Brincken, Anna-Dorothee von den (1972): *Tabula alphabetica*. Von den Anfängen alphabetischer Registerarbeiten zu Geschichtswerken. In: *Festschrift für Hermann Heimpel zum 70. Geburtstag am 19. September 1971*. Göttingen: Vandenhoeck & Ruprecht, vol. 2, pp. 900–923.

Bruner, Jerome (2009): *Il pensiero. Strategie e categorie*. Roma: Armando.

Brunton, Finn and Nissenbaum, Helen (2013): Political and Ethical Perspectives on Data Obfuscation. In: Mireille Hildebrandt and Katja De Vries (Eds.): *Privacy, Due Process, and the Computational Turn: The Philosophy of Law Meets the Philosophy of Technology*. New York: Routledge, pp. 164–188.

Brunton, Finn and Nissenbaum, Helen (2016): *Offuscamento. Manuale di difesa della privacy e della protesta*. Roma: Stampa Alternativa.

Brusilovsky, Peter et al. (2018): Social Search. In: Peter Brusilovsky and Daqing He (Eds.): *Social Information Access. Systems and Technologies*. Cham: Springer, pp. 213–277.

Buckley, Walter (1976): *Sociologia e teoria dei sistemi*. Torino: Rosenberg & Sellier.

Burrell, Jenna (2016): How the Machine 'Thinks': Understanding Opacity in Machine Learning Algorithms. *Big Data & Society*, 3(1), pp. 1–12.

Bush, Vannevar (1945): As We May Think. *The Atlantic Monthly*, July, pp. 101–108.

Bush, Vannevar (1987): Memex Revisited [orig. ed. 1969]. In: Anthony E. Cawkell (Ed.): *Evolution of an Information Society*. London: Aslib, pp. 179–191.

Bush, Vannevar (1992): Come possiamo pensare. In: Theodor H. Nelson: *Literary machines 90.1. Il progetto Xanadu*. Padova: Muzzio Editore, pp. 1/38–1/53.

Büttcher, Stefan et al. (2010): *Information Retrieval. Implementing and Evaluating Search Engines*. Cambridge: The MIT Press.

Campanella, Tommaso (1998): *La città del sole* [orig. ed. 1623]. Milano: Mondadori.

Campbell, Donald (1960): Blind Variation and Selective Retention in Creative Thought as in Other Knowledge Processes. *Psychological Review*, 67(6), pp. 380–400.

Campbell, Donald (1969a): Variation and Selective Retention in Socio-Cultural Evolution. *General Systems*, 14, pp. 69–85.

Campbell, Donald (1969b): Variazioni alla cieca e sopravvivenza selettiva come strategia generale nei processi conoscitivi. In: Vittorio Somenzi (Ed.): *La fisica della mente*. Torino: Boringhieri, pp. 205–231.

Caramuel y Lobkowitz, Juan (1664): Syntagma de arte typographica. In: Juan Caramuel y Lobkowitz: *Theologia praeterintentionalis... Est theologiae fundamentalis tomus IV*. Lugduni: Sumptibus Philippi Borde et al., pp. 185–200 (reprint in Valentino Romani: *Il "Syntagma de arte typographica" di Juan Caramuel ed altri testi secenteschi sulla tipografia e l'edizione*. Roma: Vecchiarelli, 1988, pp. 1–73).

Carr, Nicholas (2008): Is Google Making Us Stupid? *The Atlantic*, 302, pp. 56–63.

Carruthers, Mary (1990): *The Book of Memory. A Study of Memory in Medieval Culture*. Cambridge: Cambridge University Press.

Carruthers, Mary (2008): *The Book of Memory. A Study of Memory in Medieval Culture*. 2nd ed. Cambridge: Cambridge University Press.

Cattuto, Ciro et al. (2007): Semiotic Dynamics and Collaborative Tagging. *Proceedings of the National Academy of Sciences*, 104(5), pp. 1461–1464.

Cattuto, Ciro et al. (2008): Semantic Grounding of Tag Relatedness in Social Bookmarking Systems. In: Amit Sheth et al. (Eds.): *The Semantic Web – ISWC 2008*. Berlin/Heidelberg: Springer, pp. 615–631.

Cawdrey, Robert (1604): *A Table Alphabeticall...* At London: Printed for Edmund Weaver.

Cevolini, Alberto (2006): *De arte excerpendi. Imparare a dimenticare nella modernità*. Firenze: Leo S. Olschki.

Cevolini, Alberto (2008): La biblioteca cibernetica. Invito alla lettura di Heinz von Foerster. *La Bibliofilìa*, 110(1), pp. 73–79.

Cevolini, Alberto (2009): Punteggiare la comunicazione e comunicare la punteggiatura. *La Bibliofilìa*, 111(3), pp. 301–307.

Cevolini, Alberto (2014): Indexing as Preadaptive Advance: A Socio-Evolutionary Perspective. *The Indexer. The International Journal of Indexing*, 32(2) pp. 50–57.

Cevolini, Alberto (Ed.) (2016a): *Forgetting Machines. Knowledge Management Evolution in Early Modern Europe*. Leiden/Boston: Brill.

Cevolini, Alberto (2016b): Storing Expansions: Openness and Closure in Secondary Memories. In: Alberto Cevolini (Ed.): *Forgetting Machines. Knowledge Management Evolution in Early Modern Europe*. Leiden/Boston: Brill, pp. 155–187.

Cevolini, Alberto (2017a): "A Universal Index upon all Authors": Thomas Harrison's Ark of Studies and the Evolution of Social Memory. In: Thomas Harrison: *The Ark of Studies*. Ed. by Alberto Cevolini. Turnhout: Brepols, pp. 1–69.

Cevolini, Alberto (2017b): Breve saggio sulla abbreviazione. *TECA. Testimonianze, editoria, cultura, arte*, 11–12, pp. 135–153.

Cevolini, Alberto (2017c): Making notae for Scholarly Retrieval: A Franciscan Case Study. In: Mariken Teeuwen and Irene van Renswoude (Eds.): *The*

Annotated Book in the Early Middle Ages: Practices of Reading and Writing. Turnhout: Brepols, pp. 343–367.

Cevolini, Alberto (2018): Where Does Niklas Luhmann's Card Index Come from? *Erudition and the Republic of Letters*, 3(4), pp. 390–420.

Cevolini, Alberto (2019a): "Uti saepius e charta sapere, ita etiam saepissime e charta meminisse ac recordari cogimur". La carta come modo di dimenticare nell'Europa primo-moderna. *La Bibliofilìa*, 121(3), pp. 481–499.

Cevolini, Alberto (2019b): The Memory of Tags. *The Indexer. The International Journal of Indexing*, 37(3), pp. 211–222.

Cevolini, Alberto (2020): Memorias virtuales: diseñar ficheros en la primera Modernidad. In: Iveta Nakládalová (Ed.): *El arte de anotar.* Artes excerpendi *y los géneros de la erudición en la primera Modernidad*. Madrid/Frankfurt a.M.: Iberoamericana/Vervuert, pp. 75–100.

Cevolini, Alberto (2021): The Art of trascegliere e notare in Early Modern Italian Culture. *Intellectual History Review*, 31(4), pp. 519–540.

Cevolini, Alberto (2022): Remembering and Forgetting by Means of Subject Headings: A Contribution to the History of Knowledge Organization. *Journal for the History of Knowledge*, 3(1), pp. 1–13.

Chambers, Ephraim (1728): *Cyclopaedia, or an Universal Dictionary of Arts and Sciences*. 2 vols. London: Printed for James and John Knapton.

Chartier, Roger (1999): *Cultura scritta e società*. Milano: Sylvestre Bonnard.

Chatelain, Jean-Marc (1997): Les recueils d'adversaria aux XVIe et XVIIe siècles: des pratiques de la lecture savante au style de l'érudition. In: Frédéric Barbier et al. (Eds.): *Le livre et l'historien. Études offertes en l'honneur du Professeur Henri-Jean Martin*. Geneva: Droz, pp. 169–186.

Cherchi, Paolo (1998): *Polimatia di riuso. Mezzo secolo di plagio (1539–1589)*. Roma: Bulzoni.

Cherchi, Paolo (1999): La selva rinascimentale: profilo di un genere. In: Paolo Cherchi (Ed.): *Ricerche sulle selve rinascimentali*. Ravenna: Longo, pp. 9–41.

Citolini, Alessandro (1561): *La Tipocosmia*. In Venetia: Appresso Vincenzo Valgrisi.

Clanchy, Michael (1993): *From Memory to Written Record. England 1066–1307*. Oxford: Blackwell.

Clément, Claude (1635): *Musei, sive Bibliothecae tam privatae quam publicae extructio, instructio, cura, usus, libri IV*. Lugduni: Sumptibus Iacobi Prost.

Comenius, Johann Amos (1974): Prodromo della pansofia [orig. ed. 1639]. In: Johann Amos Comenius: *Opere*. Ed. by Marta Fattori. Torino: UTET, pp. 481–556.

Condorcet, Marie-Jean-Antoine-Nicolas (1989): *Quadro storico dei progressi dello spirito umano* [orig. ed. 1795]. Milano: Rizzoli.

Connerton, Paul (2008): Seven Types of Forgetting. *Memory Studies*, 1(1), pp. 59–71.

Conrau-Lewis, Kyle (2021): The Index in the Premodern and Modern World. In: *Oxford Research Encyclopedia of Literature*. Oxford: Oxford University Press, pp. 1–23.

Considine, John (2015): Cutting and Pasting Slips: Early Modern Compilation and Information Management. *Journal of Medieval and Early Modern Studies*, 45, pp. 487–504.

Cope, Edward Drinker (1896): *The Primacy Factors of Organic Evolution*. Chicago: The Open Court Publishing Company.

Corsi, Giancarlo (1993): Die dunkle Seite der Karriere. In: Dirk Baecker (Ed.): *Probleme der Form*. Frankfurt a.M.: Suhrkamp, pp. 252–265.

Corsi, Giancarlo (2001): "Geräuschlos und unbemerkt". Zur Paradoxie struktureller Kopplung. *Soziale Systeme*, 7(2), pp. 253–266.

Corsi, Giancarlo (2014a): Die Ordnung der Zahlen und die Intransparenz der Öffentlichkeit. In: Alberto Cevolini (Ed.): *Die Ordnung des Kontingenten. Beiträge zur zahlenmäßigen Selbstbeschreibung der modernen Gesellschaft*. Wiesbaden: Springer VS, pp. 63–82.

Corsi, Giancarlo (2014b): Hypertrophie der Zukunft. Scheitern als Perspektive der Karriere. In: René John and Antonia Langhof (Eds.): *Scheitern—Ein Desiderat der Moderne?* Wiesbaden: Springer VS, pp. 301–321.

Corsi, Giancarlo (2023): Sociologia dei mezzi di comunicazione. Considerazioni per una teoria generale. *Philosophy Kitchen. Rivista di Filosofia Contemporanea*, 18, pp. 213–231.

Croft, Bruce et al. (2015): *Search Engines. Information Retrieval in Practice*. Boston: Pearson.

Crupi, Gianfranco (2021): John Locke's Algorithm and the Commonplace Books. *JLIS.it*, 12(1), pp. 63–72.

Cukier, Kenneth (2010): Data, Data Everywhere. A Special Report on Managing Information. *The Economist*, 27 February, pp. 1–14.

Curtius, Ernst Robert (1972): Zum Begriff einer historischen Topik (1938–1949). In: Peter Jehn (Ed.): *Toposforschung: Eine Dokumentation*. Frankfurt a.M.: Athenäum, pp. 3–19.

Dacome, Lucia (2004): Noting the Mind: Commonplace Books and the Pursuit of the Self in Eighteenth-Century Britain. *Journal of the History of Ideas*, 65(4), pp. 603–625.

D'Alembert, Jean Baptiste Le Rond (1894): *Discours préliminaire de l'Encyclopédie publié intégralement d'après l'édition de 1763*. Ed. by F. Picavet. Paris: Armand Colin.

Darwin, Charles (1952): *The Origin of Species by Means of Natural Selection*. Chicago et al.: The University of Chicago/William Benton Publisher.

Daston, Lorraine (2017a): Introduction: Third Nature. In: Lorraine Daston (Ed.): *Science in the Archives. Pasts, Presents, Futures*. Chicago/London: The University of Chicago Press, pp. 1–14.

Daston, Lorraine (2017b): Epilogue: The Time of the Archive. In: Lorraine Daston (Ed.): *Science in the Archives. Pasts, Presents, Futures*. Chicago/London: The University of Chicago Press, pp. 329–332.
Davies, Watson (1967): The Universal Brain: Is Centralized Storage and Retrieval of All Knowledge Possible, Feasible, or Desirable? In: Manfred Kochen (Ed.): *The Growth of Knowledge. Readings on Organization and Retrieval of Information*. New York/London: John Wiley, pp. 60–65.
De Bruyn, Frans (2001): The Classical Silva and the Generic Development of Scientific Writing in Seventeenth-Century England. *New Literary History*, 32(2), pp. 347–373.
Décultot, Élisabeth (2003): Introduction. L'art de l'extrait: définition, évolution, enjeux. In: Élisabeth Décultot (Ed.): *Lire, copier, écrire. Les bibliothèques manuscrites et leurs usages au XVIIIe siècle*. Paris: Centre National de la Recherche Scientifique, pp. 7–28.
Derrida, Jacques (1996): *Mal d'archivio. Un'impressione freudiana*. Napoli: Filema Edizioni.
Descartes, René (1902): *Discours de la méthode. Pour bien conduire la raison & chercher la vérité dans les sciences* [orig. ed. 1637]. In: *Œuvres de Descartes*. Ed. by Charles Adam and Paul Tannery. Paris: Léopold Cerf, vol. 6, pp. 1–78.
Dick, Leopold (1564): *De optima studiorum ratione, idque omni facultatum genere Methodus*. s.l.: Sumptibus Joh. Georgii à Werdenstein.
Dimitrov, Dimitar et al. (2018): Tag-Based Navigation and Visualization. In: Peter Brusilovsky and Daqing He (Eds.): *Social Information Access. Systems and Technologies*. Cham: Springer, pp. 181–212.
Dohrn, Anton (1875): *Der Ursprung der Wirbelthiere und das Princip des Functionswechsels. Genealogische Skizzen*. Leipzig: Verlag von Wilhelm Engelmann.
Dolce, Ludovico (2001): *Dialogo del modo di accrescere e conservar la memoria* [orig. ed. 1562]. Ed. by Andrea Torre. Pisa: Scuola Normale Superiore.
Doyle, Lauren (1963): *Is Relevance an Adequate Criterion in Retrieval System Evaluation?* Santa Monica: System Development Corporation.
Drexel, Jeremias (1638): *Aurifodina artium et scientiarum omnium. Excerpendi sollertia, omnibus litterarum amantibus monstrata*. Antuerpiae: Apud Viduam Ioannis Cnobbari.
Du Cange, Charles Du Fresne Sieur (1886): *Glossarium mediae et infimae latinitatis*. Editio nova. Vol. 6. O-S. Niort: Favre.
Duguid, Paul (1996): Material Matters: The Past and Futurology of the Book. In: Geoffrey Nunberg (Ed.): *The Future of the Book*. Berkeley/Los Angeles: University of California Press, pp. 63–102.
Duncan, Dennis (2022): *Index, A History of the. A Bookish Adventure from Medieval Manuscripts to the Digital Age*. New York: W. W. Norton & Company.

Ebbinghaus, Hermann (2011): *Über das Gedächtnis. Untersuchungen zur experimentellen Psychologie* [orig. ed. 1885]. Darmstadt: Wissenschaftliche Buchgesellschaft.

Eco, Umberto (1962): *Opera aperta. Forma e indeterminazione nelle poetiche contemporanee*. Milano: Bompiani.

Eco, Umberto (1988): An Ars oblivionalis? Forget It! *Modern Language Association*, 103(3), pp. 254–261.

Eco, Umberto (1990): *Il pendolo di Foucault*. Milano: Bompiani.

Eco, Umberto (2007): *Dall'albero al labirinto. Studi storici sul segno e l'interpretazione*. Milano: Bompiani.

Eco, Umberto (2009): *Vertigine della lista*. Milano: Bompiani.

Edwards, Paul et al. (2011): Science Friction: Data, Metadata, and Collaboration. *Social Studies of Science*, 41(5), pp. 667–690.

Eisenstein, Elizabeth (1979): *The Printing Press as an Agent of Change. Communications and Cultural Transformations in Early-Modern Europe*. 2 vols. Cambridge: Cambridge University Press.

Eldredge, Niles and Gould, Stephen Jay (1972): Punctuated Equilibria: An Alternative to Phyletic Gradualism. In: Thomas Schopf (Ed.): *Models in Paleobiology*. San Francisco: Freeman Cooper & Co., pp. 82–115.

Erhardt, Thomas (1716): *Clavis aurea sive facilis, & perspicua methodus notandi & excerpendi nucleum rerum memoratu digniorum ex omnium scientiarum libris*. Augusta Vindelicorum: Sumptibus Joannis Strötter.

Ernst, Wolfgang (2002): *Das Rumoren der Archive. Ordnung aus Unordnung*. Berlin: Merve Verlag.

Esposito, Elena (1993): Computer als Medium und Maschine. *Zeitschrift für Soziologie*, 22(5), pp. 338–354.

Esposito, Elena (1995): Computers and the Asymmetrization of Communication. *Versus. Quaderni di studi semiotici*, 72, pp. 77–106.

Esposito, Elena (2001): *La memoria sociale. Mezzi per comunicare e modi di dimenticare*. Roma/Bari: Laterza.

Esposito, Elena (2002): *Soziales Vergessen. Formen und Medien des Gedächtnisses der Gesellschaft*. Frankfurt a.M.: Suhrkamp.

Esposito, Elena (2010): Social Forgetting: A Systems-Theory Approach. In: Astrid Erll and Ansgar Nünning (Eds.): *A Companion to Cultural Memory Studies*. Berlin/New York: Walter de Gruyter, pp. 181–190.

Esposito, Elena (2016): Tools to Remember an Ever-Changing Past. In: Alberto Cevolini (Ed.): *Forgetting Machines. Knowledge Management Evolution in Early Modern Europe*. Leiden/Boston: Brill, pp. 335–344.

Esposito, Elena (2017a): Organizing without Understanding: Lists in Ancient and in Digital Cultures. *Zeitschrift für Literaturwissenschaft und Linguistik*, 47(3), pp. 351–359.

Esposito, Elena (2017b): Algorithmic Memory and the Right to Be Forgotten on the Web. *Big Data & Society*, 4(1), pp. 1–11.

Esposito, Elena (2022): *Artificial Communication. How Algorithms Produce Social Intelligence*. Cambridge/London: The MIT Press.

Fabricius, Johann Andreas (1752): *Abriß einer allgemeinen Historie der Gelehrsamkeit*. Leipzig: In der Weidmannischen Buchhandlung.

Farnaby, Thomas (1659): *Index rhetoricus et oratorius* [orig. ed. 1625]. Amstelodami: Apud Joannem Janssonium.

Fauvel, John and Wilson, Robin (1994): The Llull before the Storm: Combinatorics and Religion in the Renaissance. *Bulletin of the Institute of Combinatorics and its Applications*, 11, pp. 49–58.

Finocchiaro, Giusella (2010): La memoria della rete e il diritto all'oblio. *Il diritto dell'informazione e dell'informatica*, 26(3), pp. 391–404.

Floridi, Luciano (2012): Big Data and Their Epistemological Challenge. *Philosophy and Technology*, 25(4), pp. 435–437.

Floridi, Luciano (2013): *The Ethics of Information*. Oxford: Oxford University Press.

Floridi, Luciano (2015): 'The Right to Be Forgotten': A Philosophical View. *Jahrbuch für Recht und Ethik/Annual Review of Law and Ethics*, 23, pp. 30–45.

Foerster, Heinz von (1948): *Gedächtnis. Eine quantenphysikalische Untersuchung*. Wien: Franz Deuticke.

Foerster, Heinz von (1969): What is Memory that it May Have Hindsight and Foresight as Well? In: Samuel Bogoch (Ed.): *The Future of the Brain Sciences*. New York: Plenum Press, pp. 19–24.

Foerster, Heinz von (1971): Technology: What Will it Mean to Librarians? (A Response). *Illinois Libraries*, 53(9), pp. 785–803.

Foerster, Heinz von (1985): Cibernetica ed epistemologia: storia e prospettive. In: Mauro Ceruti and Gianluca Bocchi (Eds.): *La sfida della complessità*. Milano: Feltrinelli, pp. 112–140.

Foerster, Heinz von (1987a): Percezione del futuro e futuro della percezione. In: Heinz von Foerster: *Sistemi che osservano*. Roma: Astrolabio, pp. 117–131.

Foerster, Heinz von (1987b): Pensieri e note sulla cognizione. In: Heinz von Foerster: *Sistemi che osservano*. Roma: Astrolabio, pp. 132–151.

Foerster, Heinz von (1987c): Note su un'epistemologia delle cose viventi. In: Heinz von Foerster: *Sistemi che osservano*. Roma: Astrolabio, pp. 152–167.

Foss, Martin (1946): *The Idea of Perfection in the Western World*. Princeton: Princeton University Press.

Foucault, Michel (1996): *Le parole e le cose. Un'archeologia delle scienze umane*. Milano: Rizzoli.

Frank, Christian (1905): Die Anlage einer Exzerptensammlung. *Bibliothek für Volks- und Heimatkunde*, 113–114, pp. 1–32.

Freeman, Linton and Winch, Robert (1957): Social Complexity: An Empirical Test of a Typology of Societies. *American Journal of Sociology*, 62(5), pp. 461–466.

Freinsheim, Johann (1638): Viro nobilissimo et doctissimo Ioanni Ludovico Peyero. In: Cornelio Tacito: *Opera omnia*. Ed. by Matthias Bernegger and Johann Freinsheim. Argentorati: Heredes Lazari Zetzneri, fol. a2r-bv.

Friedrich, Markus (2013): *Die Geburt des Archivs. Eine Wissensgeschichte*. München: Oldenburg Verlag.

Fuller, Thomas (1840): *The History of the Worthies of England* [orig. ed. 1662]. London: Printed for Thomas Tegg.

Fuller, Thomas (1841): *The Holy State and the Profane State* [orig. ed. 1642]. London: Printed for Thomas Tegg.

Furnas, George (1985): Experience with an Adaptive Indexing Scheme. In: *Human Factors in Computing Systems. CHI 1985 Conference Proceedings. ACM SIGCHI Bulletin*, 16(4), pp. 131–135.

Gadamer, Hans Georg (1960): *Wahrheit und Methode. Grundzüge einer philosophischen Hermeneutik*. Tübingen: J. C. B. Mohr.

Garner, Wendell (1962): *Uncertainty and Structure as Psychological Concepts*. New York/London: John Wiley.

Georgoudi, Stella (1988): Manières d'archivage et archives de cités. In: Marcel Detienne (Ed.): *Les savoirs de l'écriture en Grèce ancienne*. Lille: Presses Universitaires de Lille, pp. 221–247.

Gerolimos, Michalis (2013): Tagging for Libraries: A Review of the Effectiveness of Tagging Systems for Library Catalogs. *Journal of Library Metadata*, 13(1), pp. 36–58.

Gese, Hartmut (1958): Geschichtliches Denken im Alten Orient und im Alten Testament. *Zeitschrift für Theologie und Kirche*, 55(2), pp. 127–145.

Gessner, Conrad (1545): *Bibliotheca universalis, sive Catalogus omnium scriptorum locupletissimus*. Tiguri: Apud Christophorum Froschoverum.

Gessner, Conrad (1548): *Pandectarum sive Partitionum universalium... libri XXI*. Tiguri: Apud Christophorum Froschoverum.

Gierer, Alfred and Meinhardt, Hans (1972): A Theory of Biological Pattern Formation. *Kybernetik/Biological Cybernetics*, 12, pp. 30–39.

Gillespie, Tarleton (2014): The Relevance of Algorithms. In: Tarleton Gillespie et al. (Eds.): *Media Technologies. Essays on Communication, Materiality, and Society*. Cambridge: The MIT Press, pp. 167–194.

Glanvill, Joseph (1661): *The Vanity of Dogmatizing*. London: Printed by E. C. for Henry Eversden.

Glanville, Ranulph (1982): Inside Every White Box There Are Two Black Boxes Trying to Get Out. *Behavioral Science*, 27(1), pp. 1–11.

Glanville, Ranulph (1984): Distinguished and Exact Lies. In: Robert Trappl (Ed.): *Cybernetics and Systems Research 2*. Amsterdam: North Holland Publishing Company, pp. 655–662.

Glanville, Ranulph (2009): Black Boxes. *Cybernetics and Human Knowing*, 16(1/2), pp. 153–167.

Goldenweiser, Alexander (1913): The Principle of Limited Possibilities in the Development of Culture. *Journal of American Folk-Lore*, 26(101), pp. 259–290.

Golder, Scott and Huberman, Bernardo (2006): The Structure of Collaborative Tagging Systems. *Journal of Information Science*, 32(2), pp. 198–208.

Goody, Jack (1977): Literacy and Classification: On Turning the Tables. In: Ravindra Jain (Ed.): *Text and Context. The Social Anthropology of Tradition*. Philadelphia: Institute for the Study of Human Issues, pp. 205–222.

Goody, Jack (1981): *L'addomesticamento del pensiero selvaggio*. Milano: Franco Angeli.

Goody, Jack (1989): *Il suono e i segni. L'interfaccia tra scrittura e oralità*. Milano: Il Saggiatore.

Gottinger, Hans (1975): Complexity and Information Technology in Dynamic Systems. *Kybernetes*, 4(3), pp. 129–141.

Gottinger, Hans (1983): *Coping with Complexity. Perspectives for Economics, Management and Social Sciences*. Dordrecht et al.: D. Reidel.

Gould, Stephen Jay (1985): Il darwinismo e l'ampliamento della teoria evoluzionistica. In: Mauro Ceruti and Gianluca Bocchi (Eds.): *La sfida della complessità*. Milano: Feltrinelli, pp. 227–245.

Gould, Stephen Jay (1989): Punctuated Equilibrium in Fact and Theory. *Theory of Social and Biological Structures*, 12(2/3), pp. 117–136.

Gould, Stephen Jay (1994): The Evolution of Life on the Earth. *Scientific American*, 271, pp. 85–91.

Gould, Stephen Jay (2003): *La struttura della teoria dell'evoluzione*. Torino: Codice Edizioni.

Gould, Stephen Jay and Vrba, Elisabeth (2008): *Exaptation*: un termine che mancava nella scienza della forma. In: Stephen Jay Gould and Elisabeth Vrba: Exaptation. *Il bricolage dell'evoluzione*. Torino: Bollati Boringhieri, pp. 7–53.

Granka, Laura (2010): The Politics of Search: A Decade Retrospective. *The Information Society*, 26(5), pp. 364–374.

Guerrini, Mauro and Possemato, Tiziana (2013): Linked Data: A New Alphabet for the Semantic Web. *JLIS.it*, 4(1), pp. 67–90.

Halavais, Alexander (2009): *Search Engine Society*. Cambridge: Polity Press.

Halpin, Harry (2012): *Social Semantics. The Search for Meaning on the Web*. New York: Springer.

Halpin, Harry et al. (2007): The Complex Dynamics of Collaborative Tagging. In: *Proceedings of the 16th International Conference on World Wide Web*. New York: Association for Computing Machinery, pp. 211–220.

Halpin, Harry et al. (2009): Emergence of Consensus and Shared Vocabularies in Collaborative Tagging Systems. *ACM Transaction on the Web*, 3, pp. 1–30.

Harrison, Thomas (2017): *The Ark of Studies*. Ed. by Alberto Cevolini. Turnhout: Brepols.

Havens, Earle (Ed.) (2001): *"Of Common Places, or Memorial Books". A Seventeenth-Century Manuscript from the James Marshall and Marie-Louise Osborn Collection*. New Haven: The Beinecke Rare Book & Manuscript Library.

Head, Randolph (2003): Knowing Like a State: The Transformation of Political Knowledge in Swiss Archives, 1450–1770. *The Journal of Modern History*, 75(4), pp. 745–782.

Head, Randolph (2007): Mirroring Governance: Archives, Inventories and Political Knowledge in Early Modern Switzerland and Europe. *Archival Science*, 7, pp. 317–329.

Head, Randolph (2014): Spaces in the Archive, Spaces of the Archive: Material, Topographical and Indexical Articulations of Space in Early Modern Chancery Collections. In: Karin Friedrich (Ed.): *Die Erschließung des Raumes. Konstruktion, Imagination und Darstellung von Räumen und Grenzen im Barockzeitalter*. Wiesbaden: Harrassowitz Verlag, vol. 2, pp. 505–519.

Head, Randolph (2019): *Making Archives in Early Modern Europe. Proof, Information, and Political Record-Keeping, 1400–1700*. Cambridge: Cambridge University Press.

Hegel, Georg Wilhelm Friedrich (2000): *Enciclopedia delle scienze filosofiche in compendio* [orig. ed. 1830]. Ed. by Vincenzo Cicero. Milano: Bompiani.

Hesse, Carla (1996): Books in Time. In: Geoffrey Nunberg (Ed.): *The Future of the Book*. Berkeley/Los Angeles: University of California Press, pp. 21–36.

Heylighen, Francis (1999): The Growth of Structural and Functional Complexity during Evolution. In: Francis Heylighen et al. (Eds.): *The Evolution of Complexity*. Dordrecht: Kluwer Academic, pp. 17–44.

Heymann, Paul et al. (2010): Tagging Human Knowledge. In: *Proceedings of the 3rd ACM International Conference on Web Search and Data Mining*. New York: Association for Computing Machinery, pp. 51–60.

Hinman, Lawrence (2005): Esse est indicato in Google: Ethical and Political Issues in Search Engines. *International Review of Information Ethics*, 3(6), pp. 19–25.

Hirsch, Rudolph (1977): Stampa e lettura fra il 1450 e il 1550. In: Armando Petrucci (Ed.): *Libri, editori e pubblico nell'Europa moderna. Guida storica e critica*. Roma/Bari: Laterza, pp. 1–50.

Hodannus, Johann Friedrich (1713): *Adminicula sapientiae atque eloquentiae, sive exempla artis methodice excerpendi*. Hanoverae: Sumptibus Nicolai Foersteri.

Hottinger, Johann Heinrich (1664): *Bibliothecarius quadripartitus*. Tiguri: Sumptibus Melchioris Stauffacheri.

Hume, David (1975): *Enquiries Concerning Human Understanding and Concerning the Principles of Morals* [orig. ed. 1777]. Ed. by Lewis Selby-Bigge and Peter Nidditch. Oxford: Clarendon Press.

Iacono, Antonella (2014): *Linked Data*. Roma: Associazione Italiana Biblioteche.

Introna, Lucas and Nissenbaum, Helen (2000): Shaping the Web: Why the Politics of Search Engines Matters. *The Information Society*, 16(3), pp. 169–185.

Jacob, Elin (1992): Classification and Categorization: Drawing the Line. In: *Proceedings of the 2nd ASIS SIG/CR Classification Research Workshop*. Washington: ASIS Special Interest Group/Classification Research, pp. 63–80.

Jacob, Elin (1993): Communication and Category Structure: The Communicative Process as a Constraint on the Semantic Representation of Information. In: *Proceedings of the 4th ASIS SIG/CR Classification Research Workshop*. Columbus (Ohio): ASIS Special Interest Group/Classification Research, pp. 103–122.

Jacob, Elin (2004): Classification and Categorization: A Difference that Makes a Difference. *Library Trends*, 52(3), pp. 515–540.

Jacob, François (1977): Evolution and Tinkering. *Science*, 196(4295), pp. 1161–1166.

Janssen, Lydia (2012): Hieremias Drexel and the Commonplace Tradition: The Direct and Indirect Sources of 'Orbis Phaëton'. *Humanistica Lovaniensia*, 61, pp. 389–413.

Joachims, Thorsten (2002): Optimizing Search Engines Using Clickthrough Data. In: *Proceedings of the 8th ACM SIGKDD International Conference on Knowledge Discovery and Data Mining*. New York: Association for Computer Machinery, pp. 133–142.

Joachims, Thorsten and Radlinski, Filip (2007): Search Engines that Learn from Implicit Feedback. *IEEE Computer*, 40(8), pp. 34–40.

Jones, Matthew (2017): Querying the Archive: Data Mining from Apriori to PageRank. In: Lorraine Daston (Ed.): *Science in the Archives. Pasts, Presents, Futures*. Chicago/London: The University of Chicago Press, pp. 311–328.

Jones, Meg Leta and Ausloos, Jef (2013): The Right to Be Forgotten Across the Pond. *Journal of Information Policy*, 3, pp. 1–23.

Jonker, Gerdien (1995): *The Topography of Remembrance. The Dead, Tradition, and Collective Memory in Mesopotamia*. Leiden/New York: Brill.

Jungius, Joachim (1691): *Historia vermium*. Hamburgi: Typis Brendekianis.

Kassirer, Jerome (2011): Bring Back Browsing. *British Medical Journal*, 342(7801), p. 827.

Kästner, Christian August Lebrecht (1805): *Mnemonik oder die Gedächtniskunst der Alten systematisch bearbeitet.* Leipzig: Paul Gotthelf Nummer.

Kayser, Albrecht Christoph (1790): *Über die Manipulation bey der Einrichtung einer Bibliothek und der Verfestigung der Bücherverzeichnisse.* Bayreuth: Im Verlag der Zeitungsdruckerei.

Kelley, Diane and Teevan, Jaime (2003): Implicit Feedback for Inferring User Preference: A Bibliography. *SIGIR Forum*, 37, pp. 18–28.

Kerger, Martin (1689): *Methodus excerpendi Drexeliana succintior.* Vratislava: s.n.

Kipp, Margaret (2011): Tagging of Biomedical Articles on CiteULike: A Comparison of User, Author, and Professional Indexing. *Knowledge Organization*, 38(3), pp. 245–261.

Kipp, Margaret and Campbell, Grant (2010): Searching with Tags: Do Tags Help Users Find Things? *Knowledge Organization*, 37(4), pp. 239–255.

Klaus, Georg and Liebscher, Heinz (1969): Komplexität/Kompliziertheit. In: Georg Klaus and Heinz Liebscher: *Wörterbuch der Kybernetik.* Berlin: Dietz, pp. 307–308.

Klaus, Georg and Liebscher, Heinz (1979): *Wörterbuch der Kybernetik.* 2 vols. Frankfurt a.M.: Fischer Taschenbuch Verlag.

Kochen, Manfred (Ed.) (1967): *The Growth of Knowledge. Readings on Organization and Retrieval of Information.* New York/London: John Wiley.

Koselleck, Reinhart (1979): *Vergangene Zukunft. Zur Semantik geschichtlicher Zeiten.* Frankfurt a.M.: Suhrkamp.

Koselleck, Reinhart and Meier, Christian (1991): *Progresso.* Venezia: Marsilio.

Kosto, Adam (2016): "Statim invenire ante". Finding Aids and Research Tools in Pre-Scholastic Legal and Administrative Manuscripts. *Scriptorium*, 70(2), pp. 285–309.

Krajewski, Markus (2002): *ZettelWirtschaft. Die Geburt der Kartei aus dem Geiste der Bibliothek.* Berlin: Kadmos.

Krämer, Fabian (2014): Ulisse Aldrovandi's Pandechion Epistemonicon and the Use of Paper Technology in Renaissance Natural History. *Early Science and Medicine*, 19(5), pp. 398–423.

Krämer, Fabian and Zedelmaier, Helmut (2014): Instruments of Invention in Renaissance Europe: The Cases of Conrad Gessner and Ulisse Aldrovandi. *Intellectual History Review*, 24(3), pp. 321–341.

Krämer, Sybille (2000): Das Vergessen nicht vergessen! Oder: Ist das Vergessen ein defizienter Modus von Erinnerung? In: Erika Fischer-Lichte and Gertrud Lehnert (Eds.): *Inszenierungen des Erinnerns. Paragrana*, 9(2), pp. 251–275.

Krippendorff, Klaus (1975): Some Principles of Information Storage and Retrieval in Society. *General Systems*, 20, pp. 15–35.

Kroll, Neal and Klimesch, Wolfgang (1992): Semantic Memory: Complexity or Connectivity? *Memory & Cognition*, 20(2), pp. 192–210.

Kuwakino, Koji (2016): From domus sapientiae to artes excerpendi: Lambert Schenkel's De memoria (1593) and the Transformation of the Art of Memory. In: Alberto Cevolini (Ed.): *Forgetting Machines. Knowledge Management Evolution in Early Modern Europe*. Leiden/Boston: Brill, pp. 58–78.

Lamarck, Jean-Baptiste Pierre Antoine de Monet de (1809): *Philosophie zoologique*. Paris: Chez Dentu/Chez l'Auteur.

Lechner, Joan Marie (1962): *Renaissance Concepts of the Commonplaces*. New York: Pageant Press.

Leibniz, Gottfried Wilhelm (1903): Consilium de Encyclopaedia nova conscribenda methodo inventoria [orig. ed. 1679]. In: Louis Couturat (Ed.): *Opuscules et fragments inédits de Leibniz*. Paris: Felix Alcan, pp. 30–41.

Leibniz, Gottfried Wilhelm (1959): Précepts pour avancer les sciences [orig. ed. 1680]. In: *Opera philosophica quae exstant latina, gallica, germanica omnia*. Aalen: Scientia, pp. 165–171.

Levins, Richard (1973): The Limits of Complexity. In: Howard Pattee (Ed.): *Hierarchy Theory: The Challenge of Complex Systems*. New York: George Braziller, pp. 109–127.

Lewandowski, Dirk (2015): *Suchmaschinen verstehen*. Heidelberg: Springer.

Licklider, Joseph Carl Robnett (1960): Man-Computer Symbiosis. *IRE Transactions on Human Factors in Electronics*, 1, pp. 4–11.

Lilford, Richard and Chilton, Peter (2011): Does the Internet Limit or Extend the Human Mind? Probably Both. *British Medical Journal*, 343(7822), pp. 495–496.

Llull, Ramon (2002): *Arte breve*. Milano: Bompiani.

Locke, Chris (2000): Digital Memory and the Problem of Forgetting. In: Susannah Radstone (Ed.): *Memory and Methodology*. Oxford: Berg, pp. 25–36.

Locke, John (1686): Méthode nouvelle de dresser des Recueils communiquée par l'Auteur. *Bibliothèque Universelle et Historique*, 2, pp. 315–340.

Lübbe, Hermann (1994): *Im Zug der Zeit. Verkürzter Aufenthalt in der Gegenwart*. Berlin: Springer.

Luhmann, Niklas (1966): *Recht und Automation in der öffentlichen Verwaltung. Eine verwaltungswissenschaftliche Untersuchung*. Berlin: Duncker & Humblot.

Luhmann, Niklas (1976): Komplexität. In: Joachim Ritter et al. (Eds.): *Historisches Wörterbuch der Philosophie*. Basel/Stuttgart: Schwabe & Co., vol. 4, coll. 939–941.

Luhmann, Niklas (1980): Komplexität. In: Erwin Grochla (Ed.): *Handwörterbuch der Organisation*. Stuttgart: C. E. Poeschel Verlag, coll. 1064–1070.

Luhmann, Niklas (1981): Selbstreferenz und Teleologie in gesellschaftstheoretischer Perspektive. In: Niklas Luhmann: *Gesellschaftsstruktur und Semantik. Studien zur Wissenssoziologie der modernen Gesellschaft*. Frankfurt a.M.: Suhrkamp, vol. 2, p. 9–44.

Luhmann, Niklas (1984): *Soziale Systeme. Grundriß einer allgemeinen Theorie.* Frankfurt a.M.: Suhrkamp.

Luhmann, Niklas (1987): Biographie, Attitüden und Zettelkasten. In: Niklas Luhmann: *Archimedes und wir.* Berlin: Merve Verlag, pp. 125–155.

Luhmann, Niklas (1988): Observing and Describing Complexity. In: Karl Vak (Ed.): *Complexities of the Human Environment. A Cultural and Technological Perspective.* Wien: Europa Verlag, pp. 251–256.

Luhmann, Niklas (1989a): Ökologie und Kommunikation. In: Lucien Criblez and Philipp Gonon (Eds.): *Ist Ökologie lehrbar?* Bonn: Zytglogge, pp. 17–30.

Luhmann, Niklas (1989b): Ökologische Kommunikation. Ein Theorie-Entscheidungsspiel. In: Joschka Fischer (Ed.): *Ökologie im Endspiel.* München: Wilhelm Fink, pp. 31–37.

Luhmann, Niklas (1990): *Die Wissenschaft der Gesellschaft.* Frankfurt a.M.: Suhrkamp.

Luhmann, Niklas (1992a): Societal Complexity. In: György Széll (Ed.): *Concise Encyclopaedia of Participation and Co-Management.* New York/Berlin: Walter de Gruyter, pp. 793–806.

Luhmann, Niklas (1992b): Reduktion von Komplexität. In: Joachim Ritter et al. (Eds.): *Historisches Wörterbuch der Philosophie.* Basel/Stuttgart: Schwabe & Co., vol. 8, coll. 377–378.

Luhmann, Niklas (1992c): Kommunikation mit Zettelkästen: Ein Erfahrungsbericht. In: Niklas Luhmann: *Universität als Milieu. Kleine Schriften.* Ed. by André Kieserling. Bielefeld: Haux, pp. 53–61.

Luhmann, Niklas (1992d): The Form of Writing. *Stanford Literature Review*, 9(1), pp. 25–42.

Luhmann, Niklas (1993): *Das Recht der Gesellschaft.* Frankfurt a.M.: Suhrkamp.

Luhmann, Niklas (1995a): Kultur als historischer Begriff. In: Niklas Luhmann: *Gesellschaftsstruktur und Semantik. Studien zur Wissenssoziologie der modernen Gesellschaft.* Frankfurt a.M.: Suhrkamp, vol. 4, pp. 31–54.

Luhmann, Niklas (1995b): Interventionen in die Umwelt? Die Gesellschaft kann nur kommunizieren. In: Gerhard de Haan (Ed.): *Umweltbewußtsein und Massenmedien. Perspektiven ökologischer Kommunikation.* Berlin: Akademie Verlag, pp. 37–45.

Luhmann, Niklas (1996): Zeit und Gedächtnis. *Soziale Systeme*, 2(2), pp. 307–330.

Luhmann, Niklas (1997a): *Die Gesellschaft der Gesellschaft.* Frankfurt a.M.: Suhrkamp.

Luhmann, Niklas (1997b): The Control of Intransparency. *System Research and Behavioral Science*, 14, pp. 359–371.

Luhmann, Niklas (2000): *Die Politik der Gesellschaft.* Frankfurt a.M.: Suhrkamp.

Luhmann, Niklas (2005a): Komplexität. In: Niklas Luhmann: *Soziologische Aufklärung 2. Aufsätze zur Theorie der Gesellschaft*. Wiesbaden: VS Verlag für Sozialwissenschaften, pp. 255–276.

Luhmann, Niklas (2005b): Haltlose Komplexität. In: Niklas Luhmann: *Soziologische Aufklärung 5. Konstruktivistische Perspektiven*. Wiesbaden: VS Verlag für Sozialwissenschaften, pp. 58–74.

Luhmann, Niklas (2005c): Das Erkenntnisprogramm des Konstruktivismus und die unbekannt bleibende Realität. In: Niklas Luhmann: *Soziologische Aufklärung 5. Konstruktivistische Perspektiven*. Wiesbaden: VS Verlag für Sozialwissenschaften, pp. 31–57.

Luhmann, Niklas (2005d): Entscheidungen in der Informationsgesellschaft. In: Giancarlo Corsi and Elena Esposito (Eds.): *Reform und Innovation in einer unstabilen Gesellschaft*. Stuttgart: Lucius & Lucius, pp. 27–40.

Luhmann, Niklas (2008): *Ökologische Kommunikation. Kann die moderne Gesellschaft sich auf ökologische Gefährdungen einstellen?* Wiesbaden: VS Verlag für Sozialwissenschaften.

Luhmann, Niklas (2009): *Die Realität der Massenmedien*. Wiesbaden: VS Verlag für Sozialwissenschaften.

Luhmann, Niklas (2011): *Organisation und Entscheidung*. Wiesbaden: VS Verlag für Sozialwissenschaften.

Luhn, Hans Peter (1957): A Statistical Approach to Mechanized Encoding and Searching of Literary Information. *IBM Journal of Research and Development*, 1(4), pp. 309–317.

Luhn, Hans Peter (1958a): A Business Intelligence System. *IBM Journal of Research and Development*, 2(4), pp. 314–319.

Luhn, Hans Peter (1958b): The Automatic Creation of Literature Abstracts. *IBM Journal of Research and Development*, 2(2), pp. 159–165.

Luhn, Hans Peter (1959): Auto-Encoding of Documents for Information Retrieval Systems. In: Martha Boaz (Ed.): *Modern Trends in Documentation*. London: Pergamon, pp. 45–58.

Lund, John and Taube, Mortimer (1937): A Nonexpansive Classification System: An Introduction to Period Classification. *The Library Quarterly*, 7(3), pp. 373–394.

Lund, Roger (1998): The Eel of Science: Index Learning, Scriblerian Satire, and the Rise of Information Culture. *Eighteenth-Century Life*, 22(2), pp. 18–42.

Lurija, Aleksandr (1976): *La storia sociale dei processi cognitivi*. Firenze: Giunti Barbera.

MacCormick, John (2012): *9 algoritmi che hanno cambiato il futuro*. Milano: Apogeo.

MacKay, Donald (1969): *Information, Mechanism and Meaning*. Cambridge/London: The MIT Press.

Malcolm, Noel (2004): Thomas Harrison and his Ark of Studies: An Episode in the History of the Organization of Knowledge. *The Seventeenth Century*, 19(2), pp. 196–232.

Mamiani, Maurizio (1983): *La mappa del sapere. La classificazione delle scienze nella Cyclopaedia di E. Chambers*. Milano: Franco Angeli.

Manovich, Lev (2002): *Il linguaggio dei nuovi media*. Milano: Edizioni Olivares.

Manuzio, Aldo (1975): *Aldo Manuzio editore: dediche, prefazioni, note ai testi*. 2 vols. Ed. by Giovanni Orlandi. Milano: Il Polifilo.

Maron, Melvin (2008): An Historical Note on the Origins of Probabilistic Indexing. *Information Processing and Management*, 44(2), pp. 971–972.

Maron, Melvin and Kuhns, John Lary (1960): On Relevance, Probabilistic Indexing and Information Retrieval. *Journal of the ACM*, 7(3), pp. 216–244.

Marten, Maria and Piepenbring-Thomas, Carola (2015): *Fogels Ordnungen. Aus dem Werkstatt des Hamburger Mediziners Martin Fogel (1634–1675)*. Frankfurt a.M.: Vittorio Klostermann.

Martin, Henri-Jean and Febvre, Lucien (1977): *La nascita del libro*. 2 vols. Roma/Bari: Laterza.

Martin, Henri-Jean and Vezin, Jean (Eds.) (1990): *Mise en page et mise en texte du livre manuscrit*. Paris: Promodis.

Martinelli, Silvia (2017a): Diritto all'oblio e motori di ricerca: il bilanciamento tra memoria e oblio e le problematiche poste dalla de-indicizzazione. *Il diritto dell'informazione e dell'informatica*, 33(3), pp. 565–581.

Martinelli, Silvia (2017b): *Diritto all'oblio e motori di ricerca. Memoria e privacy nell'era di Google*. Milano: Giuffrè.

Maruyama, Magoroh (1960): Morphogenesis and Morphostasis. *Methodos*, 12(48), pp. 251–296.

Maruyama, Magoroh (1963a): The Second Cybernetics. Deviation-Amplifying Mutual Causal Processes. *American Scientist*, 51(2), pp. 164–179.

Maruyama, Magoroh (1963b): A Postscript to 'The Second Cybernetics'. *American Scientist*, 51(3), pp. 250A–256A.

Maruyama, Magoroh (1976): Toward Cultural Symbiosis. In: Erich Jantsch and Conrad Waddington (Eds.): *Evolution and Consciousness: Human Systems in Transition*. Reading: Addison-Wesley Publishing Company, pp. 198–213.

Mathes, Adam (2004): *Folksonomies—Cooperative Classification and Communication Through Shared Metadata*. Graduate School of Library and Information Science. University of Illinois Urbana-Champaign. Retrieved from https://adammathes.com/academic/computer-mediated-communication/folksonomies.html

Matthiae, Paolo (2008): *Gli Archivi Reali di Ebla. La scoperta, i testi, il significato*. Milano: Mondadori.

Maturana, Humberto (1986): Information—Mißverständnisse ohne Ende. *Delfin*, 7, pp. 24–27.

Maturana, Humberto (1993): *Autocoscienza e realtà*. Milano: Cortina.

Maturana, Humberto and Varela, Francisco (1999): *L'albero della conoscenza*. Milano: Garzanti.

Mayer, Katja (2009): On the Sociometry of Search Engines: A Historical Review of Methods. In: Konrad Becker and Felix Stalder (Eds.): *Deep Search. The Politics of Search Beyond Google*. Edison: Transaction, pp. 54–72.

Mayer-Schönberger, Viktor (2009): *Delete. The Virtue of Forgetting in the Digital Age*. Princeton/Oxford: Princeton University Press.

Mayr, Ernst (1960): The Emergence of Evolutionary Novelties. In: Sol Tax (Ed.): *Evolution After Darwin 1. The Evolution of Life*. Chicago: The University of Chicago Press, pp. 349–380.

McKitterick, David (2003): *Print, Manuscript and the Search for Order, 1450–1830*. Cambridge: Cambridge University Press.

Medin, Douglas (1983): Structural Principles in Categorization. In: Thomas Tighe and Bryan Shepp (Eds.): *Perception, Cognition and Development: Interactional Analyses*. Hillsdale: Erlbaum, pp. 203–230.

Meinel, Christoph (1995): Enzyklopädie der Welt und Verzettelung des Wissens: Aporien der Empirie bei Joachim Jungius. In: Franz Eybl (Ed.): *Enzyklopädien der frühen Neuzeit. Beiträge zu ihrer Erforschung*. Tübingen: Max Niemeyer, pp. 162–187.

Meiners, Christoph (1791): *Anweisungen für Jünglinge zum eigenen Arbeiten besonders zum Lesen, Excerpiren, und Schreiben*. Hannover: In der Helwigischen Hofbuchhandlung.

Mertner, Edgar (1972): Topos und Commonplace. In: Peter Jehn (Ed.): *Toposforschung: Eine Dokumentation*. Frankfurt a.M.: Athenäum, pp. 20–68.

Meyer, Heinz (1991): *Ordo rerum* und Registerhilfen in mittelalterlichen Enzyklopädiehandschriften. *Frühmittelalterliche Studien*, 25, pp. 315–339.

Meynell, Guy (1993): John Locke's Method of Commonplacing, as seen in his Drafts and his Medical Notebooks, Bodleian MSS d. 9, f. 21 and f. 23. *Seventeenth Century*, 8, pp. 245–267.

Miller, George (1956): The Magical Number Seven, Plus or Minus Two: Some Limits on our Capacity for Processing Information. *The Psychological Review*, 63(2), pp. 81–97.

Mizzaro, Stefano (1995): Le differenti *relevance* in *information retrieval*: una classificazione. In: *Proceedings of the Annual Conference AICA '95*. s.l.: s.n., vol. 1, pp. 361–368.

Mizzaro, Stefano (1997): Relevance: The Whole History. *Journal of the American Society for Information Science*, 48(9), pp. 810–832.

Mizzaro, Stefano (1998): How Many Relevances in Information Retrieval? *Interacting with Computers*, 10(3), pp. 305–322.

Moreri, Louis (1683): *Le grand dictionnaire historique ou le mélange curieux de l'histoire sacrée et profane*. A Lyon: Chez Jean Girin & Barthelemy Riviere.

Morhof, Daniel Georg (1747): *Polyhistor, literarius, philosophicus et practicus*. 4th ed. Lubecae: Sumptibus Petri Boeckmanni.

Morlet, Sébastien (Ed.) (2015): *Lire en extraits. Lecture et production des textes, de l'Antiquité à la fin du Moyen Âge*. Paris: Presses de l'Université Paris-Sorbonne.

Morville, Peter (2005): *Ambient Findability*. Sebastopol: O'Reilly Media.

Moss, Ann (1996): *Printed Commonplace-Books and the Structuring of Renaissance Thought*. Oxford: Clarendon Press.

Moss, Ann (2002): *Les recueils de lieux communs. Méthode pour apprendre à penser à la Renaisssance*. Genève: Librairie Droz.

Mouchon, Pierre (1780): *Table analytique et rainsonnée des matieres contenues dans le XXXIII volumes in-folio du Dictionnaire des sciences, des arts et des métiers, et dans son supplément*. 2 vols. Paris/Amsterdam: Chez Panckoucke/ Chez Marc-Michel Rey.

Müller, Jan-Dirk (1998): Universalbibliothek und Gedächtnis. Aporien frühneuzeitlicher Wissenskodifikation bei Conrad Gessner (mit einem Ausblick auf Antonio Possevino, Theodor Zwinger und Johann Fischart). In: Dietmar Peil (Ed.): *Erkennen und Erinnern in Kunst und Literatur*. Tübingen: Niemeyer, pp. 285–309.

Muratori, Lodovico Antonio (1723): *Delle riflessioni sopra il buon gusto nelle scienze e nelle arti* [orig. ed. 1708]. Venezia: Presso Nicolò Pezzana.

Muratori, Lodovico Antonio (1768): *Delle riflessioni sopra il buon gusto nelle scienze e nelle arti di Lamindo Pritanio* [orig. ed. 1708]. In: Lodovico Antonio Muratori: *Opere*. In Arezzo: Per Michele Bellotti, vol. 8, pp. 1–371.

Nadeau, Ray (1950): A Renaissance Schoolmaster on Practice. *Speech Monographs*, 17(2), pp. 171–179.

Nakládalová, Iveta (2016): Johann Amos Comenius: Early Modern Metaphysics of Knowledge and *ars excerpendi*. In: Alberto Cevolini (Ed.): *Forgetting Machines. Knowledge Management Evolution in Early Modern Europe*. Leiden/Boston: Brill, pp. 188–208.

Naudé, Gabriel (1627): *Advis pour dresser une bibliothèque*. A Paris: Chez François Targa.

Navarro Bullock, Beate et al. (2018): Accessing Information with Tags: Search and Ranking. In: Peter Brusilovsky and Daqing He (Eds.): *Social Information Access. Systems and Technologies*. Cham: Springer, pp. 310–343.

Nevizzano, Giovanni (1525): *Index librorum omnium in utroque iure*. In Venetiis: Per Gregorium de Gregoriis.

Nietzsche, Friedrich (1874): *Unzeitgemäße Betrachtungen. Zweites Stück: Vom Nutzen und Nachteil der Historie für das Leben*. Leipzig: Verlag von E. W. Fritzsch.

Nunberg, Geoffrey (1996): Farewell to the Information Age. In: Geoffrey Nunberg (Ed.): *The Future of the Book*. Berkeley/Los Angeles: University of California Press, pp. 103–138.

Ong, Walter (1958): *Ramus, Method, and the Decay of Dialog. From the Art of Discourse to the Art of Reason*. Chicago/London: The University of Chicago Press.

Ong, Walter (1961): Ramist Method and the Commercial Mind. *Studies in the Renaissance*, 8, pp. 155–172.

Ong, Walter (1970): *La presenza della parola*. Bologna: Il Mulino.

Ong, Walter (1976): Commonplace Rapsody: Ravisius, Textor, Zwinger and Shakespeare. In: Robert Ralph Bolgar (Ed.): *Classical Influences on European Culture A.D. 1500–1700*. Cambridge: Cambridge University Press, pp. 91–126.

Ong, Walter (1986a): *Oralità e scrittura. Le tecnologie della parola*. Bologna: Il Mulino.

Ong, Walter (1986b): Writing is a Technology that Restructures Thought. In: Gerd Baumann (Ed.): *The Written Word. Literacy in Transition*. Oxford: Clarendon Press, pp. 23–50.

Pariser, Eli (2012): *The Filter Bubble. What the Internet is Hiding from You*. New York: Penguin Books.

Parkes, Malcom (1976): The Influence of the Concepts of *ordinatio* and *compilatio* on the Development of the Book. In: Jonathan Alexander and Margaret Gibson (Eds.): *Medieval Literature and Learning*. Oxford: Clarendon Press, pp. 115–141.

Parkes, Malcom (2008): Layout and Presentation of the Text. In: Nigel Morgan and Rodney Thomson (Eds.): *The Cambridge History of the Book in Britain*. Cambridge: Cambridge University Press, vol. 2, pp. 55–74.

Parlangeli, Oronzo et al. (2003): Delete Memories: Learning Through Deliberate Forgetting. *Cognitive Technology*, 8(1), pp. 25–33.

Pasi, Gabriella (2014): Implicit Feedback through User-System Interactions for Defining User Models in Personalized Search. *Procedia Computer Science*, 39, pp. 8–11.

Pellegrini, Letizia (1995): Indici per predicare: le tavole nei manoscritti di sermoni fra XIII e XV secolo. In: Claudio Leonardi et al. (Eds.): Fabula in tabula. *Una storia degli indici dal manoscritto al testo elettronico*. Spoleto: Centro Italiano di Studi sull'Alto Medioevo, pp. 135–143.

Perotti, Niccolò (1499): *Cornucopia*. Venezia: Aldo Manuzio.

Peters, Isabella (2009): *Folksonomies: Indexing and Retrieval in Web 2.0*. Berlin: Walter de Gruyter.

Petrarca, Francesco (1975): *De remediis utriusque fortunae*. München: Wilhelm Fink.

Petrucciani, Alberto (1998): L'indicizzazione per soggetto. In: Paola Geretto (Ed.): *Lineamenti di biblioteconomia*. Roma: Carocci, pp. 151–200.

Philomusus (1684): *Industria excerpendi brevis, facilis, amoena, a multis impedimentis quibus adhuc tenebatur, exsoluta*. Constantiae: Typis Joannis Jacobi Labhart.

Pievani, Telmo (2009): *Exaptation*: la logica evolutiva del vivente tra funzioni e strutture. *Discipline Filosofiche*, 19(1), pp. 137–152.

Pitkow, James et al. (2002): Personalized Search. *Communications of the ACM*, 45(9), pp. 50–55.

Placcius, Vincent (1689): *De arte excerpendi. Vom gelehrten Buchhalten liber singularis*. Holmiae/Hamburgi: Apud Gottfried Liebezeit.

Pomian, Krzysztof (1997): Les archives. Du Trésor des chartes au Caran. In: Pierre Nora (Ed.): *Les lieux de mémoire*. Paris: Gallimard, pp. 3999–4067.

Posner, Ernst (1972): *Archives in the Ancient World*. Cambridge: Harvard University Press.

Pringle, John William (1951): On the Parallel Between Learning and Evolution. *Behaviour*, 3(3), pp. 174–215.

Quensted, Johann Andreas (1678): *Ethica pastoralis & Instructio cathedralis... accedit Ratio seu Methodus, Scriptores Sacros & Ecclesiasticos cum fructu legendi et excerpendi*. Wittenbergae: Typis Christiani Schrödteri.

Quillian, Ross (1966): *Semantic Memory*. Cambridge: Bolt Beranek & Newman.

Rabnett, Mark (1982): The First Printed Indexes: A Study of Indexing Techniques in Some Incunabula. *Cataloging & Classification Quarterly*, 2(3–4), pp. 87–102.

Radcliffe-Brown, Alfred (1947): Evolution, Social or Cultural? *American Anthropologist*, 49(1), pp. 78–83.

Rawley, William (1670): To the Reader. In: Francis Bacon: *Sylva Sylvarum, or a Natural History in Ten Centuries*. London: William Lee, s.n.

Ridolfi, Pierluigi (1994): Tecnologia e memoria: l'evoluzione dei calcolatori e la conservazione delle informazioni. In: Tullio Gregory and Marcello Morelli (Eds.): *L'eclisse delle memorie*. Roma/Bari: Laterza, pp. 247–255.

Rieder, Bernhard (2012): What is in PageRank? A Historical and Conceptual Investigation of a Recursive Status Index. *Computational Culture. A Journal of Software Studies*, 2. Retrieved from http://computationalculture.net/what_is_in_pagerank/

Rieff, David (2019): *Elogio dell'oblio. I paradossi della memoria storica*. Roma: Luiss University Press.

Rizzo, Francesca et al. (2003): Remembering and Forgetting in Analyzing Search Engine List Results. In: *Proceedings of the 9th European Conference (CSAPC 2003) on Cognitive Science Approaches to Process Control*. Amsterdam: ACM Press, pp. 83–88.

Robertson, Stephen (1977a): The Probability Ranking Principle in IR. *Journal of Documentation*, 33(4), pp. 294–304.

Robertson, Stephen (1977b): The Probabilistic Character of Relevance. *Information Processing and Management*, 13(4), pp. 247–251.

Rocchio, Joseph (1971): Relevance Feedback in Information Retrieval. In: Gerard Salton (Ed.): *The SMART Retrieval System: Experiments in Automatic Document Processing*. Englewood Cliffs: Prentice-Hall, pp. 313–323.

Rolla, Peter (2009): User Tags versus Subject Headings. Can User-Supplied Data Improve Subject Access to Library Collections? *Library Resources & Technical Services*, 53(3), pp. 174–184.

Rosch, Eleanor (1998): Principles of Categorization. In: George Mather et al. (Eds.): *The Motion Aftereffect. A Modern Perspective*. Cambridge: The MIT Press, pp. 251–270.

Rosch, Eleanor et al. (1976): Basic Objects in Natural Categories. *Cognitive Psychology*, 8(3), pp. 382–439.

Rosen, Jeffrey (2010): The Web Means the End of Forgetting. *The New York Times Magazine*, July 21. Retrieved from https://www.nytimes.com/2010/07/25/magazine/25privacy-t2.htm

Rossi, Paolo (2000): *Clavis universalis. Arti della memoria e logica combinatoria da Lullo a Leibniz*. Bologna: Il Mulino.

Rothenberg, Jeff (1995): Ensuring the Longevity of Digital Documents. *Scientific American*, 272(1), pp. 42–47.

Rouse, Richard (1976): Cistercian Aids to Study in the Thirteenth Century. In: John Sommerfeldt (Ed.): *Studies in Medieval Cistercian History*. Kalamazoo: Cistercian Publications, vol. 2, pp. 123–134.

Rouse, Richard (1977): La diffusion en Occident au XIIIe siècle des outils de travail facilitant l'accès aux textes autoritatifs. In: George Makdisi et al. (Eds.): *L'enseignement en Islam et en Occident au Moyen Âge*. Paris: Librairie Orientaliste Paul Geuthner, pp. 115–147.

Rouse, Richard and Rouse, Mary (1979): *Preachers, Florilegia, and Sermons. Studies on the* Manipulus florum *of Thomas of Ireland*. Toronto: Pontifical Institute of Medieval Studies.

Rouse, Richard and Rouse, Mary (1982a): *Statim invenire*. Schools, Preachers, and New Attitudes to the Page. In: Robert Benson and Giles Constable (Eds.): *Renaissance and Renewal in the Twelfth Century*. Cambridge: Harvard University Press, pp. 201–225.

Rouse, Richard and Rouse, Mary (1982b): La naissance des index. In: Henri-Jean Martin et al. (Eds.): *Histoire de l'édition française 1. Le livre conquérant*. Paris: Promodis, pp. 77–85.

Rouse, Richard and Rouse, Mary (1990): Concordances et index. In: Henri-Jean Martin and Jean Vezin (Eds.): *Mise en page et mise en texte du livre manuscrit*. Paris: Promodis, pp. 219–228.

Sacchini, Francesco (1613): *De ratione libros cum profectu legendi libellus*. Romae: Apud Bartholomaeum Zannettum.

Sagittarius, Caspar (1703): *Commentariolus modos excerpendi omnium ordinum studiosis summa cum cura monstrans*. Helmstadii: Süstermann.

Salarelli, Alberto (2014): Diritto all'oblio e archivi online dei quotidiani: alcune considerazioni sulla memoria sociale ai nostri tempi. *JLIS.it*, 5(1), pp. 1–20.

Salarelli, Alberto (2015): Ancora sul diritto all'oblio: cosa cambia dopo la sentenza della Corte di Giustizia Europea contro Google. *JLIS.it*, 6(1), pp. 147–160.

Saracevic, Tefko (1975): Relevance: A Review of and a Framework for the Thinking on the Notion in Information Science. *Journal of the American Society for Information Science*, 26(6), pp. 321–343.

Schmidt, Adolf (1896): Zeilenzählung in Druckwerken. Inhaltsverzeichnisse und alphabetische Register. *Zentralblatt für Bibliothekswesen*, 13, pp. 13–30.

Schmidt, Johannes (2015): Der Zettelkasten Niklas Luhmanns als Überraschungsgenerator. In: Friedrich Meschede (Ed.): *Serendipity. Vom Glück des Findens*. Köln: Snoeck, pp. 153–167.

Schmidt-Biggemann, Wilhelm (1983): *Topica universalis. Eine Modellgeschichte humanistischer und barocker Wissenschaft*. Hamburg: Felix Meiner.

Schubert, Johann Balthasar (1699): *Sciagraphiam de studio excerpendi*. Lipsiae: Literis Joh. Andreae Zschauens.

Schurink, Fred (2010): Manuscript Commonplace Books, Literature, and Reading in Early Modern England. *Huntington Library Quarterly*, 73(3), pp. 453–469.

Seifert, Arno (1983): Der enzyklopädische Gedanke von der Renaissance zu Leibniz. In: Albert Heinekamp (Ed.): *Leibniz et la Renaissance*. Wiesbaden: Franz Steiner Verlag, pp. 113–124.

Shannon, Claude and Weaver, Warren (1963): *The Mathematical Theory of Communication* [orig. ed. 1949]. Urbana: University of Illinois Press.

Shirky, Clay (2005): *Ontology is Overrated: Categories, Links, and Tags*. Retrieved from www.shirky.com/writings/ontology_overrated.html

Sica, Salvatore and D'Antonio, Virgilio (2014): La procedura di deindicizzazione. *Il diritto dell'informazione e dell'informatica*, 30(4/5), pp. 147–176.

Sidelius, Fridericus and Schubart, Paulus Sigismundus (1713): *Positiones XXXIV de studio excerpendi*. Ienae: Fickelscher.

Silva, Ana Margarida Dias da (2017): Folksonomies in Archives: Controlled Collaboration for Specific Documents. *Ariadne. Web Magazine for Information Professionals*, 77. Retrieved from http://www.ariadne.ac.uk/issue/77/margaridadiasdasilva/

Simon, Herbert (1956): Rational Choice and the Structure of the Environment. *Psychological Review*, 63(2), pp. 129–138.

Simon, Herbert (1971): Designing Organizations for an Information-Rich World. In: Martin Greenberger (Ed.): *Computers, Communication, and the Public Interest*. Baltimore: The John Hopkins University, pp. 37–72.

Simon, Herbert (1997): The Future of Information Systems. *Annals of Operations Research*, 71, pp. 3–14.

Sinclair, James and Cardew-Hall, Michael (2008): The Folksonomy Tag Cloud: When is it Useful? *Journal of Information Science*, 34(1), pp. 15–29.

Sinha, Rashmi (2005): *A Cognitive Analysis of Tagging (Or, How the Lower Cognitive Cost of Tagging Makes It Popular)*. Retrieved from https://rashmi sinha.com/2005/09/27/a-cognitive-analysis-of-tagging/

Sixtus of Siena (1566): *Bibliotheca Sancta*. Venetiis: Apud Franciscum Franciscium.

Smith, Gene (2008): *Tagging. People-Powered Metadata for the Social Web*. Berkeley: New Riders.

Smith, Margaret (1988): Printed Foliation: Forerunner to Printed Page-Numbers? *Gutenberg-Jahrbuch*, 63, pp. 54–70.

Soden, Wolfram von (1965): *Leistung und Grenze sumerischer und babylonischer Wissenschaft*. Darmstadt: Wissenschaftliche Buchgesellschaft.

Solla Price, Derek de (1967): Networks of Scientific Papers. In: Manfred Kochen (Ed.): *The Growth of Knowledge. Readings on Organization and Retrieval of Information*. New York/London: John Wiley, pp. 145–155.

Sommerhoff, Gerd (1974): *Logic of the Living Brain*. New York/London: John Wiley.

Sorel, Charles (1673): *Supplement des Traitez de la connoissance des bons livres*. Paris: Chez André Pralard.

Sparrow, Betsy et al. (2011): Google Effects on Memory: Cognitive Consequences of Having Information at Our Fingertips. *Science*, 333(6043), pp. 776–778.

Spencer, Herbert (1898): What is Social Evolution? *The Nineteenth Century*, 44(259), pp. 348–358.

Spencer, Herbert (1937): *First Principles*. London: Watts & Co.

Spencer Brown, George (1979): *Laws of Form*. New York: E. P. Dutton.

Spiteri, Louise (2006): The Use of Folksonomies in Public Library Catalogues. *The Serials Librarian: From the Printed Page to the Digital Age*, 51(2), pp. 75–89.

Spiteri, Louise (2007): Structure and Form of Folksonomy Tags: The Road to the Public Library Catalogue. *Information Technology and Libraries*, 26(3), pp. 13–25.

Sprat, Thomas (1667): *The History of the Royal Society of London for the Improving of Natural Knowledge*. London: Printed for Martyn.

St. Victor, Hugh of (1880): Eruditionis didascalicae libri septem. In: *Opera omnia*. Ed. by Jacques-Paul Migne. Paris: Garnier, vol. 1, coll. 739–839.

Stebbins, Ledyard (1969): *The Basis of Progressive Evolution*. Chapel Hill: The University of North Carolina Press.
Stock, Wolfgang (2007): Folksonomies and Science Communication: A Mash-Up of Professional Science Databases and Web 2.0 Services. *Information Services & Use*, 27, pp. 97–103.
Stolberg, Michael (2013): Medizinische loci communes. Formen und Funktionen einer ärztlichen Aufzeichnungspraxis im 16. und 17. Jahrhundert. *Zeitschrift für Geschichte der Wissenschaften, Technik und Medizin*, 21(1), pp. 37–60.
Stolberg, Michael (2014): John Locke's 'New Method of Making Common-Place-Books': Tradition, Innovation and Epistemic Effects. *Early Science and Medicine*, 19, pp. 448–470.
Stolberg, Michael (2016): Medical Note-Taking in the Sixteenth and Seventeenth Centuries. In: Alberto Cevolini (Ed.): *Forgetting Machines. Knowledge Management Evolution in Early Modern Europe*. Leiden/Boston: Brill, pp. 243–264.
Stübel, Andreas (1684): *Exercitatio academica de excerptis adornandis*. Lipsiae: Literis Johannis Coleri.
Sturm, Johann (1581): *Linguae Latinae resolvendae ratio*. Argentorati: Excudebat Nicolaus Wyriot.
Swanson, Don (1977): Information Retrieval as a Trial-and-Error Process. *The Library Quarterly*, 47(2), pp. 128–148.
Swanson, Don (1979): Libraries and the Growth of Knowledge. *The Library Quarterly*, 49(1), pp. 3–25.
Swanson, Don (1986): Undiscovered Public Knowledge. *The Library Quarterly*, 56(2), pp. 103–118.
Swanson, Don (1988): Historical Note: Information Retrieval and the Future of an Illusion. *Journal of the American Society for Information*, 39(2), pp. 92–98.
Swanson, Don (1989): Online Search for Logically-Related Noninteractive Medical Literatures: A Systematic Trial-and-Error Strategy. *Journal of the American Society for Information Science*, 40(5), pp. 356–358.
Swanson, Don (1993): Intervening in the Life Cycles of Scientific Knowledge. *Library Trends*, 41(4), pp. 606–631.
Swanson, Don and Smalheiser, Neil (1996): Undiscovered Public Knowledge: A Ten-Year Update. In: Evangelos Simoudis et al. (Eds.): *Proceedings of the Second International Conference on Knowledge Discovery and Data Mining*. Portland: AAAI Press, pp. 295–298.
Swanson, Don and Smalheiser, Neil (1997): An Interactive System for Finding Complementary Literatures: A Stimulus to Scientific Discovery. *Artificial Intelligence*, 91, pp. 183–203.
Tanaka, James and Taylor, Marjorie (1991): Object Categories and Expertise: Is the Basic Level in the Eye of the Beholder? *Cognitive Psychology*, 23(3), pp. 457–482.

Taube, Mortimer (1954a): The Problem of Machine Association of Ideas. In: *Studies in Coordinate Indexing*. Washington: Documentation Incorporated, vol. 2, pp. 72–80.

Taube, Mortimer (1954b): The Actual and Potential Association of Ideas in Information Systems. In: *Studies in Coordinate Indexing*. Washington: Documentation Incorporated, vol. 2, pp. 81–84.

Taube, Mortimer (1954c): Networks of Association. In: *Studies in Coordinate Indexing*. Washington: Documentation Incorporated, vol. 2, pp. 100–111.

Taube, Mortimer and Wachtel, Irma (1953): The Logical Structure of Coordinate Indexing. In: *Studies in Coordinate Indexing*. Washington: Documentation Incorporated, vol. 1, pp. 73–76.

Taylor, John (2003): *La categorizzazione linguistica. I prototipi nella teoria del linguaggio.* Macerata: Quodlibet.

Tesauro, Emanuele (1669): *Il Cannocchiale aristotelico.* In Venetia: Presso Paolo Baglioni.

Theisohn, Philipp (2009): *Plagiat. Eine unoriginelle Literaturgeschichte*. Stuttgart: Alfred Kröner Verlag.

Thomas of Ireland (1494): *Manipulus florum*. Venetia: s.e.

Titius, Johann Petrus (1676): *Manuductio ad excerpendum*. Gedani: Typis David-Friderici Rhetii.

Toobin, Jeffrey (2014): The Solace of Oblivion. In Europe, the Right to Be Forgotten Trumps the Internet. *The New Yorker*, September 29. Retrieved from https://www.newyorker.com/magazine/2014/09/29/solace-oblivion

Turner, Eric (1977): *The Typology of the Early Codex*. Philadelphia: University of Pennsylvania Press.

Udenius, Christoph Just (1687): *Excerpendi ratio nova, das ist eine neue Art und sonderbare Anweisung, wie die studirende Jugend in jeden Wissenschaften... ihre Locos Communes füglich einrichten*. Northusae: Sumptibus Johannis Daeterstadii Bibliopolio.

Vaidhyanathan, Siva (2011): *The Googlization of Everything (and Why We Should Worry)*. Berkeley/Los Angeles: University of California Press.

Vavra, Ashley Nicole (2018): The Right to Be Forgotten: An Archival Perspective. *The American Archivist*, 81(1), pp. 100–111.

Vecce, Carlo (1998): Aldo e l'invenzione dell'Indice. In: David Zeidberg (Ed.): *Aldus Manutius and Renaissance Culture. Essays in Memory of Franklin D. Murphy*. Firenze: Leo S. Olschki, pp. 109–141.

Vezin, Jean (1990): Manuscrits 'imposés'. In: Henri-Jean Martin and Jean Vezin (Eds.): *Mise en page et mise en texte du livre manuscrit*. Paris: Promodis, pp. 423–426.

Vine, Angus (2011): Commercial Commonplacing: Francis Bacon, the Waste-Book, and the Ledger. In: Richard Beadle et al. (Eds.): *English Manuscript Studies 1100–1700*. London: The British Library, vol. 16, pp. 197–218.

Vine, Angus (2019): *Miscellaneous Order. Manuscript Culture and the Early Modern Organization of Knowledge*. Oxford: Oxford University Press.
Wachtel, Irma (1953): Classification and Categorization in Information Systems. In: *Studies in Coordinate Indexing*. Washington: Documentation Incorporated, vol. 1, pp. 65–72.
Wagner, Claudia et al. (2014): Semantic Stability in Social Tagging Streams. In: *Proceedings of the 23rd International Conference on World Wide Web*. New York: Association for Computing Machinery, pp. 735–746.
Walker, Alan (2001): Indexing Commonplace Books: John Locke's Method. *The Indexer. The International Journal of Indexing*, 22(3), pp. 114–118.
Walker, Obadiah (1673): *Of Education. Especially of Young Gentlemen*. Oxon: At the Theatre.
Weick, Karl (1995): *Der Prozeß des Organisierens*. Suhrkamp: Frankfurt a.M.
Weijers, Olga (1995): Les index au Moyen Âge sont-ils un genre littéraire? In: Claudio Leonardi et al. (Eds.): Fabula in tabula. *Una storia degli indici dal manoscritto al testo elettronico*. Spoleto: Centro Italiano di Studi sull'Alto Medioevo, pp. 11–22.
Weinberger, David (2005): Taxonomies to Tags: From Trees to Piles of Leaves. *Release 1.0*, 23(2), pp. 1–32.
Weinberger, David (2007): *Everything is Miscellaneous. The Power of the New Digital Disorder*. New York: Times Books/Henry Holt and Company.
Weinberger, David (2008): *Das Ende der Schublade: Die Macht der neuen digitalen Unordnung*. München: Carl Hanser.
Weinrich, Harald (2004): *Lethe. The Art and Critique of Forgetting*. Ithaca/London: Cornell University Press.
Weiss, Paul (1967): Knowledge: A Growth Process. In: Manfred Kochen (Ed.): *The Growth of Knowledge. Readings on Organization and Retrieval of Information*. New York/London: John Wiley, pp. 209–215.
Wellisch, Hans (1978): Early Multilingual and Multiscript Indexes in Herbals. *The Indexer. The International Journal of Indexing*, 11(2), pp. 81–102.
Wellisch, Hans (1986): The Oldest Printed Indexes. *The Indexer. The International Journal of Indexing*, 15(2), pp. 73–82.
Wellisch, Hans (1994): Incunabula Indexes. *The Indexer. The International Journal of Indexing*, 19(1), pp. 3–12.
Wells, Herbert George (1938): *World Brain*. New York: Doubleday, Doran & Co.
Welter, Jean-Thiébaut (1927): *L'exemplum dans la littérature religieuse et didactique du Moyen Âge. La Tabula exemplorum secundum ordinem alphabeti. Recueil d'exempla compilé en France à la fin du XIIIe siècle*. Paris/Toulouse: Occitania/E. H. Guitard (reprint Genève: Slaktine Reprints, 2012).
Werro, Franz (2009): The Right to Inform v. the Right to Be Forgotten: A Transatlantic Clash. In: Aurelia Colombi Ciacchi et al. (Eds.): *Haftungsrecht*

im dritten Millennium. Liability in the Third Millennium. Liber Amicorum Gert Brüggemeier. Baden-Baden: Nomos, pp. 285–300.

Weston, Paul (1970): To Uncover; To Deduce; To Conclude. *Computer Studies in the Humanities and Verbal Behavior*, 3, pp. 77–89.

Wheatley, Henry (1878): *What is an Index? A Few Notes on Indexes and Indexers*. London: Longmans, Green & Co. for the Index Society.

Wheatley, Henry (1902): *How to Make an Index*. London: Elliot Stock.

Wiener, Norbert (1948): *Cybernetics. Or Control and Communication in the Animal and the Machine*. New York/Paris: John Wiley/Hermann.

Witty, Francis (1965): Early Indexing Techniques: A Study of Several Book Indexes of the Fourteenth, Fifteenth, and Early Sixteenth Centuries. *The Library Quarterly*, 35(3), pp. 141–148.

Witty, Francis (1973): The Beginnings of Indexing and Abstracting: Some Notes Towards a History of Indexing and Abstracting in Antiquity and the Middle Ages. *The Indexer. The International Journal of Indexing*, 8(4), pp. 193–198.

Wood, David et al. (2014): *Linked Data. Structured Data on the Web*. New York: Manning Publisher.

Wu, Harris et al. (2006): Harvesting Social Knowledge from Folksonomies. In: *Proceedings of the 17th Conference on Hypertext and Hypermedia*. New York: Association for Computing Machinery, pp. 111–114.

Yates, Francis (1966): *The Art of Memory*. London: Routledge & Kegan Paul.

Yedid, Nadina (2013): Introducción a las folksonomías: definición, características y diferencias con los modelos tradicionales de indización. *Información, cultura y sociedad*, 29, pp. 13–26.

Yeo, Richard (2001): *Encyclopaedic Visions. Scientific Dictionaries and Enlightenment Culture*. Cambridge: Cambridge University Press.

Yeo, Richard (2004): John Locke's "New Method" of Commonplacing: Managing Memory and Information. *Eighteenth-Century Thought*, 2, pp. 1–38.

Yeo, Richard (2014): *Notebooks, English Virtuosi, and Early Modern Science*. Chicago/London: The University of Chicago Press.

Yeo, Richard (2020): Thinking with Excerpts: John Locke (1632–1704) and his Notebooks. *Berichte zur Wissenschaftsgeschichte/History of Science and Humanities*, 43(2), pp. 180–202.

Zedelmaier, Helmut (1992): *Bibliotheca universalis und Bibliotheca selecta. Das Problem der Ordnung des gelehrten Wissens in der frühen Neuzeit*. Köln et al.: Bohlau Verlag.

Zedelmaier, Helmut (2007): *Facilitas inveniendi*: The Alphabetical Index as a Knowledge Management Tool. *The Indexer. The International Journal of Indexing*, 25(4), pp. 235–242.

Zedelmaier, Helmut (2008): Navigieren im Textuniversum. Theodor Zwingers *Theatrum vitae humanae*. In: Flemming Schock et al. (Eds.): *Dimensionen der*

Theatrum-Metapher in der Frühen Neuzeit. Ordnung und Repräsentationen von Wissen. Hannover: Wehrhahn Verlag, pp. 113–135.

Ziccardi, Giovanni (2019): The Right to Data Oblivion. In: Didier Bigo et al. (Eds.): *Data Politics. Worlds, Subjects, Rights*. London/New York: Routledge, pp. 231–247.

Index

A. Cevolini, *Indexing Systems*
https://doi.org/10.1007/978-3-032-13813-2

Kolibri 360 GmbH
Ferdinand-Jühlke-Straße 7
99095 Erfurt, Deutschland
produktsicherheit@kolibri360.de